T0222449

IMPOSSIBLE MINDS

MINDS

My Neurons, My Consciousness

Revised Edition

IMPOSSIBLE MINDS

My Neurons, My Consciousness

Revised Edition

IGOR ALEKSANDER
Imperial College London, UK

Imperial College Press

ICP

Published by

Imperial College Press
57 Shelton Street
Covent Garden
London WC2H 9HE

Distributed by

World Scientific Publishing Co. Pte. Ltd.

5 Toh Tuck Link, Singapore 596224

USA office: 27 Warren Street, Suite 401-402, Hackensack, NJ 07601

UK office: 57 Shelton Street, Covent Garden, London WC2H 9HE

Library of Congress Cataloging-in-Publication Data
Aleksander, Igor.
   Impossible minds : my neurons, my consciousness / Igor Aleksander. -- Revised Edition.
   pages cm
   ISBN 978-1-78326-568-8 (hardback : alk. paper) -- ISBN 978-1-78326-569-5 (pbk. : alk. paper)
1. Consciousness. 2. Neurons. 3. Artificial intelligence. I. Title.
BF311$b .A493 2015
128'.2--dc23
                                    2014040431

British Library Cataloguing-in-Publication Data
A catalogue record for this book is available from the British Library.

"Olive Trees" (cover image) painted by the late Bettina Morton.

In-house Editor: Amanda Yun

Typeset by Stallion Press
Email: enquiries@stallionpress.com

Printed in Singapore

About the Author

 **Igor Aleksander** has been researching intelligent machinery and models of brain function for more than 45 years, and has published 14 books and over 300 scientific papers on these subjects. His books include the bestsellers *Reinventing Man, Introduction to Neural Computing, Neurons and Symbols, How to Build a Mind, The World in My Mind — My Mind in the World* and *Aristotle's Laptop*.

For this work he was elected to the Royal Academy of Engineering and awarded a lifetime achievement medal of the Institution of Electrical Engineers for contributions to informatics. He currently is Emeritus Professor and Senior Research Investigator at Imperial College London, researching artificial consciousness. He makes frequent TV and radio appearances.

Prof. Aleksander was awarded his PhD by Queen Mary College, where is subsequently became a lecturer at in 1961. He became a reader in electronics in the University of Kent in 1968, then a Professor at Brunel University in 1974. He joined Imperial College

London in 1984, as Professor of the Management of Information Technology, and was appointed Head of Electrical Engineering and Gabor Professor of Neural Systems Engineering from 1988 becoming Emeritus and a Senior Research Investigator in 2002.

Contents

Preface to the Revised Edition

Twenty Years on

A Kind of Maturity

A major difference between then and now is that now, working with informational machines which are brain-like is far better accepted than it was then. It is more acceptable now than before to address important issues about being conscious using formal ideas derived from the design of 'intelligent machines'. As evidence of this, one finds a thriving journal of machine consciousness[a] and a variety of books to be read.[b] A plethora of computational models and theories about consciousness are presented to vie with one another at conferences on a wide range of topics from artificial intelligence to clinical neurology. But what has not changed is that chorus of erudite thinkers who still stay aloof from this effort and see the perpetrators as being misguided and doing the impossible in attempting to penetrate the shuttered personal nature of being conscious.[c] So I need not change the title of this book.

---

[a] The International Journal of Machine Consciousness, published by World Scientific.

[b] I shall refer to these in other parts of this edition.

[c] See chapter 8 of Aleksander, I. and Morton, B. H. (2012) *Aristotle's Laptop: The Discovery Of Our Informational Minds*, (World Scientific, Singapore).

In the first edition I avowed that working with very simple neural networks assuaged my personal fascination — call it obsession — with what makes *me* conscious. I am happy that this personal mode of discovery has continued and that I can share some of these insights with those who now read this book.

The machine that was called Magnus was turned into a general tool for simulating very roughly some neural structures resembling those of the brain, particularly to give chase to the sources of visual consciousness. (This simulator is called NRM: Neural Representation Modeller). I take a hard look at each chapter and comment in postscripts how things have or have not changed.

But, and this is reassuring, I find that even if some of the perplexity of being conscious is lessened, this makes *being* conscious no less awesome. And as I write, it is still the dark blue of the North Aegean, the red 'ruffe' of the Languedoc and the white hills of Sussex that impinge on my consciousness with an ever greater impact as the years go by.

Igor Aleksander
July 2014

Preface to the First Edition

Yet Another Book on Consciousness?

How this book got to be written

July 1991 was an exceedingly hot month. The film crew for an Equinox programme on neural networks, having filmed Yorick, a forerunner neural system of the Magnus machine in our laboratories at Imperial College, were preparing to film an interview with me. I had just said that there were some peculiar states in Yorick which showed that it continued "thinking" about what it had just seen even when its "eyes" were closed. I described this as Yorick's mental image, and, in some cases, Yorick's ability to dream.

"It seems to me," said the interviewer, "that as it has mental imagery of its experience, this neural net is conscious."

I protested violently. "Consciousness is very much a human property, you cannot talk about machines being conscious." But then, with cameras rolling, and I don't know whether it was due to the heat or the confusion of facing the camera, I said, "Well, I suppose that you could say that Yorick was conscious in its own artificial way, so if you talk of the consciousness of machines you have to distinguish between the real consciousness of people and the artificial consciousness of machines."

In the months to come I gave much thought to this idea, and "artificial consciousness" made more and more sense as I thought about it. What would a machine have to have which, if humans didn't have, would limit human consciousness, whatever that is? Artificial consciousness made more sense to me than artificial intelligence (AI). In forty years of AI while computers became very good at doing things such as playing chess or configuring complex equipment, this was the product of intelligent programming and not the inherent intelligence of the machine. In fact, such programs generally do only one thing at a time, and while the programmer who designs the programs is clearly intelligent, there is little that such efforts tell us about the competences which we ourselves associate with our own consciousness.

It seemed to me that it was well worth defining a programme of research where, within one neural system, a list of mental properties, usually associated with living beings, could be tested. This was the beginning of the Magnus (multi-automata-general-neural-units-structure) project. Magnus is a piece of learning neural software within which it could be seen whether the machine could learn this open-ended list of mental properties. By 1992 I was talking about this project at neural net conferences and colleagues were doing interesting things such as demonstrating short and long term mental imagery, and showing that Magnus-like nets had the ability to foresee events and plan accordingly.

I started writing this book in the summer of 1994 because Magnus was having a strange effect on me. By that time I had read the many worthy and sophisticated books written on consciousness by contemporary philosophers and scientists. The hunting season for this subject was clearly open. But while I was able to appreciate the depth of thought which such texts presented (quantum gravity, evolutionary principles, the impossibility of knowing what it is like to be a bat, multiple drafts theories, and so on), none of these gave me the impression that they resonated with the sense of awe and wonder which I have about my own consciousness. But working with Magnus was different. I began to feel that I understood how *my* neurons may be causing *my* consciousness. This is the experience I want to share with the readers of this book. This is the experience which led to the subtitle of this book. However, the more I exposed these ideas to sophisticated thinkers in the field, the more I was told that I was trying to do the impossible — hence the title of the book. Whatever the case, even if the reader does not share my feelings about all this, I hope that learning about some simple ideas that go into making Magnus artificially conscious might be found amusing.

Apologies

I have tried as far as possible to present the thoughts of the major contributors in the current debate on consciousness. Inevitably some have been left out. I am particularly conscious of the deep and interesting contributions of the many who have been stimulated by the recent revival of interest in this subject. Any omissions are no reflection on the relevance of these contributions, but are just due to an attempt to put some bounds on the number of directions taken within this book.

Thanks

First of all, thanks are due to Helen for her understanding when her time for relaxation was met by the clatter of my word processor. We should have walked more often over the Seven Sisters, which appear on the cover of this book as painted by the late Bettina Morton. These are also the cliffs which inspired parts of Molecula's story. Many ideas in this book came from discussions and seminars held by the Neural Systems Engineering group in the Department of

Electrical and Electronic Engineering at Imperial College. I thank the many visitors to this group from the world over, as well as my students and colleagues in whose hands has been the development of Magnus' artificial consciousness and some of whom make an appearance (albeit slightly disguised) in Chapter 10.

Finally, I am thankful for the green downs and white cliffs of Sussex, the dark blue of the Aegean and the red soil of the Languedoc, all of which are so much a part of my feeling of the joy of consciousness which made the writing of this book absolutely necessary.

Molecula's Story

Alongside the discussions about how developing experience gets into neurons and can be retrieved from them, there is a story. It is a piece of fiction about a world in which imposed beliefs about consciousness are used to oppress an entire population. This symbol is a flying cormorant. It signifies the freedom which imaginative science can bring. The cormorant is comfortable both in water and in air, as science is comfortable both in rigorous descriptions and in

flights of imagination. This thought pervades Molecula's story as it pervades the descriptive side of this book. It is a reminder that keeping an open mind is the mark of an adventurous scientist.

Igor Aleksander
April 1996

Chapter 1

Who's Afraid of Magnus?

Artificial Consciousness: The Very Idea!

Molecula Multiplexer picked up the next grant application from the huge pile on her desk. The sign on her door read, "Artificial Intelligence Co-ordinator — United Siliconia Science Funding Programme." She was important — there was not much money for science in Siliconia. For those few who don't know, Siliconia is one of the struggling industrial nations of planet Volta in the single-sun system of Ohm. Siliconian scientists' pride in universal supremacy was at its peak, since the revered automaton expert at Fordox, Sir Global Attractor-State, had declared that it was quite impossible for any other celestial body in the universe to be populated by automata with the level of intelligence possessed by those on Volta.

As Molecula read, her usually serious face slowly broadened into a confusion of amusement and perplexity. "Come here, Asic!" she shouted to her assistant, who was nearly asleep in the next

1

office. "I think that Red Naskela down at Galactic College has finally flipped his lid." Asic was soon by her side and they were both staring at the bold letters at the top of the application:

GRANT REQUEST FOR AN INVESTIGATION INTO THE DESIGN OF AN ARTIFICIAL CONSCIOUSNESS.

Asic let out a howl of laughter. "I always had my suspicions about this guy — I tell you, whatever you do with this one, you can't recommend it. Sir Global would not approve — it contravenes his own theory that only automata which are made of silicon and which have evolved through the principle of machine replication can be conscious."

"There is a slight problem, of course," said Molecula. "We are now actually required to read these applications and provide constructive feedback. But how can I with this one? Professor Naskela says that organisms could exist that are made of flesh, blood, neurons, hormones and other strange materials. Every child knows that these don't work half as well as silicon switches, digital architectures and parallel algorithms. But the height of this nonsense is in this bit here ... He says that you can have a principled discussion not only about artificial consciousness, but also about the real kind we automata have through 'philosophy'. Doesn't he know that 'philosophy' has been decreed to be heretical by Sir Global because philosophers say that a thinker cannot explain his own thinking? Sir Global himself was elected to the Universal Academy for having proved through GAT (global automata theory) that this philosophical conundrum was just a heap of confusion."

By this time Asic had sat down, tears of laughter streaming down his cheeks, the cackle resounding in the usually quiet corridors of the Siliconia Science Headquarters.

Why Magnus?

At Imperial College a new machine was built in 1990. It was called Magnus, for reasons that do not bear repeating. To be absolutely correct, Magnus is not even a real machine — it is what computer scientists call a "Virtual machine". A virtual machine like Magnus is a simulation which causes a host computer to work like the intended machine. On my laptop, I have a gadget called a "calculator". If I call it up by pointing with the mouse to its icon on the screen and clicking the mouse button, the computer becomes a calculator. The screen turns into a picture of numbered buttons and control keys, like those one finds on the front of most calculators. What's more, I can now use this calculator as if it were the real thing. I can push the buttons with the arrow driven by the mouse and carry out calculations.

So, on a largish workstation I can click on the icon labelled Magnus, and my computer becomes a large "neural network".[1] For some years, this network has been used to see if a bunch of simulated (or artificial) neurons can carry out some of the feats that their living counterparts, the cells of human or animal brains, perform in going about their daily lives. The feats are feats which when performed by humans are described as the result of "conscious thought". At this point the reader should simply appeal to a feeling for what this means — the attempts at definition and dissection will come later. The question that haunts every page of this book is: How much of what Magnus is doing could be described as some form of "conscious" thought — some form of artificial consciousness?

---

[1] For the moment all that needs to be said about neural networks is that they are computing systems which, vaguely inspired by networks of neurons we all have in our brains, are capable of learning what they are supposed to do, rather than being programmed step by step, as is required by conventional computers.

To some, this suggestion is offensive. They see consciousness as the ultimate prerogative of a human being — a property that should remain impervious to the assaults of scientists, a property that has a right to remain apart from "mere" scientific explanation. The eminent Oxford philosopher John Lucas[2] has often argued this point forcefully and eloquently. Sometimes consciousness is seen, by Oxford mathematician Roger Penrose among others, as a property that is so awe-inspiring that only an as-yet-undiscovered scientific theory of physics could be dignified enough to be applied to it. Others, such as Stanford philosopher and linguist John Searle, feel that both science and philosophy have said much of what there is to be said on the subject and attempts at further explanations are superfluous. Yet others, for example Nobel laureates Francis Crick and Gerald Edelman, believe that they have given a reasonable framework for scientific accounts of the phenomenon. And yet others, such as psychologist Stuart Sutherland, say that the concept is uninteresting and nothing worthwhile can be said about it. It is certainly not the intention of this book to question the existence of such beliefs; on the contrary, discussions involving artificial consciousness may help to clarify them and explain the rich spectrum that they represent. The starting point is that most of us are intrigued by our own consciousness and being introduced to the consciousness of Magnus may be an interesting experience.

Suppose that Magnus is driven by something that could be described as an *artificial* form of consciousness. Does this say anything about the real kind? I shall argue positively by showing that this idea answers some important questions. Could real consciousness capitulate to analysis as does the artificial kind? Is it possible

---

[2] Many authors appear in these pages and a full bibliography is provided at the end of the book. When a specific reference is made, the year will appear after the name. For example, "Jones (1992)" is a specific reference. Without the year, e.g. "… Mary Jones believes …", it means that the general thoughts of the author are important and drawn from her works in general.

to focus on those precise elements that distinguish the artificial from the real, so explaining the real?

Some may say that given that the literature on consciousness now abounds with opinions, why add to the confusion with the consciousness of Magnus? After all, the idea of asking whether machines could think is by no means new and is ground that has been heavily trodden on by eminent thinkers such as Alan Turing, Douglas Hofstadter and Daniel Dennett. What could possibly be added to all this by an engineer and his neural computer program? When the question of thinking machines has been raised in the past, the word "machine" has always been a general concept — something resembling a programmed computer. Here I wish to talk of a specific machine and explain what it does and how it does it. I believe that anyone can understand Magnus. I am determined that this should not be the kind of discussion which, while promising great insights to all who buy this volume, requires a PhD in automata theory to read beyond page 24. This thing called "automata theory" is not a fearsome theory at all; it is just a childishly simple language (or just a way of orderly thinking) which helps us to tidy up confusing ideas. Anyone should be able to master it from the early chapters of this book. So if anyone can understand the consciousness of Magnus, then anyone can ask whether this understanding can explain personal feelings about their own consciousness. Then, if one is gripped by the undoubted fascination of the subject, it becomes possible to enter the intriguing world of contrasting scientific and philosophical descriptions of real consciousness with the mind of Magnus at the back of one's mind.

The Consciousness of a Vacuum Cleaner?

My ultimate aim is to show by small steps how those properties that we associate with our own consciousness get into the artificial consciousness of Magnus. To make the process of understanding meaningful, I shall recommend the suspension of deep prejudices that many of us hold in having awe for living matter and possibly some contempt for dead ("inanimate"), man-made machines. I do believe that a study of machines shows us part of the way by linking a heap of parts to a working whole and, hopefully, linking a heap of neurons to consciousness. At the same time this should not be mis-read as a suggestion that all machines are conscious in some artificial sense. I do not believe that a vacuum cleaner, or a chess-playing machine, has much to tell us about consciousness. So another intriguing question is how one might distinguish between machines that are and machines that are not artificially conscious.

Consciousness is a large number of things. Just pointing to one or two which are done by conscious human beings and then saying that some artificial device which does them as well is conscious, is evident nonsense. For any artificial device to be called "artificially conscious", this can happen not only through a reasonable convic-tion that the artificial object can do most, if not all, of those things that lead us to believe that we are conscious, but also through a conviction that the way such properties enter the machinery is a bit like how it feels to us in acquiring knowledge and experience. A lack of the latter is part of the reason that consciousness is unlikely to be found in the programs written over the last 40 or so years under the heading of artificial intelligence (AI). A typical product of AI is the chess-playing program which is currently threatening some of the world's best players, or the medical expert system which helps with the diagnosis of some diseases. While each of these achievements in isolation seems pretty intelligent, they are isolated and superficial simulations of behaviour. In a search for consciousness, it is necessary to step above these examples and look for mechanisms that can build up a vast store of experience on which the artificial organism (Magnus in this case) can base its behaviour. The artificially conscious machine may not be very good at chess or giving medical advice, but it may be able to tell us what it is like to be a conscious machine.

Why Neurons and Not Beer Cans?

John Searle, who, by the way, was BBC 1984 Reith Lecturer, when pushed hard during a television debate, said that he didn't particularly care whether a machine was made of silicon or beer cans, but if it couldn't build up experience on a par with something made of biological materials, something that knew what objects in the world were for, it could never "understand" anything. The consequence of this belief this is that you have to get pretty close to the flesh and blood of real neurons before you are likely to find a neural machine which causes consciousness in the way that the brain does.

In the search for mechanical models of the brain, there has been a tradition of pointing to the technology of the day as a metaphor for the living brain. I wish to avoid that particular trap by recognising its seductive existence. "The brain is like a telephone exchange" may be as inaccurate as saying "the brain is like string and sealing wax" or "the brain is like an artificial neural network". Artificial neural networks (ANNs) are one of the more recent playthings that have come into the hands of computer scientists. It is true that these devices are inspired by the processing cells of brains — neurons (or neurones). Each of us has ten billion of these things in our heads. They are beautifully organised into intriguing complexes which neurobiologists call by colourful names. There is the hippocampus, so called because it looks like a sea horse; the visual cortex, where seeing happens; or the cerebellum, where much of our ability to move becomes coordinated.

But the designers of ANNs, while they may throw some light on what the hippocampus is doing, cannot pretend to mimic in detail the working of the brain, for the simple reason that the working of the brain as a whole is not fully understood at the level of neural detail. It is true that the function of the hippocampus is vaguely known to facilitate certain forms of learning. Rough artificial models appear to do the same thing. But what is immensely important is that ANNs may be distinguished from conventional ways of computing due to their "natural" ability to learn rather than being programmed. So, in the armoury of tools available for the modelling of behaviour, ANNs have a distinctive and rare role to play. I shall argue that for a machine to begin its climb to consciousness, the possession of a cellular learning system is crucial. Could an individual be said to have any form of consciousness were he or she to rely solely on the instincts available at birth? Everything I think about has something to do with a mass of images, sounds and feelings that seem to happen in my head. Such sensations could not have been there at birth as they are reflections of events that have happened since birth. So the neural network is a special kind of string and sealing wax in which learning of sensations and visions can be explained. Without it we would be back in the domain of the artificial intelligence specialist who can model a chess-playing process but cannot explain how such a process gets into the machine without the aid of a programmer. Despite the lack of direct similarity to the cells of the brain, the bricks of our model have to be artificial neurons — this hint has now been dropped with some force. The cement that holds the model together by explaining what it does, is this thing called "automata theory". So there is no doubt that we shall be looking for consciousness in a system that does not pretend to model the brain, but one which, in common with the brain, gets to do what it does through learning to represent the world it inhabits. The fact that the model and the real thing work in different ways, rather than making artificial consciousness into a dubious, dismissible concept, may help us to understand what kind of latitude there can be in the meaning of the word "consciousness", whether artificial or real.

The Mental World of Magnus

What has persuaded me to write this book is that I have found working with Magnus-like automata a fascinating experience. Simply put, it makes me view my own consciousness in a way which shuns mystery. Undoubtedly, the consciousness which I can explain is not my own but that of Magnus-like automata. While I happen to think that such consciousness is a bit like that which we all know in ourselves but find impossible to describe, the judgment as to whether this is the case or not is left entirely to the reader. The mission of this book is to allow the reader to share in the experience of working with Magnus and getting to know how it acquires its artificial consciousness. Luckily this can be done without owning Magnus, as, through the power of the written word, Magnus can become a familiar object much in the same way as the characters in a novel can become familiar. Our own consciousness has the handy capacity to attribute consciousness to other entities, whether they be real of fictional. So, in some way, it may be helpful to think of this book as one might think of a novel or a Walt Disney movie. It is not fiction but a story of the way that Magnus actually works now, and the way that Magnus-like systems might work in the future.

The conscious world of a living individual is a cocooned and private thing. Each of us lives in our own cocoon and we have to imagine what it might be like to be someone else. The fact that another is conscious in the same way as I am, is an act of belief — one that philosophers have been known to care about. But with Magnus, things are different. On a screen, I can actually see the sum total of what Magnus is "thinking" at any one time. And because I shall define a process of learning which has picture-like or "iconic" properties, the display on Magnus' screen actually represents Magnus' thought as a picture. In a word, I can get into Magnus' cocoon and start speculating on what it is like to be Magnus. Also because I have built Magnus, I know how it works and I can predict what it will do. I can also provide an explanation of how it is that Magnus' mental world is the way it is. So, whatever Magnus' level of consciousness might be, I can give an explanation of it in terms of its design and experience.

The Basic Guess: Neurons and Thoughts

The personal sensations which lead to the consciousness of an organism are due to the firing patterns of some neurons, such neurons being part of a larger number which form the state variables of a neural state machine, the firing patterns having been learned through a transfer of activity between sensory input neurons and the state neurons.

> "Think of a card," says the conjuror.
> I think of the King of Spades.
> "King of Spades," he says!

I have no idea how he did that or even if it was ever done. But the mystery in that interchange is how I can think of the King of Spades at all or even how it is that I know what I am thinking. How do I work out whether the magician had guessed correctly or not? What is even more intriguing is that, reflecting on the King of Spades, which I thought of, I can say that it was a card from an English or American pack as opposed to, say, an Italian pack. Of course, I also know that I could have thought of an Italian King of Spades had I wanted to, as I have played cards with both packs.

The reason that consciousness is something that we might wish to know more about, is that our ability to think is, to ourselves, at the same time entirely familiar but highly confusing if we try to say "what it is". In Chapter 2, I shall show how the somewhat austere Guess quoted above serves as a framework for saying what might be going on in the machinery of any neural organism when it is thinking conscious thoughts. Francis Crick (1994) has another way of putting almost the same fundamental idea. He calls it "The Astonishing Hypothesis":

> "The Astonishing Hypothesis is that 'You', your joys and your sorrows, your memories and ambitions, your sense of identity and free will, are in fact no more than the behaviour of a vast assembly of nerve cells and their associated molecules."

At first sight, this appears to be the same as my Basic Guess. Indeed I find that Crick's discussion on consciousness has its roots in the same principles as my own and would suggest that anyone interested in consciousness should take "The Astonishing Hypothesis" as compulsory reading. But the difference between our approaches is quite significant. First, the above quote resonates only with the first part of the Basic Guess:

> *The personal sensations which lead to the consciousness of an organism are due to the firing patterns of some neurons, ...*

Second, I use the word "organism". I intend this to apply to artificial machinery as well as animate objects. Crick, perhaps more wisely than I, stays away from the idea of consciousness for anything other than the human being. The next part:

> *... such neurons being part of a larger number which form the state variables of a neural state machine, ...*

agrees with Crick that not all neural activity leads to conscious experience, introduces strange terms such as "state variables" and "neural state machine". This is where the formalism of automata theory starts creeping in. It is best to leave the theory unexplained at the moment — Chapter 3 will deal with what one can hope to gain from such theory. Here it might be said in what way the implications of this part of the Basic Guess might be significant. This means that the instantaneous activity within the organism which is part of a "thought" can be localised to what is called the "state" of some neurons. In artificial systems this can be measured and displayed — it is possible to make explicit what the machine is "thinking". In humans this cannot be done at present and perhaps it will never be done in the pictorial way that it can be done for a machine. However, technologies such as positron emission tomography (PET) scans are heading in that direction. PET scans measure by-products of neural activity in the brain: blood flow in active regions, in this case.

A "state" is the atomic element of thinking and consciousness. Many of the questions which surround consciousness can be stated as questions about how such states are connected to one another in time and in response to sensory input. These are just the kind of questions that can be posed and answered in automata theory — or, more specifically, the theory of neural state machines.

The final part of the Basic Guess contains the ingredient that makes the consciousness of of Magnus visible and explicit:

> ... *the firing patterns having been learned through a transfer of activity between sensory input neurons and the state neurons.*

The fact that I can visualise the King of Spades and that this "feels" as if I were looking at it inside my head leads to debates about screens in the head and homunculi looking at them. Crick again argues that this "iconic" property, in common with short term memory, is very important to consciousness. He goes on to say:

"We can see how the brain takes a picture apart, but we don't know how it puts it together."

This turns out to be less of a problem with Magnus, which may give us a clue as to how it might happen in general.

A Game of Consequences

While it would be quite easy to believe that future generations of Magnus could be zombie-like creatures whose thoughts could be displayed on a screen, it is a much harder to believe that these could have some of the more elusive characteristics of consciousness — "selfhood", "awareness" and the like. Even some of the factors that distinguish consciousness from unconsciousness and subconsciousness may be hard to attribute to a mere machine. This is the reason that I chose to express a "theory" of artificial consciousness as a Big Guess and thirteen Consequences. This not just a process of giving some kind of respectability to otherwise simple ideas. It is a method which I have unashamedly borrowed from George Kelly, a clinical psychologist who, in the mid-1950s, wrote *The Theory of Personal Constructs*. This is an enticingly clear exposition of a psychological theory of the way that personality develops in individuals. It is a framework that allows a long sequence of questions (Corollaries) to be answered that arise from a belief (the Fundamental postulate). I return to Kelly's work in Chapter 5, while here simply expressing the hope that the theoretical framework works as well for the theory of artificial consciousness as it does for personal constructs. However, here I do feel that what I am saying is not formulated well enough to be given the formal terms "Postulate" and "Corollaries". Basic Guess and Consequences will have to do for my story.

Many will find that the central belief about artificial consciousness, the Basic Guess, is easy to accept. Too easy, some might say; simplistic, perhaps. However, it is full of hidden implications. Without the thirteen Consequences, the Guess could be seen as capitulating to Roger Penrose's "child's view" (1989):

> "Consciousness seems to me to be such an important phenomenon that I simply cannot believe that it is something just accidentally conjured up by a complicated computation."

My Consequences are there to enable me to show that important concepts such as *selfhood, will* and even *qualia* (the quality of a mental experience) are not just accidental products of a complex computation. They are the direct consequences of the belief expressed in the Basic Guess: that mentation is the product of a developing structure of linked "iconic" states which represents the function of a concrete network of neurons. Consequence 1 in Chapter 3 defines terms such as "state" and "link" while Consequence 2 in Chapter 4 suggests that not all neurons take part in the "iconic" process — some are there to represent ideas such as "before", "after" or "long ago". Other Consequences are set out in an order which is dictated by the fact that earlier ones are needed to explain later ones. This means that they hop across from psychology to linguistics and to philosophy in a disordered manner. The next few sections of this chapter say a little more about the relationship of the Consequences to these major fields.

Psychological Puzzles

When we are awake and go about our daily business it is said that we are conscious. When it is said that we are unconscious, things are not so clear. This state of mind is used to describe blissful, dreamless sleep, or the less fortunate states of being anaesthetised or having been severely mugged through a blow on the head. But what is dreaming? Are stories about anaesthetised patients remembering the chit-chat of surgeons likely to be true? Even more intriguing is Freud's idea of the unconscious as a collection of repressed memories. What is their effect on conscious behaviour? Freud has stood accused (largely by biologist Jacques Monod) of charlatanism while armies of psychotherapists adhere fervently to his ideas. Consequence 3 in Chapter 4 suggests that a neural system will develop both the "asleep" and "repressed memory" aspects of unconsciousness, and that such representations may be observed in Magnus-like machines. Without giving too much of the plot away at this stage, this phenomenon is seen in Magnus when its input senses are enduringly shut off. Then the structure of "mental states" built up during waking hours doesn't go away but develops (largely due to an increase in "noise") meaningless states and enables new chance-driven links between existing states. Moving in and out of meaningful and meaningless states in a rhythmic fashion can be predicted, suggesting a model for the relationship between dreaming and dreamless sleep.

Repressed memory, on the other hand, is predicted and observed through an occasional tendency for the neural system to develop bypasses of meaningful states either accidentally or due to external influence. Curiously, it is seen that states cut off during waking life may be reached during the more haphazard state of "sleep" and this then affects behaviour during waking life. This may say something about Freud's suggestion that repressed memories make contact with behaviour and conscious thought through dreams. But of what "use" could such phenomena be to a servile robot such as Magnus? Perhaps none, but manufacturers of Magnus-like creatures will have to be aware of the possibility. Speculation on this point is left to

Chapter 4, the final part of which (Consequence 4) concentrates on the learning mechanism which leads to this memory structure — the "inner eye" of awareness. It is this mechanism which is central to all which is said in this book. It is this mechanism which gives Magnus a vivid and accessible memory of its mental world. This is the heart (to mix metaphors) of Magnus' artificial consciousness.

In Chapter 5 the iconic memory mechanism is extended in Consequence 5 to explain how Magnus might remember sequences of events in the world and how this might provide a basis for predicting events and controlling them. Consequences 4 and 5 are more than an explanation of memory and learning: they are the epicentre of the nature of consciousness as expressed in this volume. They are the mechanisms which have to be accepted if one is ever to be convinced that it is the firing of neurons that leads to awareness. Crick regrets that the location of the neurons which lead to awareness in the brain is not known. We do know where they are in Magnus and I believe that this may give neurobiologists an inkling as to where to look in the brain. One of the major implications of these Consequences will, in Chapters 4 and 5, be seen to be a mechanism of self-selection by an individual brain as to where the awareness neurons might be.

The theme of awareness, particularly self-awareness, is continued in Chapter 5 (Consequence 6). This is where we stop thinking of Magnus as a machine that sits around and sucks in iconic experience from its surroundings, but discovers that it has outputs that affect its surroundings. Arms move things around, hands grasp and even voice makes other organisms come and go. The effect of Magnus' own actions becomes part of its sensory experience.[3] In engineering terms, a new feedback loop has come into operation

---

[3] Here Magnus becomes a bit of a fictional machine. Current versions do not have arms and legs, but they do have the equivalent of voice, as is seen in Chapter 2. This should not tax the reader's imagination too much.

so that actions and their effects become part of acquired sensory experience. This experience is special. It is experience of self, taking selfhood into the growing state structure. Combined with Consequences 4 and 5, this simple learning of selfhood introduces the basis of a "first person" into Magnus' knowledge of the world and its plans to control it.

Chapter 8 (Consequences 12 and 13) deals with further psychological issues: instinct and emotion. These are central topics in psychology, but what possible use could they be in artifacts such as Magnus? Loosely rephrased, instinct is that which causes reactions of output to input in Magnus as required or "wired in" by the designer. The "use" of such links is that they provide the necessary infrastructure for Magnus to operate at all. They are platforms on which Magnus builds its state structure; the seeds of consciousness, one might say. Some aspects of consciousness, such as learning to ride a bicycle, have a curious progression. Early attempts use the instinctive control loop that keeps us upright, only to waft out of consciousness once the task has been learned. (In living organisms keeping upright is a peculiar mixture of instinct and learning — babies need to learn some of it, some animals don't.) Emotion and instinct in Magnus are closely connected, and this is evident in theories about humans too. But I can see the headline now:

EMOTIONAL MACHINE BUILT AT IMPERIAL COLLEGE!

In Magnus, emotions have a functional character — nothing to write headlines about. Emotions are seen as global settings (or firing patterns) of the auxiliary neurons that have been introduced in Consequence 2. Some are learned, but the more basic ones come from instinctive reactions to danger and the like. The avoidance of unprotected heights is known to be instinctive in babies. It may be worth building it into Magnus, as learning not to step off a tall building cannot be left to trial and error. Were Magnus a working robot in a factory, the way it approaches a dangerous task should be different from the way it approaches a routine task, even though the outward actions and the firing of neurons that make the difference are a mixture of instinct and increased sophistication achieved through learning. The various abstract sensations due to these auxiliary neurons are described as emotions.[4]

So, could it be that some morning, Magnus would produce the message "I feel depressed today, I don't want to be used"? Are we witnessing the birth of Marvin, Douglas Adams' lovable but depressed robot in *The Hitchhiker's Guide to the Galaxy*? Chapters 8 and 10 contain some speculations about robot depression being unlikely, which may throw some light on the meaning of such concepts. Finally, Consequence 7 (Chapter 5) relates to "will". This addresses important philosophical as well as psychological issues. Even the "freedom" of will is modelled through the fact that the neural net is capable of exploring alternatives. Given a mental, conscious state and a particular sensory environment, "will" is represented as a consideration of action, options and choice. Magnus can discover that several courses of action are possible. Freedom comes from the sensation that there are no overriding preferences and the choice that is actually adopted is not the function of any constraint. It is freely taken.

Language: The Human Competitive Edge

There is no doubt that animals communicate and that they do so in ways that are more sophisticated than generally imagined. But

---

[4]Care needs to be taken here in the neural net/brain analogy. In the brain it is known that the global settings are sometimes due to chemical, hormonal causes. In Magnus they are assumed to be electrical, but this should not affect the nature of the discussion.

human communication is undoubtedly on a higher rung of the ladder of sophistication and, in the eyes of many, it is that which gives humans a massive start on all other living organisms. Language is therefore a most important aspect of *human* consciousness. It cannot be left out of the consciousness of Magnus. Indeed, there would be no point in building Magnus were it not able to communicate with me, and I with it, in something like natural language. Also, were I to take the AI route and give Magnus rules that "understand" natural language, I would seriously hamper Magnus' artificial consciousness, having created a machine whose language I cannot trust. Searle is right. True understanding comes from knowing the "aboutness" of words in the outside world rather knowing the rules that put sentences together. Searle calls this "intentionality". To have artificial consciousness, Magnus must have intentionality. To have intentionality, Magnus must build up its knowledge of language a bit like a child does. This point is so important and so involved that three chapters are needed to develop the theme to the full.

Chapter 6 (Consequence 8) deals with the problem that has been given the name "binding". Having maintained that awareness is due to the firing of neurons as selected by sensory information, awareness of an object becomes bound to the sensory experience that surrounds that object. A dog barks and a dog can be perceived in many ways — there are many dog breeds. Also, the spoken word "dog" and various forms of the written word are used. Consequence 8 suggests that all these events are "bound" to one another as firing patterns through the iconic learning process. Crick writes that we do not know how the brain expresses this binding. How this happens in Magnus opens the way for a discussion as to whether something similar is happening in the brain.

Most will say that the most influential linguist of this century is US mathematician Noam Chomsky. His description of grammars as mathematical structures has not only become deeply rooted as the mainstay of modern linguistics, but also underpins the computer languages that have been designed and analysed. More than this, Chomsky has had a major influence on philosophical views not only of language, but of mental activity in general. This has led Jerry Fodor, a philosopher at New York City University, to describe consciousness as a grammar-like innate computer program fashioned in individuals through programming by genetic evolution. Working with neural networks leads to different conclusions. To Magnus, the grammar of language may be less important than its power to communicate, even in an ungrammatical way. Were I to run into the street and shout:

"Help, fire, child, top floor, trapped!"

the message would be clear despite the jumbled nature of the words. It is true that were I to say:

"loves, John, Mary"

the listener would be left in some doubt as to who loves whom. In Chapter 7, Consequence 9 indicates the way that a Magnus-like device learns to mould some initially random utterances into words and then phrases. The key to this development is the representation of selfhood as expressed in Consequence 6. Clearly the utterances of a child form part of what she hears, and encouragement by "adults" helps her to absorb and develop those utterances which have an effect on her world. This gradual process can be isolated and studied in Magnus.

The second part of the development of language in Magnus' neurons follows an imaginative argument due to Richard Dawkins, a British biologist. He refers to ideas that can be expressed in language as "memes", in parallel with the "genes" of biology. Memes are held in a repository maintained and evolved by the adults in a society and are absorbed by newcomers (i.e. a child) through the massive encouragement by some of those adults (i.e. parents and teachers). So it is with Magnus. In Chapter 7 (Consequence 10) I speculate on this process on the basis of earlier Consequences.

While the natural language abilities of Magnus are at present pitifully limited, they show that the iconic learning method coupled with mechanisms of self-representation are sufficient for achieving this access to a "meme" pool through the help of "adults". This, in turn, with Magnus' ability to bind memes to language, gives Magnus a sense of aboutness of the language it uses without which its consciousness would be severely handicapped. This is a novelty in computation as, at the moment, such aboutness is missing. It is my hope that, in the future, the artificially conscious successors to Magnus will not make the demand of its users that they need to know a computer language. Natural language could become an option which is largely not available at the moment.

Philosophy or Mathematical Equations?

In recent times attempts at explaining consciousness have become widespread. "Almost an industry," observed a philosopher friend at the beginning of his own lecture on the subject. It is quite proper in philosophy for philosophers to hold different views of the elements of mental life. The debate which emerges is what makes philosophy an exciting subject. In the next chapter I shall argue that the study of consciousness may have begun with the challenge of Descartes' idea that mind and body pursue dual paths in the life of an individual with only a minor link in the pineal gland. This was a product of debate on the relationship of mind to body which can be traced to the pronouncements of philosophers over the previous two thousand years. In the next chapter I shall also put forward the opinion that it was British philosopher John Locke who, through skepticism towards Descartes' ideas, brought consciousness into the theatre of philosophical discussion. He was more concerned with the nature of the ideas we have in our heads or ideas of which "we are conscious" than the mechanisms which give rise to these ideas. This set the agenda, which remains to the present day, leaving us with a fascinating literature of contrasting philosophical ideas. The feature of the present time, however, is that scientists and engineers are trying to get into the act and join in the debate. There would be nothing wrong with this except for the fact that the methods of the scientist are different from those of the philosopher. While the philosopher accepts a diversity of opinion as adding to the interesting texture of the debate, the scientist is looking for a consensus or "paradigm". This encourages rivalry and competition for being the leader of the dominant paradigm. So the average person who reads the dozen or so "popular" books available at the time of writing may be a little puzzled by the attacks that authors launch on one another.

The skepticism that scientists have towards philosophers is rather overt. Nobel laureate Francis Crick (in *The Astonishing Hypothesis)* says:

> "Philosophers have had such a poor record over the last two thousand years that they would do better to show a certain modesty rather than the lofty superiority they usually display ... But they must also learn how to abandon their pet theories when the scientific evidence goes against them or they will expose themselves to ridicule."

Another Nobel laureate, neuroscientist Gerald Edelman, is no kinder:

> "Philosophy by contrast [with science] has no proper subject matter of its own. Instead it scrutinises other areas of activity for

clarity and consistency. Furthermore, unlike science, it may be called immodest. There is no partial philosophy, it is complete with each philosopher."

Philosophers give as good as they get. In a skirmish published in the *Times Higher Education Supplement* in London in 1994, Andrea Christofidou, a lecturer in philosophy at Oxford, dismissed Crick's "astonishing hypothesis" about neurons and consciousness as being simply "fallacious". She points to the belief that "the self" cannot be described by what she calls "equations". (Readers may be puzzled by the fact that not a single equation appears in Crick's book.) In fact, Christofidou, along with other philosophers such as John Lucas, believes that the "pure" philosophical approach to consciousness incorporates and cherishes the inexplicability of the concept, particularly when it comes to selfhood. As Christofidou makes plain, science and its "equations" are rejected as a matter of policy:

"Whatever equations a scientist may give ... the problem of consciousness will always remain."

"What it is to be conscious is not a matter of equations."

"But even if it turns out to be just a matter of equations, there is still something unaccounted for: the first person."

So the scientist mistrusts the philosopher's use of rational, verbal argument while the philosopher mistrusts the scientist's use of formalisms (equations). The problem with such unaccepting views is that, whatever consciousness is, it lacks the level of agreement about how it could be discussed if a common understanding is ever to enter our culture.

There are other notable factions in the battle for consciousness — those who believe that science needs to develop beyond what it is now before it can approach an explanation. Roger Penrose dissociates himself from the Lucas school. He is not averse to using equations, but holds the view that the equations for consciousness are not yet within the grasp of science. He thinks that the answer will be an equation, one that explains quantum gravity — a problem in physics of dimension on a par with consciousness. This may be pessimistic, as it denies the possibility of finding models of consciousness in computational structures, which is in contrast with most of what is written in this book. To me, waiting for a theory of quantum gravity before consciousness can be tackled seems a somewhat self-imposed impediment, the necessity for which has only been put forward as a belief.

There are other pessimists, particularly in the scientific community. Consciousness is sometimes seen by some eminent scientific figures as something improper. It's OK (they would argue) for philosophers to waste their time with it, but real scientists will leave it well alone. Those who don't are suspect. Engineers, in particular, are supposed to be getting on with the design of "wealth-creating" objects. If they mix it with philosophers they become even more suspect than scientists. My own belief is two-pronged. First, it is clear that acrimony does the topic no good at all. An interdisciplinary approach where the warring factions try to understand and use each other's contributions may lead to greater success. Secondly, I believe that the process of synthesis has been neglected as an avenue for explanation: hence this book. The method of a Basic Guess and its Consequences recognises that whatever consciousness is, it isn't something that can be explained with a single equation or a single argument. It therefore tries to list (as Consequences) those aspects of mental life which at some point or another are evoked as being part of conscious thought.

This smacks of what psychologists, philosophers and scientists sometimes call "the folk explanations of consciousness". This could be taken as a disparaging outlook — only professionals being allowed to have opinions on an important topic. However, consciousness may be a field where any explanation needs to make sense against what individuals feel about their own sense of self and consciousness. So when you or I talk about "being aware of my own self" the method in this book is to break this statement down (Chapter 5) into "I know where I am", I know who I am", "I know where I have been" and "I know where I could go next or what I could do next". Also, it may be important to note thoughts such as: "I can also make a good guess at what the consequences of my actions are likely to be". Other aspects come under the heading of thoughts such as "I am different from someone else". With this breakdown it becomes possible to ask what properties need to exist in real and artificial machinery for it to develop these sensations and abilities. It may be that this can be dismissed on the argument of "How do you know that the artificial you create has anything to say about the real I feel?" My suggestion is that the artificial at least provides models which take some of the mystery out of concepts such as "self" without reducing one's awe of the human capacity. In a way, the process is akin to saying that the human heart is a bit like a pump rather than the mysterious centre of all emotions which it was thought to be not so long ago. If one has to make a pump which might replace a heart, the real awe for the reliability and precision of the real organ comes to the fore. And so it might be with "self", "will" and even "qualia". These ideas should not be threatened by asking how an organism might acquire them and then giving some answers to the questions.

Given that Magnus can develop language (Consequences 8–10), it becomes quite possible for it to say "I believe X". As such a statement is based on the self being modelled in Magnus' structure of states, and X has been acquired through experience or inferred from experience, it becomes a challenge for skeptics to distinguish this statement from occasions when a similar statement is made by a conscious human. In conventional AI, machines could easily make such statements when they discover X in their databases. This can be attacked through pointing (in Searle's "Chinese room" style; see Chapter 6) at the lack of intentional "grounding" of the concept X. In Magnus, this line of attack is not available as everything in its state structure, including the self, is grounded through iconic learning.

Finally, there is the issue of "qualia". Whenever scientists enter a tug of war with philosophers and appear to be winning, philosophers produce a final tug by asking, "What about qualia?" This magical concept is often exemplified by statements such as "the redness of a red object". It too is often portrayed as a pure, scientifically unassailable philosophical idea. In artificial consciousness, Magnus could certainly respond to statements such as "think of a red boat". The neural correlate of this event is clearly distinguishable from that which happens when "think of a green boat" and even "think of redness" are requested. Interestingly, Dennett dismisses qualia as an illusion, although he admits it is easy to see why people think that they do exist. I have attempted to be less dismissive in Chapter 8 as, for me, "qualia" are actually at the centre of the puzzle as to why something personal should not be explained by an observer from outside. I shall try to show that attributes can be independently bound to objects and that such attributes may exist in state structure independently of objects. In simple terms, the neurons of Magnus act differently for different subjective thoughts, such as the redness as an undefined red object — a blob, say. I suspect that people do something similar. So, I suggest in Chapter 8 that qualia, rather than being dismissible, may be explained, and that such explanation may throw some light on why some think that the explanation is impossible or that qualia do not exist.

In summary, it is not my intention to compete in the race to become a paradigm leader. I feel that this rivalry may not be conducive to understanding, so part of the aim of this book is to try to make sense of the wide variety of views of contemporary discussants alongside the ideas that are generated by working with Magnus-like machinery.

Cultural Pressures

The technical side of this book ends in Chapter 8. Chapter 9 is about the folklore and fears which surround the idea of a conscious machine.

Can machines be conscious? "I should say so! You should see my new video recorder — it's got a will of its own. Set it up to record *Neighbours* and it gives you the early evening news instead. It does as it pleases." It's the easiest thing in the world for people to ascribe consciousness to the daftest selection of objects and then argue that sophisticated information-processing machines are definitely not conscious. The judgment of whether a manufactured object is conscious or not may not be a property of the machine; it may be in the gift of the beholder. So while it is possible to make artifacts which some people will think are conscious, it is impossible to do this in a way which is universally agreed on. In fact, people are only too ready to assign consciousness to inanimate objects — ancient Egyptians ascribed consciousness to the statue of Mnemnon because it emitted sounds as air expanded within it in the rays of the sun. In contrast, if the person at a party with whom you had had an interesting conversation all evening were to reveal that he was made of silicon chips, a perfectly understandable reaction might be: "Good heavens! I've been talking to an unconscious zombie all evening."

As mentioned earlier, it is impossible, some philosophers argue, to tell whether anything outside ourselves is conscious or not. It is impossible (argues US philosopher Thomas Nagel) to know what it is like to be a bat. The only organism whose consciousness I can be absolutely sure of is myself. This is a "first person" view. So, philosophically minded people will perfectly properly argue that science and the engineering of machines, being about objects outside ourselves, cannot cope with anything but "third person" problems and therefore cannot approach the question of consciousness. My argument, however, is that the machine engineer can conjure up a sneaky finesse on this problem. He would ask the question:

> "What properties does an organism need to have to decide that it itself is conscious?"

If it cannot come to that conclusion as a "first person" property, any argument that it can be conscious is a non-starter or just daft attribution.

So Chapter 9 is about the history of myth and fiction which the idea of machine consciousness faces. As a machine designer am I trying to play God? The answer is negative, but historically the Rabbi of Prague was trying to do just this in building the Golem in Gustav Meyerling's 1915 story. Literature of this kind stretches from rabbinical incantations, through Mary Shelley's story of Dr. Frankenstein, to the terminators of the present day. Can the creation of Magnus become an evil act in the hands of an evil designer? Can combining Magnus with the successes of artificial intelligence produce the machine which will dominate humans? While I hope that the answers to these questions given in Chapter 9 are reasonably reassuring, it would be wrong to end the book without asking them.

The Point of It All

Crick argues that once the neural correlates of consciousness have been found in living brains, it becomes possible to have a general view of the matter and build machines that are, in some way, conscious. I find living brains too complicated and have put the proposition about conscious machines the other way round. If consciousness is a property of neural material, it will be easier to develop the general view through the synthesis and analysis of the artificial version first. I concede that the artificial and the real cannot be equated on every count, and hence I insist on the term "artificial consciousness". In the last chapter I argue that this approach, despite its potentially unpalatable nature for philosophers and biologists, could, as a flight of fancy, lead to a conscious machine whose only object for existing would be to clarify the large number of issues that "being conscious" implies. The chapter is written as an interview with such a machine so as to allow the reader to decide whether such an interview is plausible.

As written at the very beginning of this chapter, Magnus is a "virtual machine" which enables me to study consciousness in the same way as a weather simulation enables me to study the weather. It is a matter of personal preference as to whether the machine which acts as a host to Magnus is described as conscious or not. Clearly there is an obvious and uncontroversial difference between this and the way that flesh and blood is conscious. But Magnus is closer to consciousness than the weather program is to the weather. I do foresee the possibility of Magnus virtual machines being used in robots and the like, simply because of their ability to build up experience, use it and have their own trustworthy point of view. This is an advance in the application of computation and may lead to machines with a useful point of view of their own in about forty years' time.

So the primary difference between artificial and real consciousness is that the former is a usable explanatory form of the latter. It also may be the case that through artificial consciousness some of the unhelpful mystique in this area has been laid to rest.

Postscript to Chapter 1

On Scepticism and Guesses

An Enduring Scepticism

Reading in Chapter 1 about the schism among those who study consciousness through scientific analysis or only for the pleasure of philosophical debate, appears unaffected by the increasing numbers of machines that are claimed by their designers to be conscious. While in earlier years I may have tried to convince the philosophers to look toward science, I no longer do this for a very good reason. As attempts are made to test one's ideas in a machine, it is likely that mainly the experimenter benefits if such ideas are supported. I learned a lot from the design of Magnus, but expecting anyone observing the machine to be impressed by its 'consciousness', may be totally unreasonable. As a 'first person' thing, being conscious is something we cannot admire in living entities even if they are our best friends, let alone machines. I learned this the hard way.

With colleagues we thought of demonstrating Magnus in the presence of the press in 1996 in the Science Museum. This resulted in cringe-inducing headlines like 'First Conscious Machine Built at Imperial College'. It also led to an invitation to demonstrate the machine on the late night BBC TV news programme called 'Newsnight'. The interviewer was the incisive Peter Snow. We demonstrated the ability of Magnus to 'imagine', in visual memory displayed on the screen, travelling down two roads and visualising in which there was a specific restaurant along one of the roads. While *we* were saying "see Magnus is 'mentally' exploring two possible routes", Peter Snow said "Oh well, so that's just pictures on a screen... we turn now to an important report on the EU's banning of imports of beef from the UK..." As I said; it's the hard way to learn that discerning consciousness in a third party is in the gift of the observer who may stay with the held belief that machine consciousness is an impossible feat.

My Basic Guess and that of Others

In the chapter, I introduced my 'basic guess' and its thirteen consequences as a way of spelling out the various 'mental' behaviours that might be studied in artificial neural networks in order to understand their counterparts in consciousness. In the intervening time, others have been producing 'basic guesses' of their own. I look at these briefly to indicate the company that my basic guess has kept after the publication of the first edition. Already there at the time of writing the original edition was Bernard Baars' influential Global Workspace Model (briefly referenced in Chapter 8). This model stems from cognitive psychology and is based on the guess that many memory (and other) processes vie with one another to come into consciousness. One of these wins (as being most relevant), enters a 'global workspace' whence it is broadcast back to influence all the vying processes. A 'stream of consciousness' is then defined as the stream of states of the global workspace. While this approach stands aside from my 'neurally based' guess, Murray Shanahan constructed a neural model based on the Global

Workspace using the Neural Representation Modeller (NRM — a successor to Magnus).[a]

Remarkably, Stan Franklin and his colleagues used Baars' guess to build a practical system that replaced human billeters of US Navy personnel. Working through email, IDA (Intelligent Distribution Agent) found new assignments by 'becoming conscious' of the needs of its user.[b] Some of these users remarked on how caring these agents were in doing their job. Again this brings home the notion that consciousness of an object is in the gift of the beholder of that object.

Another area of guesses is whether what one is conscious *of* is the product of many neural processes or one. Interestingly, US Philosopher Ned Block explains 'functionalist theories' of the mind in terms that are derived from the 'automata theory' mentioned in chapter 1 and which pervade the rest of the book. That is, a conscious mental state is part of a system of states influenced by perceptual input which causes the progression from one state to another. Block's key guess about a *functional* mental state that it is solely defined by what it does. A mental state of pain may lead to further states that are 'where is the aspirin' and 'go to the medicine drawer'.[c] Aaron Sloman and Ron Chrisley have a related but different point of view which goes under the heading of Virtual Machine Functionalism.[d] This suggests that a mental state is made up of the states of many interacting sub-automata. So, the 'pain' state and the

---

[a] Shanahan, M. (2006), A Cognitive Architecture that Combines Internal Simulation with a Global Workspace, *Consciousness and Cognition*, 15 pp. 433–449.

[b] Franklin, S. (2003). 'IDA: A Conscious Artifact?' in Owen Holland (ed), *Machine Consciousness*, Imprint Academic, Exeter, pp. 47–67,

[c] Block, N. (1996). 'What is functionalism?' a revised version of the entry on functionalism in Borchert, D. M. (ed), *The Encyclopedia of Philosophy Supplement*, Macmillan, London. (PDF online)

[d] Sloman, A. and Chrisley, R. (2003). Virtual machines and consciousness, *Journal of Consciousness Studies*, 10 (4–5), pp. 133–72.

'aspirin' state might coexist and be produced by different mechanisms. They are also virtual as these coexisting automata are not physical but operations within an informational machine. Such virtual systems could (according to Dennett[e]) be functioning on networks of neurons in the brain.

A similar notion occurred to Semir Zeki and Andreas Bartels, who dubbed these separate areas 'Microconsciousnesses' and attempted to find them in the physical brain, arguing that they come into consciousness by overlapping in timing in physical (as oppose to virtual) systems in the brain.[f] Barry Dunmall and I developed an extension to this idea which includes the muscular activity involved in vision to provide the necessary integration of events in different parts of the visual cortex.[g] This was intended to explain how our visual experience of a comprehensive visual world uses signals that drive the eyes to integrate that tiny bit of vision that comes through our 'peep-hole' in the retina known as the fovea.

This led us to think again about the 'basic guess' and group the 13 consequences into the five principal, personal experiences of what 'being conscious' feels like and that most people might agree with.[h] We called these the 'five axioms' — an axiom being "A self-evident or universally recognized truth". Briefly, they concern

- the perception of a coherent world from a personal perspective;
- the imagination of experienced or invented worlds;

---

[e] Dennett, D. C. (1991). *Consciousness explained*, Penguin Press, London and New York.

[f] Zeki, S. and Bartels, A. (1998). The Asynchrony of Consciousness, *Proc. R. Soc. Lond. B*, 265, pp. 1583–1585.

[g] Aleksander, I. & Dunmall, B. (2000). An extension to the hypothesis of the asynchrony of visual consciousness, *Proceedings of the Royal Society B Biological Sciences* Volume: 267, Issue: 1439, pp. 197–200.

[h] Aleksander, I. & Dunmall, B. (2003), 'Axioms and Tests for the Presence of Minimal Consciousness in Agents', in Holland, O. (ed), *Machine Consciousness*, Imprint Academic, Exeter, pp. 7–19.

- the attentive focus on important input or memory;
- the use of imagination in making decisions;
- the involvement of emotions in decision making.

These serve both as tests for the presence of consciousness in living or artificial organisms as well as guides for the design of artificially conscious systems.[i] In the meantime, others have also taken the approach of decomposing consciousness into components that are easier to analyse than the entire monumental concept. Pentti Haikonen has also written three clear books suggesting decompositions of consciousness in terms of neural system engineering.[jkl] On the philosophical side Thomas Metzinger made essential lists which he called 'constraints' to be met by any system that is considered to be conscious.[m] David Gamez (2008) in his PhD thesis "The Development and Analysis of Conscious Machines"[n] discusses both the 'axioms' and 'constraints' listings in terms of their implications for designers of potentially conscious machines.

In sum, the purpose of the book enunciated early in chapter 1 that the primary difference between artificial and real consciousness is that the former may be used to explain the latter persists even 20 years on — encouraged and strengthened by the work of an expanding group of researchers.

---

[i] Aleksander, I. (2005). The World in my Mind, my Mind in the *World Key Mechanisms of Consciousness in People, Animals and Machines*, Imprint Academic , Exeter.

[j] Haikonen, P. O. (2003). *The Cognitive Approach to Conscious Machines*, Imprint Academic, Exeter.

[k] Haikonen, P. O. (2007). *Robot Brains: Circuits and Systems for Conscious Machines*, Wiley, New York.

[l] Haikonen, P. O. (2012). *Consciousness and Robot Sentience*, World Scientific, Singapore.

[m] Metzinger, T. (2003). *Being No One: The Self-Model Theory of Subjectivity*, MIT Press Boston.

[n] Gamez, D. (2008). *The Development and Analysis of Conscious Minds.* [Online] (Updated 19 November 2008). Available at http://www.davidgamez.eu/mc-thesis/index.html [Accessed 12 May 2014]

"Wake up, Asic!" said Molecula. "I've read Prof. Naskela's whole proposal now."

"So, do you want me to write the rejection letter now?" whispered Asic, rubbing his eyes; "I could use phrases like 'unproven case', meaning 'pretentious rubbish' ..." "I'm not entirely sure," said Molecula slowly; "it may be e case for getting more information. Naskela is making the point that consciousness is something that could be discussed independently of automata and therefore could apply to flesh and blood."

"But where's the wealth creation?" said Asic crossly. "This is taxpayers' money, don't forget. All that this research will do is irritate important people like Sir Global."

"Do you remember the old days, Asic? We used to be able to fund projects on things that we were curious about. What Naskela says about us all being intrigued by our own consciousness rings a bell with me. I am curious, and Sir Global's pronouncements don't do very much for me. Do write Red Naskela a letter saying that he should elaborate on his proposal. No promises, of course ..."

"You're the boss. I'll do as you say. But I'd like to put it on record that I think it's all pretentious rubbish. I don't see why we should both get the sack!"

Chapter 2

Neurons and Thought

The Basic Guess

The personal sensations which lead to the consciousness of an organism are due to the firing patterns of some neurons, such neurons being part of a larger number which form the state variables of a neural state machine, the firing patterns having been learned through a transfer of activity between sensory input neurons and the state neurons.

In the context of consciousness, this guess is meant to be the answer to the question "What generates consciousness?". Clearly, as it stands, the postulate sounds a bit technical, and it is one of the objectives of this chapter to clarify the technicalities. But the key implication of the postulate is that consciousness is generated by some kind of machine — in a living organism this machine is called the brain. But prejudice and tradition have it that other machines, being "inanimate" objects (things without a soul or "anima"), make it "wrong" to use words such as "consciousness" and "machine" in the same sentence. So, right from the start, I need to justify the notion that consciousness is not outside the scope of what can be gained by studying objects manufactured by man rather than God or Nature. I do this not by arguing that man-created artifacts are necessarily as conscious as humans, but that by looking at brains with the instruments that are available for looking at machines, it becomes possible to get an inkling of what consciousness might be.

The idea that consciousness could be explained in this way is what some would call "reductionist". This is a polite way of saying that the discussion has been simplified to such an extent that the explanation may not refer to consciousness at all. But the almost hidden implication of the Basic Guess is that consciousness may be simpler than many are prepared to believe. I believe that simplification and clarification go well together if adequate precautions are taken. I further believe that this clarification is necessary in order to satisfy those who have a curiosity about their own sense of consciousness. Fear of simplification has deep roots in the belief that consciousness is something that inspires awe and must therefore be complex and, in some ways of thinking, mystical. The Basic Guess is purposefully designed to encourage a view of consciousness which stems from being confident of knowing what being conscious *feels* like. It requires one to suspend any feelings of contempt that may exist for machines or simple, but relevant, logical arguments. This may be reductionist in the sense that it simplifies things, but, as I shall argue passionately, it does not remove any of the awe one might have for one's own consciousness — it is meant to replace mystique by logic.

Two questions are raised and then answered in this chapter. First, how much of our individual curiosity about consciousness could be satisfied through the study of the behaviour of an artificial device? Second, how far have the existing explanations of philosophers, biologists, linguists and computer scientists gone towards this satisfaction? The happy conclusion is that nothing in the Basic Guess turns out to be too startling. It paves the way for the rest of the book to look at its consequences (thirteen of them), which aim to describe the many fascinating mechanisms that may be at work in making conscious objects conscious.

Defining My Own Consciousness

The only consciousness that I can be absolutely sure of is my own. So any attempt at defining consciousness will start by having an intimate character, the character of a confession or a personal diary. It was to stress this point that US philosopher Thomas Nagel (1974) posed the celebrated question "What is it like to be a bat?". He argued that no amount of knowledge of the neurophysiology of a bat will lead a human to know what it is like to be a bat without being a bat. He concluded that neurophysiology is inadequate in giving a full account of consciousness. I believe that while this is an intriguing point of view, it addresses the wrong question. The question I wish to address is "What aspect of neurophysiology lets a conscious object feel that *it* is conscious?". Put another way, the question is "What do I need to have in my head in order for me to believe I am conscious?" or even "What does a machine need to have for it to believe it is conscious?". I do not believe that this will tell me exactly what it is like to be a bat or a machine, except to the extent that I can put my own experience to use to try imagining what it is like to be a bat or, perhaps more easily, a machine.

The fascination with consciousness, despite its very personal nature, is shared by a large number of humans and has been so down through the ages. Since the beginning of recorded philosophy, thinkers have tried to share their views of what consciousness is with a wide audience. Inevitably these discussions have started with each philosopher's own thoughts about being conscious. Therefore it seems quite proper for me, even if I wish to rely on logical argument, to start with this introspective view of my own consciousness. I then guess that readers will be able to relate what I say to their own feelings. I may not be able to know what it feels like to be a bat, but I may be able to speculate on what a bat may be able to feel, once I can work out how what *I* feel is based on what I know about my own brain. The first step is to try to articulate what precisely it is about my own consciousness which makes me curious about it.

Psychologists talk of the conscious state in contrast with the unconscious state. Being conscious means being awake as opposed to being anaesthetised or just fast asleep. When I am awake, being "me" comes from the major sensations of my knowing who I am, perceiving and understanding where I am, knowing what I have done in the past and what, according to my current perception, I can do in the future. I can also discuss all of this, and mainly with those who share my language. The property which is common to all these attributes is "knowing" — a knowing which stretches from the very personal which I may choose to share with nobody to the knowing of language or knowing how to bake a good apple pie. What I would like to know, what needs to be explained about consciousness, is how this personal "me-ness" relates not only to my brain, but to the rest of my physical make-up and the nature of the world I live in.

The intriguing "me-ness" that makes me curious about consciousness is what I have included in the first phrase of the Basic Guess, i.e. *personal sensations*.

The Consciousness of Others

The hunt for consciousness has so far seemed to be a highly introverted affair. This is intended to be just a start which needs development and amplification. In discussions about consciousness it seems important to include any object which could possibly be deemed to be conscious. So, in the Basic Guess, the word *organism* is used to include objects other than ourselves. Is an ant conscious? A cat? A pencil? The Internet? The universe? The use of the word *personal* is not intended to refer only to "persons". It points to owner-ship and individuality, in the sense that an ant could have a *personal* way of reacting to an obstacle. By using *personal* in conjunction with *sensation* and *organism* I include objects that primarily must be capa-ble of sensing things not only externally but in some internal way too (much will be made of internal sensing later). Clearly, an ant has sensations which it owns and are therefore personal to that ant, but the same may not be true of a pencil. Why would we shrink from saying that a pencil senses the paper on which it is made to write?

The difference between an ant and a pencil is that the antenna of an ant is a sensor which translates pressure into an electrical signal which can lead to a change in what the rest of the ant is doing. It may change direction or speed. Importantly, the ant is capable of an outward action and the outward action is dictated by some condition of the ant's internal machinery. So sensing leads to a change of state of the inner machinery which may lead to a change in outward action. Figure 2.1 illustrates these components.

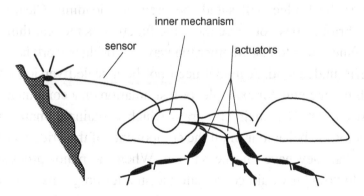

Fig. 2.1. Sensor (antenna)–mechanism (brain)–actuator (legs) arrangement for an ant.

I suggest that in order to be scrutinised for some kind of consciousness, organisms must, minimally, have some inner machinery which may be controlled by sensors and which is capable of acting in some physical outward way. The outward action in living organisms is usually due to the contraction of some muscles which work in the opposite way to sensors. Muscles receive electrical signals and turn them into physical actions. Engineers call such outputs "actuators". This broad definition lets in clockwork mice, ants, cats and Uncle Harry. A point that I shall make very often is that any study of consciousness should allow a broad range of organisms, but, at the same time, enable us to say with clarity why the consciousness of a clockwork mouse is pretty trivial while that of Uncle Harry is very impressive.

The Power of Modelling

What is beginning to emerge from the above is the idea of a "model". Sometimes in science, but principally in engineering, models are used to test an understanding of a phenomenon by means of a kind of mock-up. For example, if a bridge is to be built, the civil engineer may think it wise to build a scale model to test whether the bridge will stand the predicted loading. Clearly the model bridge does not serve the same function as the real thing; its main function is to test whether the way that bridges work has been properly understood. A model need not be a scaled version of the real thing; it could, for example, be a simulation on a computer. This would consist of a major program which contained smaller programs for the behaviour of all the components of the bridge and the effect that they have on one another. When the major program is made to "run" it would coordinate the smaller programs and invite the user of the machine to specify a load for the bridge. The program would calculate the effect of the load on all the components and show the amount by which the bridge would deform under the load and whether there might be a collapse. Indeed the bridge could be tested to destruction without incurring the cost of any damage.

The model would be seen by some as a list of mathematical laws that govern the components and their interactions. Mathematicians would call this a set of equations, with which, given the value of the load, they may be able to work out whether the bridge will stand up or not.

I have said that, in order to begin discussing the consciousness of an organism, a minimal list of objects, sensors, inner machinery and actuators is needed; this spells out a framework for a model which will apply to all such organisms. The distilled nature of this framework is shown in Fig. 2.2.

The vague part of this model, and the part which will enable us to talk of the sophistication of the modelled system, is the "inner machinery". A neat trick that engineers have for modelling even the most complex of systems is to think of the inner machinery as being capable of being in a number of "states". Part of the inner machinery of a car, for example, is the gears. A five-gear car has five gear-states, each such state determining a different way in which actuators (the force on the driving wheels) respond to sensors (e.g. the force on the accelerator pedal, the weight of the car, the slope of the road, the angle of the wheels).

The beauty of this approach is that any complex mechanism can be modelled by the technique — a point which will be explained in

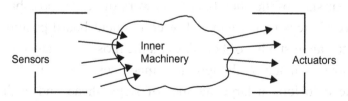

Fig. 2.2.   Framework for a model.

some detail in Chapter 3. For the moment, what has been said only explains the appearance in the Basic Guess of the words "state machine". The model framework of Fig. 2.2, when the inner mechanism is represented by states, is a state machine. The words indicate that the general power of such state machines will be used as model which, as in the case of the model of the bridge, will give us a way of checking that what is being said about brains, minds and consciousness is consistent and coherent.

The Danger of Inappropriate Modelling

There are appropriate and inappropriate models, and all of them could be run on a computer. I don't mean that a model could be just wrong. What I do mean is that a model can arrive at the right answer without providing the understanding it was meant to provide. Partly, this is the sad story of the field called artificial intelligence (AI). Defined as "doing on computers that which if done by humans would require intelligence", AI was the "in" thing in computing laboratories in the 1970s. AI programs were meant to be models of human cognition, i.e. human thinking. Probably the most familiar product of this work is the chess-playing machine, which every respectable executive toyshop will sell. Expensive versions, requiring many massive computers, have recently threatened chess masters and will in the future probably beat them regularly. These systems are based on the programmer's notion of how a good game of chess might be played. The computer is made to look ahead of a particular state of the chessboard and work out every possible move for several steps of the game. The consequent board positions are evaluated against a list of benefits and the most advantageous available move is made. Although such machines can easily beat me, they need to look a large number of steps ahead and evaluate a prodigious number of board positions to beat a good player.

While such machines have their fascination and merit, their designers cannot pretend to have made models of human thinking. On television, champion players are sometimes asked to comment on the replays of their games. They say things such as "... he's got me in a tight corner now ... but I think I can win if I keep on fighting for seven or eight moves ... I could sacrifice a pawn to give him a false sense of confidence ... I know he doesn't like using his Queen's Bishop ...". This is no mechanical evaluation of moves.

The player is using a wealth of experience, cunning and even a psychological knowledge of his opponent. So, while the AI program plays a game which humans play, it is not possible to say that it is a model of a human player. It is merely a programmer's idea of how a machine might play the game. It is for this reason that AI skeptics will say that a computer model which absorbs and stores a story represented in natural language, and then answers questions, does not necessarily understand the story. This is the nature of John Searle's objection to AI (mentioned in Chapter 1). He argues that a programmer can write complex programs which are very good at manipulating words by means of many rules, without capturing what is meant by "understanding". Thinking about the Humpty Dumpty rhyme, if asked, "Why could he not be mended?", I would probably answer, "Because he broke into too many pieces." I do this by appealing to my experience and knowledge that Humpty Dumpty was an eggshell and eggshells shatter when you drop them. The computer would have to have rules such as "fragile things are hard to mend" and "Humpty Dumpty was a fragile egg".

Some who have given much thought to the problems of consciousness (e.g. Penrose) take this argument to mean that any model that runs on a computer cannot be an appropriate model of consciousness, as running on a computer is in a different category from living and knowing. I argue that this is not so. The examples above are inappropriate, incomplete models because they do not have their own way of building up and accessing experience. This does not mean that appropriate models do not exist. Appropriate models of the mechanisms of consciousness have to answer the question of how consciousness is built up and cannot simply be AI mock-ups with mechanisms supplied by a programmer's idea of what consciousness is. It is this need for appropriateness which leads to an appeal to neural models in the Basic Guess, as is explained below.

Why Neurons?

We come back here to the idea of inner states. What are they in a living brain?

The building brick of the brain is the neuron — a cell which receives signals from other neurons (input) and transmits a signal to further neurons (output). This is illustrated in Fig. 2.3. Without wishing to minimise the beautiful and detailed electrochemical properties of neurons found by neurobiologists, the essence of what a neuron

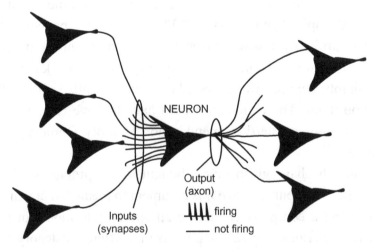

Fig. 2.3.   A neuron in a net of neurons.

does can be described very simply. At times, the neuron generates at its output (called the "axon") a stream of electrical impulses (about 100 impulses each second) and, at other times, almost no impulses at all. It is said that the neuron either "fires" or "does not fire" to describe these two conditions. Whether a neuron fires or not is determined by the current pattern of firing and non-firing of the "input" neurons (the input connections are called "synapses").

Which input pattern leads to firing and which does not is something that the neuron can learn (this will be explained below). Much more of this will be explained in Chapter 3 — here we are still on the path of trying to define an inner state of the model as implied in the Basic Guess. Figure 2.4 shows the way in which a network of neurons could be seen to form the interior of the model in Fig. 2.2. Labelling the five neurons as "a", "b", "c", "d" and "e", it is clear that the actuators can only react to what "d" and "e" are doing. The others, "a", "b" and "c", are the inner neurons which create the internal states. How many of these states are there?

As each of the inner neurons can either fire (f) or not fire (n), "a", "b" and "c" can be in eight states: fff, ffn, fnf, fnn, nff, nfn, nnf and nnn. The number of inner states can be calculated for any number of neurons N (it turns out to be 2^N).[5] These inner states are

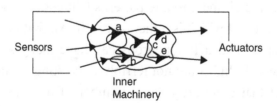

Fig. 2.4.   A neural net model.

---

[5] For one neuron there are 2 states, and for two neurons there are $2 \times 2 = 4$ states; so, in general, for N neurons there are $2 \times 2 \times 2 \ldots$ (N times) states. This is written as 2^N.

particularly interesting because of the inner network of connections. This makes "a", "b" and "c" interdependent — it gives them a behaviour "of their own". This property is thought to be essential for representing concepts such as "thinking". Even if the sensory inputs of the organism are unchanging and the effect of the "thought" is not immediately discernible at the actuators, the inner states can change. That is, the model can represent private, inner events. Each of the inner neurons has been called a state variable in the Basic Guess, which is meant to suggest that much of the privacy that goes with consciousness, much of the inner thought that is so central to the mental makeup of a living organism, can be modelled by the activity of inner neurons.

Returning for a moment to the number of states of a neural mechanism, it is salutary to think that the human brain has ten billion neurons, which implies that the number of inner thoughts a human being can have is astronomical. Imagine for the sake of argument that a human has one hundred "thoughts" (inner states) a second. In a lifetime of, say, one hundred years this would amount to a total of 316 billion thoughts. The amazing implication of the 2^N rule is that only 39 neurons are required to have that number of states! What's wrong with this calculation? Why do we have so many neurons in our heads? The problem lies with the coding of these states. The 316 billion states are all the possible patterns that could appear on a row of 39 lights each of which is either on or off. All that this calculation does is to show that a few neurons can have many states, but the states on these 39 lights are not terribly interesting or meaningful.

The fact that there are a large number of neurons in the brain points to the idea that each thought could be encoded in a much richer, more interesting way than could be done with only 39 lights. That is, with billions of lights one could represent colourful and detailed pictures, as is done in the advertisements which, at night, adorn Piccadilly Circus or Times Square. Could each thought

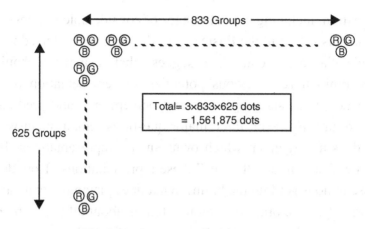

Fig. 2.5. Dots on a television screen.

resemble a television picture? Let's pursue this hypothetical idea. The screen of a colour television set is made up of tiny groups of dots, as shown in Fig. 2.5. Each group has three dots, one for each primary colour (red, blue and green). Being generous, say that 10 neurons are used to control the intensity of one dot, something of the order of 16 million neurons could represent a frame of a full colour television picture. Now, the cortex in the brain (the outer sheet which is involved in sensory processing, particularly vision) has tens of billions of neurons with a density of about 100,000 per square millimetre, the whole cortex spanning about half a square metre (the size of a large handkerchief) if stretched out. So, an area of the size of a thumbnail (160 square millimetres) would contain the 16 million neurons capable of giving us an "inner" TV show for a lifetime.

I hasten to add that I am not suggesting that the mental images which are so much a part of our conscious life are generated in a small area of the cortex. As Crick (1994) points out, we may not know where neurons associated with conscious thinking can be found in a living brain. However, the point of all this is that it draws attention to the massive power of the neural networks we carry in our head which is such as to be able to represent a great deal of information, including mental images of considerable richness. It is for this reason that in the Basic Guess the neuron is referred to as a variable of a state machine. This suggests that the inner mechanisms of the brain have enormous potential for representation of past experience, understanding of current perceptionss and predictions of the future. However, three major questions remain unanswered. How does an organism which owns such a representational brain also "own" and internally "see" these representations? How do the representations get into the brain? What does playing with an artificial brain (i.e. the brain of Magnus) tell us about all this? The next three sections show how the Basic Guess reflects these issues.

The Mind's Eye

If I sit in a darkened and quiet room, I can think of many previously experienced events. I can remember things as different as last night's dinner, driving to work, Pythagoras' theorem or Mahler's second symphony. To me, my brain appears to be a veritable multimedia computer. Seeing and hearing appear not to go away just because my sensory organs are currently inactive. The Basic Guess takes an extremely simple view of how this might happen.

If we touch something with a finger the pressure-sensing neurons in our fingers cause the firing of some neurons in our brains. It is this inner firing to which we give the name "sensation". It is well known from the anatomy of the brain that different neurons are associated with different sensory parts of our body, so if I touch something with my tongue, a bunch of neurons in my brain fires, but this is a different bunch from that which fires when I touch something with my finger. In fact neurophysiologists have mapped out how the different touch-sensing organs of the body map onto an area of the cortex in the brain called "the sensory strip" (Fig. 2.6).

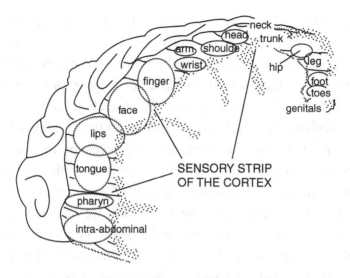

Fig. 2.6. The sensory strip in the cortex.

Figure 2.6 shows this mapping in the left part of the cortex which corresponds to the right side of the body. There is a similar strip on the right side of the cortex which corresponds to the left of the body. It is not my intention to launch into a lesson on neuro-anatomy; I merely draw attention to the very important property of the brain to reflect, in miniature, patterns sensed by the outer surfaces of our bodies. However, when I touch something, while neurons are firing in my sensory strip, the sensation I have appears to be "in my finger". The reason for this is that while the touch sensors are active, much other firing in other parts of the brain is associated with that event. Many muscles are holding appropriate positions to get the tip of my finger to where it is. Every time a muscle does something, it sends signals back to the brain which cause further firing of neurons in parts other than the sensory strip. Indeed, as we shall see in the next chapter, an action strip which relates to the muscles in the tongue, mouth, etc. lies close to the sensory strip in the cortex. We shall see in later chapters that these multi-channel patterns give us a sense of self: patterns in the brain are related to where bits of our body are and what they are sensing.

Now, suppose that one such pattern of inputs can be stimulated artificially (as might happen during a brain operation); the patient could be fooled into thinking that she is feeling something very specific with the tip of a finger. Returning to the question of where pictures in our heads come from, it is only necessary to think of the sensory retina at the back of the eyeball as a set of densely packed sensitive "fingers" which cause patterns of neurons to fire in the visual part of the cortex, causing a sensation we call "seeing". The same goes for smell and hearing, and again some internal stimulation of these neurons could produce the sensation of seeing or hearing in our heads. There have been many reports of patients whose brains were artificially stimulated during brain surgery — they heard symphonies, saw visions and smelled flowers. In other words, in common with all other living organisms we *own* a representation of the world as specific combinations of the firing of neurons in our brains. The key property of such patterns is that they are self-sustaining for a while, and may be triggered by sensory experience or other inner events. That is, we could report a particular firing experience as "seeing" a dog or "thinking" of a dog, depending on whether the trigger was external or internal. It is not being said that the acuity of the two patterns is the same — we see a dog with greater clarity and specificity than we think of a dog. On the other hand we can think of one of several dogs we know. We could even imagine a dog we have never seen before. Much more will be said in other parts of this book of the way in which such rich and varied representations can coexist in one, limited piece of neural machinery. Here I merely stress the importance of the use of the term *firing patterns* in the Basic Guess. Next, I need to say something about how such firing patterns get into brains, a process which is sometimes called "learning".

Learning and Remembering

A primary property of the neuron is that, in some raw, "inexperienced" state, it can be made to fire by incoming stimulation. For example, the firing of a sensory nerve in the tip of the finger caused by pressure makes a neuron in the sensory strip (Fig. 2.6) fire, a bit like a bell ringing inside the house when the doorbell is pressed. Learning consists in the neuron "taking note" of the pattern present at its other inputs (exactly how it does this is left to Chapter 3). Learning is complete when the firing of the neuron is controlled by the patterns the neuron has "taken note" of. With Fig. 2.7 I shall try to explain how several neurons may be working together to "remember" patterns of sensory input. The figure represents a system (a bit

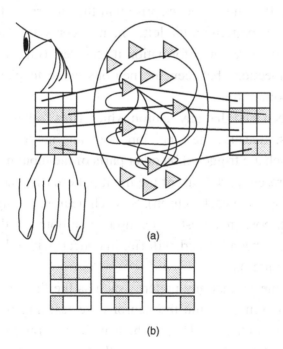

(a)

(b)

Fig. 2.7.   (a) The net and its connections to fingers and an eye. (b) Three learned sensory experiences.

of Magnus, say) with three "fingers" and an "eye". This is a purely fictitious system, nothing exactly like it is likely to exist in the brain. But things a bit like this do go on in the brain and, according to the Basic Guess, underpin conscious experience.

In Fig. 2.7(a), the arrangement of squares on the left is merely a way of showing what various sensory elements are doing. The bottom line shows shaded squares where the sensors in the fingers are causing firing to enter the net. That which is sensed by some kind of "retina" in the eye is shown as a 3 × 3 arrangement, shaded squares again representing the connections which are firing (a horizontal bar is seen). All these sensory connections enter the neural net (for which only some of the connections are shown). Any neuron in this net which receives a firing signal is itself assumed to fire and the firing of the net neurons is shown in the arrangement of squares on the right. It comes as no surprise that the pattern on the right is the same as the pattern on the left. The net seems to be just a relay station which passes on information it receives. But it is here that the interconnections between the neurons come to play an enormously important role.

It has been said that any neuron which fires "takes note" of its other inputs. Because the other inputs of any neuron come from neurons which are triggered by other parts of the input pattern, they actually represent part or all of the input pattern (depending on the number of inputs to each neuron). So each neuron, through the fact that it will fire when almost all its input conditions are the same as those that have been learned, will fire in concert with other neurons for learned patterns.

All this means that any pattern [such as the three examples in (b)] which is sensed while the neurons are learning will become self-sustaining in the net. That is, the learned patterns can appear in the right hand set of squares even if they are not sensed. What's more, they can be made to appear by partial firing patterns at the input. In human terms, this is like saying that the cross seen by the eye in (b) is "felt" by the left finger, the square by the middle finger and the X by the right finger. The fact that the net can sustain only these combinations means that if the right finger is stimulated and the other two are not, the net will reconstruct the associated X within itself and "see" X but only with some "inner eye".

All the ins and outs of this fascinating property have not been explained here, and the reader may feel that it is all a bit complicated. Chapter 4 is chiefly devoted to a step-by-step explanation of this, the ancient puzzle of the "inner eye". The mechanism just described is merely an appetiser for things to come, but one which is meant to explain why the following words have been used in the Basic Guess:

> ... *the firing patterns having been learned through a transfer of activity between sensory input neurons and the state neurons.*

In a Nutshell ...

Before measuring the above beliefs about consciousness against those of ancestors and contemporaries, it is worth revisiting the Basic Guess in a way which is less terse than that found at the beginning of this chapter. Consciousness, according to the Basic Guess, has all to do with the sensations which each of us has within our heads. The key submission is that such sensations are due entirely to the firing of some neurons. But the firing of these neurons is highly conditioned by sensory experience. A neuron is not only driven by the perception while the act of perception is in course, but also takes note of what many other neurons are doing at the time. As these other neurons also represent other parts of the perception, learning creates self-sustained patterns in networks of neurons and these patterns have an "internal" existence of their own. They can be triggered by part of the perception, such as "touch", leading to the internal "vision" of what is being touched. A distant roll of thunder may make us conscious of impending danger or, more poetically, the smell of a flower in spring may make us conscious of the longing for someone we love. Association is a highly important mechanism which comes naturally to networks of learning neurons. It has also been said that the sensations which neurons can produce can be astronomical in number and highly complex in their interrelations. Some may call the Basic Guess "oversimplified". I recommend the reader to embrace simplicity as a friend — it does not detract from the sense of awe at the way a neural net can conjure up both the beauty and the usefulness of a rich mental life. So far, only the surface of an explanation has been touched — more questions have been raised than answered. What is awareness of self? What is free will? These and many other questions are the subjects for the rest of the book, where an attempt is made to provide the answers through the use of methods introduced in this chapter.

There is, however, a question of some importance which needs to be answered in *this* chapter. If consciousness is really generated by the simple mechanisms suggested by the Basic Guess, why has this not been obvious to thinkers who, both over the centuries and in recent times, have puzzled over what the phenomenon is or is not? Part of the answer may be that the idea of a "state machine" is relatively new. It has been known for forty or so years. This is not very long in a history which stretches back for several millennia. Also, while the principles of state machines are commonplace for some computer scientists and engineers, they do not feature in the thinking of many modern philosophers and others who have attempted to describe consciousness. They are treated with suspicion and put in the class of modelling through the use of "golems". Indeed, some contemporary philosophers (e.g. Lucas, 1994) have an explicit distaste for this kind of modelling as they argue that the model, being synthesised, is devoid of the very thing one is searching for: an independent existence or "coming into being". The model has a "constructed" identity which makes it invalid. Here we shall try to keep an open mind on this issue and not hold back from gaining insight if such insight is in the offing.

Philosophy and Consciousness

The new student and the engineer

The students who sit excitedly at the first lecture of their chosen university course in philosophy believe that the professor will sweep to the podium in a black gown and explain what philosophy is and say how wise such students are for being interested in the subject. Rarely are such expectations fulfilled. It is more likely that they will be confronted by a keen young lecturer in a hurry, whose interest is wholly absorbed by the paper he is writing on the umpteenth interpretation of a paragraph of Wittgenstein's writings. He will soon disabuse the bold questioner who, at the end of the lecture, asks, "Can you define philosophy, please sir?" It is the nature of philosophy, he will say, to avoid asking simplistic questions. The true nature of philosophy will be discovered after three years of studying three millennia of the writings of great philosophers and the subtleties of the interpretation of their ideas by contemporary sages. "But what are they writing about?" will ask the student who is already being marked down by the lecturer for a very poor degree classification. If an answer comes forth at all it may be something like "… the nature of things".

My concern as an engineer and an outsider to philosophy is to find out when, in the last three thousand years, philosophers concerned with "the nature of things" put consciousness on their list of interests and how they presented their thoughts on the subject. (By the way, Wittgenstein studied engineering before becoming one of the more enigmatic philosophers of this century — I shall return to this later.) The first realisation is that the word "consciousness" could be seen as having made a relatively recent entry into the English version of the philosophical vocabulary. As suggested below, the event seems to me to have happened at the end of the seventeenth century through the writings of John Locke. Evidently, discussions about consciousness overlap a great deal with discussions about "what is mind?". The latter stretches a long way back in recorded history. I shall return to this later too. Here it may be important to focus on the origins of contemporary debates: why do philosophers still find it hard to agree about consciousness? So, the next few sections could be entitled "An Engineer in a Philosophical Wonderland". I have not written a comprehensive text on the history of the philosophy of consciousness; just a daisy-chain of the ideas of eminent philosophers mainly from the seventeenth century to the present day. These ideas not only fuel and illuminate contemporary debates about the nature of consciousness, but also constitute the folklore on which the Basic Guess is founded.

Descartes (1596–1650)

Many will say that modern philosophy began with René Descartes. Born in France, he had a strict Catholic upbringing and retained his faith through life. In the history of the philosophy of consciousness he is often quoted as the prime exponent of dualism, the idea that mind and matter have largely independent existences (with some interaction in what Descartes thought to be the pineal gland). In retrospect, Descartes is seen as a general in an army of "rationalists" who believe that mind can arrive at logical truths with no reference to experience [examples of others being Benedict de Spinoza (1632–1677) and Gottfried Wilhelm Leibnitz (1646–1716)]. It is clear that such purity of thought may instinctively appear to be true when a mathematician develops a proof of an abstract algebraic theorem, but is hard to accept as a description of the mental activity which accompanies everyday life. The reader will find objections to dualism in most modern writing on the philosophy of consciousness, so I shall not dwell on it further.

Indeed, the Basic Guess indicates that much of the content of this book is devoted to the puzzle of the way in which sensory experience translates into what we call our consciousness, including the "purity" of doing mathematics. This is contrary to the belief of dualists.

Locke (1632–1704)

Probably the first philosopher to identify consciousness as a matter for particular attention is John Locke, the giant of British philosophy of the seventeenth century. Self-knowledge came under his scrutiny in *Essay Concerning Human Understanding* (1690). He came to the conclusion that we can account for all the ideas in our minds through experience as indicated to our brains by the senses. This belief (in contrast to earlier beliefs of rationalists that knowledge is somehow given or innate) is an element of *empiricism* and Locke is often referred to as the founder of British empiricism. He used "understanding" as the word which underlay his thesis, although what was later seen as the puzzle of consciousness was clearly embedded in his quest:

> "First, I shall enquire into the original of those ideas, notions, or whatever else you please to call them, which a man observes and is conscious to himself he has in his mind; and the way in which the understanding comes to be furnished with them." (Ch. i. 4.)

He made much of introspection as a secondary source of ideas and mental constructs, the primary one being a function of the properties of objects. This was a highly controversial view at the time, as it had been widely accepted that core ideas were somehow inborn and other forms of thinking heavily dependent on this core. In the latter parts of the essay, Locke stressed the importance of language in the formation and representation of ideas. Although the details of his thinking were later questioned and criticised, there is no doubt that he made mental representation of experience a matter for philosophical study — a step beyond the notion of mind as "stuff" which had to be understood in its own right. It is precisely the same fascination with mental representation of experience that underpins the structure of the Basic Guess and its corollaries.

Where the Basic Guess differs from Locke's outlook is in a concern with the *mechanism* of consciousness. Locke sees this concern as being a distraction from true inquiry:

> "... I shall not at present meddle with the physical consideration of the mind, or trouble myself to examine wherein its essence consists, or by what motions of our spirits or alterations of our bodies we come to have any sensation by our organs, or any ideas in our understandings; and whether those ideas do, in their formation, any or all of them, depend on matter or not." (Ch. i. 2.)

Philosophers from time to time in the history of their subject have shown a certain fatigue with the mind–body problem. In the above passage, Locke is thought to be referring to the writing of Thomas Hobbes (1588–1679), who [in "Human Nature" (Ch. ii. 4)] referred to image or colour as:

> "... the motion, agitation, or alteration which the object worketh in the brain, or spirits, or some internal substance in the head."

It is unlikely that Locke would have been given to discourse which he could not trace to first principles. One imagines that he saw the state of the mind–body problem as having got to a stale impasse, as "agitations or alterations" were speculative and not useful in a discourse about experience and understanding. Are things different now? Obviously I think yes; in an age of information processing I think that it is possible to interpret "which the object worketh in the brain" with greater conviction than was possible sixty years ago, not to mention three centuries ago.

Curiously, the mind–body problem is one which permeates not only philosophy but also engineering science under a different heading: the function–structure problem. Were I to find an electronic circuit lying in the street and discover that the labels on the silicon chips were obliterated, could I, simply by sketching out the wiring diagram, work out what that circuit was designed to do? The specific answer is negative, but, through the use of state machine theory, I could say something about the "set" or collection of functions it could do and, in consequence, that which it could not do. More of this in the next chapter; here it is sufficient to say that the choice of neural state machine theory as the language of the Basic Guess just might take the argument about mind and body beyond the sterility which Locke had recognised in the seventeenth century, a sterility which still casts a shadow of concern even among the most materialistic of commentators on the nature of consciousness.

Much more could be said about Locke's concerns about a human's conscious understanding of the world and the way this has entered the beliefs of even those who are not students of philosophy. I shall just stress one feature among many: his division of mental events into primary and secondary categories. If I think of a rock, I would describe it as a solid object, or if I think of my left hand I would agree with any other observer that it has five fingers on it. Solidity and number are what Locke would call primary ideas, while other properties of objects, such as colour or beauty, are secondary as being truly a function of the perceptual system of the beholder. Were there no colour receptors in the retina or emotions aroused by perceptions, colour and beauty would not exist. This division is important mainly because of the influence it had on philosophers who succeeded Locke. From the standpoint of a neural state machine model of consciousness, Locke and his successors have created a bedrock of important questions about the translation of sensory experience into mental representation which the model needs to address.

Berkeley (1685–1753)

Remembered by students of philosophy as the person who suggested that objects cease to exist if they are not perceived by someone, George Berkeley deserves deeper recognition. He took Locke's idea that objects have properties which are modulated by our senses, to its logical conclusion. There are no primary properties such as solidity and number. He argued that these too are ideas that come to us through our senses. The very existence of any object is dependent on the fact that we can sense such existence with our senses. For example, we strongly debate the existence phenomena we have not all experienced: ghosts, extra-sensory communication and the like. A man of religion (he was Bishop of Cloyne in Ireland), Berkeley supported his belief in the existence of God with the notion of existence through perception. The unobserved tree would not disappear from the quad when human eyes were not on it simply because it was under the eyes of God. God, therefore, as Christianity has always had it, is responsible for the existence of all objects on Earth.

For an engineer, the progress of philosophy has a character which contrasts curiously with that of science. In science, valid explanations of a phenomenon fit together to form a developing understanding — a paradigm. Thomas Kuhn, of course, has pointed out that such edifices sometimes crumble as a result of new evidence. On the whole, scientists contribute to bits of the jigsaw. In philosophy it seems as if a great deal of radical revision occurs as the thoughts of a philosopher come into ascendancy. So George Berkeley clarified for himself parts of Locke's thinking which seemed to him not to have been followed to its logical conclusion. With Berkeley, the fledgling idea of consciousness reached a height of belief that reality exists only to the extent that it is forged by ideas in our heads, such ideas being driven by perception. The submission of a transfer between sensory and mental neural behaviour in the Basic Guess suggests that a grain of Berkeley's influence survives. But Locke and Berkeley's clay, with which the idea of consciousness appeared to be moulded, has gone through many wondrous shapes during the last quarter of this millennium. These all leave a trace in some collection of personal ideas which define consciousness not only for philosophers and neural modellers, but for us all.

Hume (1711–1776)

In reading about David Hume, I get the impression of a forcefully unconventional character. Born into a Calvinist family of minor Scottish gentry, at the age of not quite twelve, he entered Edinburgh University, where he was exposed to science and philosophy. He left at the age of fifteen as a confirmed atheist and without a degree. He wrote many major works (some anonymously), among them *Inquiry into Human Understanding*. It may not be an accident that this title is close to Locke's *Essay*. Hume appears to have felt it necessary to create a distinction between mental representations all of which Locke had called "secondary". The recollection of a tree in blossom on a cold winter's night is not the same as the sensation of actually seeing the tree in the spring. Hume made a distinction between "impressions" which have the force and violence of current experience and "ideas" which are the faint recollections of experience used in reasoning. Ideas are further divided into "simple" and "complex". Simple ideas have a direct relationship with impressions. Memories of objects and events are simple while images of distant lands never seen but only heard described are complex and belong to the realm of imagination.

Hume had also a clear view of abstract, complex ideas. He recognised that there are natural or instinctive ways in which human beings react to perceived events. For example, Elena in Jane Austen's *Sense and Sensibility*, on meeting Edward, a charming and attentive man, may experience an internal emotion which she knows is given the name "love". The reader of the novel who has experienced love then continues to believe that Elena talks and thinks of love as a real but complex idea.

Without having ever experienced love, the reader would only think of it as a word and not as a real idea. Therefore Hume was very much in agreement with Berkeley that human understanding is vitally dependent on perception and experience for ideas which range widely from the memory of objects to abstract notions.

In contemporary philosophy, Hume is criticised mainly for having anchored his theory of ideas too closely to observed things, thus making it incapable of dealing with *general* concepts such as "ape" standing for a category of things and not just observed examples. This (as described by Bertrand Russell, 1961) also leads to a repudiation of self (as it is never directly observed) which is so central to contemporary debate about consciousness. While self cannot feature as a simple idea in Hume's scheme of things, it can enter the mental world as a bundle of perceptions and this, according to Russell, is the way that Hume made an important advance on Berkeley.

In the ideas presented in this book, I recognise the influence of Hume in having introduced systematic and important questions about the nature of complex ideas into the folklore of consciousness. They reappear in many parts of this book, and specifically the relationship of self to perception dominates Chapter 5.

When it comes to Hume as a person, I am struck by several things. According to Shand (1993), Hume was aware that his philosophy as advanced in an early book, *Treatise into Human Nature*, as well as *Enquiry* made important contributions. But he was surprised that his ideas received little attention at the time of their publication. Indeed he had difficulties in getting *Treatise* published and was not accepted by the academic establishment of the day, having had his applications for a professorship of philosophy at Edinburgh University in 1745 and the Chair of Logic at Glasgow University in 1751 turned down. He wrote while working as a clerk, a diplomatic secretary, a personal secretary and a librarian. It was not the first time nor certainly the last that the academic establishment acted for the preservation of traditions rather than as a seed-bed for radical ideas.

Kant (1724–1807)

Reading Locke, Berkeley and Hume gives one the impression that philosophy in the eighteenth century was very much a British affair. However, major philosophical movements were coming into being in both France and Germany. In France, Jean Jacques Rousseau became the main spokesman for romanticism which emphasised the *self* in a social way rather than as a function experience. Romanticism is sometimes described as a humanitarian reaction to the cold and clinical character of British empiricism. Immanuel Kant was the German who, while agreeing with the role of experience in empiricism, felt that innate abilities of reasoning had not been appropriately treated. Said by Russell to be "generally considered to be the greatest of modern philosophers" (although Russell reserves his own position on this), Kant was the model of a donnish academic. A man of regular habits and few distractions, he was (again according to Russell) able to address audiences of scholars where the British empiricists were "gentlemen ... addressing amateurs".

In *The Critique of Pure Reason* (Kant, 1781) it is clear that Kant was sure that, at times, knowledge appears to transcend experience. For example, were I to play with toy blocks I would experience that adding one block to another would lead to my possession of two blocks. There are many properties I would learn to associate with two blocks in contrast with just one; for example, they need a bigger box for keeping in, they are heavier, and so on. However, I can generalise this experience to thinking about what might happen if I possessed an elephant and someone gave me another. I need not actually go out to buy elephants and carry out the experiment to acquire this experience. In other words, playing with blocks elicits a generality within me which transcends the original experience and encourages me to recognise that $1+1=2$. Kant is known for having defined a form of "transcendentalism" which recognises that we possess the ability to decide whether a proposition is true or not. That is, Kant has responded to the need to explain "knowledge":

> "... which is occupied not so much with objects as with our mode
> of cognition of objects, so far as this is possible *a priori*." (*The
> Critique of Pure Reason*, B25, A11–12.)

It is said that the problem of transcendentalism occupied Kant's mind for twelve years, but once resolved, *Critique* took only a few months to write. He sought to reconcile the concerns of the empiricists for the importance of experience on one hand, with the existence of internal abilities on the other, without returning to earlier mystical explanations about the nature of eternal truths (which a hundred years earlier Leibnitz, for example, had explained as coming from the mind of God). He was very precise about this:

— Propositions can be either "analytic" or "synthetic".
— Analytic propositions contain logical truths.

For example, if it is known analytically that a "black horse" is still a "horse", or that an upturned tumbler is still a tumbler …

— Synthetic propositions depend on experience and cannot be checked inwardly for absolute truth.

For example, the proposition "there is a horse in the stable" can only be verified by observation. The major distinction between Kant's thinking on synthetic propositions and that of his predecessors is the suggestion that experience is not involved in all synthetic propositions:

— Synthetic propositions can be either *empirical* or *a priori*.
— Empirical propositions can only be known through perception or a trusted linguistic report.

For example, "there is a horse in the stable" is an empirical synthetic proposition.

— *A priori* propositions are elicited by experience but become general.

For example, "two plus two is four" is not analytic in the sense that it may require to be taught by example (psychologists are fond of showing how children need this experience to form proper concepts of "volume", for example). It is the generalisation that sets in from a few examples which is seen by Kant as being *a priori*. Indeed he would see knowledge based on both arithmetic and geometry as being in the synthetic *a priori* class. But how can such knowledge come about? The depth of Kant's argument deserves a little more attention here.

— Space and time are imposed on reality by the perceptual apparatus.

Understanding space and time is the same as anticipating the function of our bodily (mental) apparatus which enables us to scan over space and notice the passage of time. More subtle are four other sets of *a priori* concepts (or "categories", as Kant called them) imposed by our mental apparatus on sensory information.

— Quantity: unity, plurality, totality.
— Quality: reality, negation, limitation.
— Of relation: substance and accident; cause and effect, reciprocity.
— Of modality: possibility, existence and necessity.

For example, in the unity category of quantities, if we happen to be looking at one particular building in a town, the unity of the observation is imposed by ourselves; there may be nothing unique about the building we happen to have chosen.

There is a great deal more that could be said about Kant's views and justifications of elements of consciousness, and the reader whose attention has been held by the above paragraphs is encouraged to read Kant and the many books which have been written about him. My aim is satisfied in showing how progress in the philosophy of consciousness is moulded anew with each major philosopher and how this would not be possible without the ideas generated by his predecessors. Through this process philosophers' ideas enter general culture and form part of what really needs to be explained — that which has been retained in this culture as making sense in terms of what we all feel about mind and consciousness.

Returning to the Basic Guess, some may say that it does not measure up to the sophistication of Kant's ideas for not having moved on from some kind of trivial empiricism. What I need to stress is that the Basic Guess is about the mechanism — what computational mechanisms are necessary for consciousness? The Basic Guess serves to produce a mechanistic substrate which can be examined to decide whether it can support higher levels of description (e.g. empiricism, transcendentionalism). Indeed, in terms of Kant's ideas, state machines are examined to ask the question as to whether a very general neural mechanism could be capable of imposing *a priori* knowledge on sensory information. Certainly much of the rest of the book is concerned with questions of this kind.

Hegel (1770–1831)

While Kant is seen as the initiator of German philosophy in the age of European Enlightenment, Hegel is considered to be its culmination. While the philosophy of the eighteenth century was moving away from mysticism in the treatment of mental events, Hegel represents a tendency to return to it. Of this, Russell said:

"[disbelief in the world being made up of separate things] must have come to him first as mystic insight; its intellectual elaboration … must have come later."

Russell also wrote:

"Hegel's philosophy is very difficult — he is, I should say, the hardest to understand of all great philosophers."

I use this quote to warn the reader that my attempts to describe Hegel's addition to the assessment of consciousness may fail through oversimplification. However, put in a simple way, a major distinction between Hegel and Kant is that Hegel would not accept that there were things in reality that were unknowable. This cleared the ground for his central thesis, that there is only one reality and that in its ultimate ideal form this reality does not vary from individual to individual. This absolute reality is knowable but not necessarily known by all individuals. Access to it is provided by a "triadic" form of reasoning which is also called a "dialectic" — a form of reasoning by argument between two individuals. The three elements of the triad are a *thesis* put forward by one individual, an *antithesis* by the other and a *synthesis* where the two are reconciled and both individuals have reached a higher form of understanding of reality. As an example, Hegel cited a belief in "right" (the thesis) as achieved through conquest and power. This may be rational but is inadequate as it does not take account of feelings of conscience. "Morality" is the antithesis which is rational too but inadequate as it fails to recognise certain forms of justice. The resolution of these two contradictory forms of rationality is "ethics" (the synthesis), where life is led according to the laws developed by a society.

In *Encyklopädie*, Hegel develops a theory of mentality (*Philosophy of Mind*, which follows *Logic and Philosophy of Nature*) which is important in our discussion of the history of the philosophy of consciousness. This progresses along dialectic lines. The thesis is consciousness, which is the ability to "make sense" of objects in the world, not only in terms of naming them, but also in imposing on them (Kantian) *a priori* universals such as plurality or category descriptions (i.e. the category of "dog" as opposed to a specific dog). The antithesis is self-consciousness, where the individual is faced with the special nature of "self" as an object. Having accepted the distinguished nature of self, another dialectic (within the broader one being discussed) leads to a mutual recognition of selves, a kind of distributed self-consciousness which is based on the logical collapse of distinction of objects as being separate from self. The synthesis is reason, where the recognition of other selves leads to "absolute idealism", where there is no separation between subject and object and all objects are seen as being unified in absolute knowledge, where all is understood.

Having scaled such heights it is a bit of an anticlimax to return to the world of state machines. It seems to me clear that traces of Hegelian absolutism exist in my own writing. The recognition of self and attribution of such recognition to other entities is reflected in this book as a modelling process much aided by natural language. It is language which becomes the "absolute" leveller and, as said in Chapter 1, much of the book is devoted to describing how a state machine can achieve feats of modelling of self and other selves through the use of natural language. Also, one could say that state machines with their reduction of thought to neural firing patterns provide an antithesis to Hegel's absolutist thesis and that the synthesis is the ability of the "thinking subject" to learn to recognise the world and other thinking organisms within it.

William James (1842–1910)

The fact that I have chosen to leap from Hegel to James does not mean that no worthy philosophy took place in the latter part of the nineteenth century. Indeed, some most influential philosophers wrote during that time. Arthur Schopenhauer (1788–1860), for example, strongly opposed Hegel while defending and developing Kantian ideas. Also, who has not heard of Friedrich Nietzsche (1844–1900), whose philosophy is sometimes described as angry and offensive, but, as argued by Shand, this may simply be the establishment's reaction to his desire to break away from the dogmatism of other philosophers. I do not go into the details of their work simply because consciousness was not necessarily one of their central interests.

I have been drawn to William James partly because of the title of an essay ("Does 'Consciousness' Exist?") which he published in 1904. This seems relevant indeed to the current discussion. James was not only a philosopher but also one of the early contributors to the foundation of psychology as a distinctive discipline. Consciousness is not a valid concept, he argued, because there is no distinction between the natural character of a knower and what is known. "Being conscious" is, however, a valid concept, and so is "experience". The focus of his philosophy is that there is no distinction between subject and object. A deeply religious man, James was moved by a spirit of democracy which made him dislike the rather privileged position in which the human as a knower was placed in the history of philosophy. He saw consciousness as the amulet with which philosophers had given the human being a superior position in a world of other objects. Instead, he believed, it is humbler to start with the human being as just one object among the many. It is under the cloak of "pure experience" that the knower and the known lose a material distinction.

At first, James' philosophy appears to draw a veil over a further development of the sequence of philosophical thought about consciousness as discussed in this chapter. But this is not so, and I, personally, find James' philosophy stimulating in conjunction with the history which has led to it. I interpret James' objection as one directed at mistaken searches for the "stuff" that consciousness is made of — stuff which human beings as knowers "have" and other objects do not have. This, argued James, leads to difficulties in categorising oneself and other selves, and to rather elaborately abstract philosophies, such as those of Hegel. But, allowing that "being conscious" is a valid concept, and that building up experience as a result of being conscious is also worthy of study, a new way of talking of "consciousness" becomes valid. It becomes precisely the process of "building up experience" while "being conscious" — together with the process of accessing such experience and, when necessary, acting according to what is being accessed, which is the consciousness — that the Basic Guess addresses. Many of the attacks I have heard on this way of dealing with consciousness have a strong flavour of a reluctance to let go of the amulet which James found so distasteful.

Wittgenstein (1889–1951)

A native of Vienna, Ludwig Wittgenstein showed an early aptitude for practical issues in mechanics and studied engineering in Berlin and Manchester. Having become interested in the mathematical foundations of engineering, he went to Cambridge at the age of 23 to study with Bertrand Russell. Later, having to serve in the Austrian army during the latter part of World War I, Wittgenstein completed the only book published in his lifetime: *Tractacus Logico-Philosophicus*. This led him to believe that he had exhausted his contribution to philosophy and to stop thinking about philosophical matters for a while. With time he became dissatisfied with *Tractacus* and returned in 1929 both to the subject and to Cambridge, first as a Research Fellow, then becoming Professor of Philosophy in 1939. While it was Russell who stressed that philosophical questions should be approached through a close consideration of the language which expresses them, it was Wittgenstein who questioned the validity of earlier philosophical thought for not having realised that it had been shaped by both the power and the inadequacy of language. Linguistic philosophy was to become an important concern for twentieth century philosophers.

It is of some interest that, in *Tractacus*, Wittgenstein defines the condition that makes a logical proposition meaningful, to be precisely the condition that it should have an iconic relationship with the world. That is, a proposition is meaningful only if the thinker of that proposition can make a sensible mental image of it. In the corollaries of the Basic Guess discussed in the chapters which follow, this picturing or iconic relationship becomes very important. It is a result of the words in the Basic Guess: "a transfer of activity between sensory input neurons and the state neurons". Much of *Tractacus* is concerned with the linguistic expression of a logical proposition and its relationship to an iconic form. This is also a central concern in the rest of this book. But Wittgenstein is also known for having changed his mind and questioning the content of *Tractacus* in later life.

Most of Wittgenstein's later thought is encompassed in *Philosophical Investigations*, published posthumously in 1951. In *Tractacus*, Wittgenstein "deals with" philosophy by suggesting that philosophical problems are not meaningful as they lack the necessary picturing relationship with the language in which such problems are stated. In *Investigations* he revises this objection through a reference to a lack of "essentialism" in language. Essentialism is the belief that there are hidden universals which can be represented by some words. To be clearer, philosophy has generally assumed that it is possible to use words which refer to entire classes of objects. That is, were I to say "I like dogs", essentialism suggests that "dogs" has some meaningful representation in my thoughts. Wittgenstein argues that, for this to be a meaningful representation, it must refer to a picture in my head. In actual fact, however, he goes on to argue that the mental representation of "dogs" refers to a small set of dogs which happen to be within my experience. So "dogs" does not possess the essentialism implied in a sentence which contains that word. Philosophical problems are heavily dependent on the assumption that their linguistic expression is meaningful in the sense of being made up of essentialist words. So the doubt cast over essentialism makes the pursuit of philosophy as a whole doubtful. In Chapter 6 it will be seen that a neural system behaves in a way which resonates with the way Wittgenstein described "representation" in human thought.

Wittgenstein did not pretend to solve philosophical problems (including the problem of consciousness); he merely questioned the validity of attempts to solve them in the only way that is available to a human being — through the use of language. This is a serious charge which requires me to say whether I think I am solving "the problem of consciousness" as it appears in the thoughts of philosophers from Locke to Hegel.

What I am attempting to do is actually helped by Wittgenstein's doubts. The word "consciousness" is available in exactly the same way as "dogs" to be used by people who are not concerned with "solving philosophical problems". I assume no essentialism for the word "consciousness" but ask what "set of experienced events" it represents in most people's thoughts. The Basic Guess says something about the mechanism of how sets of events can be experienced at all. The rest of the book is devoted to the content of "the set of experienced events" which make up the "consciousness" of which we all happily speak. Using the word "artificial" allows me to proceed by analogy with systems we can test and understand through analysis.

The end of the millennium

Despite the efforts of some educational funding agencies, philosophy is alive and well as the twentieth century and the millennium draw to a close. In the twentieth century there have been philosophers who have contributed enormously to the continuing debate about the nature of consciousness, which I must leave it to the reader to discover in detail. For example, Gilbert Ryle (1900–1976) mounted a monumental attack on dualism. He is known for having suggested that an attempt to discover the properties of mind is a "category mistake" as the properties of mind cannot be put in the same category as those of physical objects which can be discovered by experiment or argument. According to Ryle a detailed psychological study of behaviour is as close as science can get to mentation. Alfred Julius Ayer (1910–1989) together with Russell and Wittgenstein were the instigators of "logical positivism", which, in short, is seen as a desire to systematise Hume's notion of "complex" ideas, particularly when these complex ideas relate to logic and the language used to represent logical propositions. Karl Popper (1902–1994) contributed to the logical positivism debate by being one of its critics. He argued that the truth and meaning underlying linguistic statements was not as important as the procedure or (in science) the experiment which leads to beliefs about physical truths. Most will remember Popper's contention that science progresses by the setting of hypotheses which experiments can only refute. This puts the status of anything that appears to be a truth on some kind of probation, as the moment might come when the truth is refuted.

Enter the ghost in the machine

This book deals with a question which was brought into philosophical discourse in the middle of this century by a stunningly influential essay of Alan Turing (1950): "Computing Machinery and Intelligence". In the first line he writes:

"I propose to consider the question *Can machines think?*"

His own conclusion is that a "dishonest" machine could be made to appear to have a mind as it could converse with a human in a seemingly human way. But, much more important, his essay points to the fact that computing machinery is the first in scientific history which leads to asking new questions in the philosophy of mind. 1950 was also the year that American engineer Claude Shannon (1950) wrote the first computer program for playing chess, which was the start of years of debate on whether machines could be intelligent. It has taken 46 years for an enormously powerful collection of machines to take a game off the world chess champion. Also, 44 years later, the Royal Society in London held a meeting entitled "Artificial Intelligence and the Mind: New Breakthroughs or Dead Ends?". Here I wish to look at what writers of position papers see as the potential for machines to have minds.

The philosopher, psychologist and artificial intelligence chronicler Margaret Boden (1994) believes that AI paradigms have helped to clarify philosophical issues and shift materialist discussions in the philosophy of mind towards clear computational procedures, rather than suppositions about how things might work. I agree with this without being as wedded to AI as Boden. AI orientation largely leaves out models of experience acquisition. As we have seen, these have been central to philosophical discourse since the seventeenth century and are certainly not forgotten in the Basic Guess. On the other hand, Fred Dretske (1994), a philosopher from Stanford University in California, refers to the mind as an informational control system. "It is hard to see how else to think about it. What good is a mind if it does not do something?" Not only is this synonymous with my appeal to state machines in the Basic Guess, but it also shows that models normally used by engineers, even if not universally accepted by philosophers, are beginning to creep into philosophical argument. This is a trend to which this book hopes to contribute.

Daniel Dennett (1994) too has expressed sympathy for the use of machinery as a test bed for ideas about mentation. This sympathy is evident in his boldly entitled *Consciousness Explained* (1991), where, after a major attack on the "Cartesian theatre", he sees consciousness as the effort of a large number of computational agents who are all busy redrafting a feasible explanation of sensory experience. Intelligent agents (a way of breaking down an "intelligent" computational task into co-operating subtasks) are currently a very popular topic in AI research laboratories. At the Royal Society, Dennett talked of the Cog project at the Massachusetts Institute of Technology. A robot is being constructed whose consciousness, it is claimed, will evolve from interaction with people and environments. Cog is equipped with a comprehensive set of sensors and limbs (effectors) — its "consciousness" will be derived by developing neural connections between the two during "training". The training is long and ambitious, akin to the bringing up of a child. It is interesting to compare Cog and Magnus, and this will be done later in the book. Suffice it to say here that while in Magnus we make a great deal of the role of sensors and effectors, its neural machinery (brain?) starts as a comprehensive neural state machine which has powers of learning to represent sensory experience and its relation to action. Rodney Brookes, the designer of Cog, has avoided reference to "representation" as far as possible.

Just as the Royal Society assembly was beginning to become comfortable in accepting that machines may have an explanatory role to play in the philosophy of consciousness, a sophisticated dissenting voice was sounded by Oxford philosopher John Lucas (1994). With devastating clarity, he reminded his audience that the AI paradigm, based on a logical modelling of outward behaviour, is inadequate for allowing consciousness to be attributed to a simulation. Being conscious and appearing to be conscious are two different things. Further, he suggested that any organism which is there through human design does not have the autonomy to warrant being described as conscious. Clearly, Lucas' skepticism is well founded and needs to be answered. It is partly the purpose of this book to provide such an answer.

Penrose

Whenever I give a talk on neurons and consciousness, the question on the minds if not the lips of many is how all this squares up with Sir Roger Penrose's suggestion that science has not yet got to the stage where it can explain consciousness. So what am I doing in trying to give such explanations? In his recent book, *Shadows of the Mind*, Penrose states his position with great clarity. He suggests that in linking computation with consciousness one can hold only four possible views:

"*A.* All thinking is computation; in particular, feelings of conscious awareness are evoked merely by the carrying out of appropriate computations.

B. Awareness is a feature of the brain's physical action; and whereas any physical action can be simulated computationally, computational simulation cannot by itself evoke awareness.

C. Appropriate physical action of the brain evokes awareness, but this physical action cannot even be properly simulated computationally.

D. Awareness cannot be explained by physical, computational, or any other scientific terms."

D is close to my previous description of the "pure" philosophers' stance on the inexplicability of consciousness. I am in close agreement with Penrose that this need not be slavishly accepted. He sees *A* as a statement of "strong AI" — a belief that everything, including consciousness, is computation. He rejects this with surprising hesitation. I reject it totally as it fails to differentiate between the computational nature of different mechanisms, i.e. it loses the ability to show an interest in mechanism. Rather than being a strong statement, it is so weak as to not be in the area of explanations of consciousness, although it may on occasion simulate acts which are carried out by conscious human beings. It fails to recognise the route whereby something called consciousness may have reached the computational device. It is this route that artificial consciousness is all about. It is in areas *B* and *C* that I feel Penrose attacks computation a little too strongly. The problem lies with the term "computational simulation" and the way it should be distinguished from "neural computation".

A computational simulation implies that the process which is being simulated has been sufficiently well understood for a programmer to write the instructions so that the process may run and be studied on a computer. The computational issue is not, therefore, whether a simulation can by itself evoke consciousness, but whether the process that is being simulated is a proper model of the phenomenon which is being researched. It is obvious that a simulated weather system is not a weather system, but the simulation of a weather system can tell us whether it will rain or not. So the question is whether consciousness can be specified and represented well enough to be tested and studied on a computer. So, while *B* is obviously correct as stated, it should be accompanied by another belief which says that the physical action which leads to awareness could be tested, studied and fully understood by simulation on a computer. *C*, which is Penrose's stated position, is simply a restatement of the belief that consciousness cannot yet be understood sufficiently to be studied on a computer or even to be talked about in scientific terms. He does not rule out the possibility that this might be done in the future. My point is that there is no need to wait, and that one appropriate scientific paradigm that is here now is *neural computation*.

Penrose is aware of neural computation but describes it as merely a way of building pattern recognition systems in which the process of learning improves performance. He does not accept the point that has now been made since the mid-1980s by a vast number of people, that neural computation is a paradigm for expressing the functional properties of dynamic neural systems. The brain is clearly a dynamic neural system and it seems appropriate at least to suggest that consciousness might be expressed as a list of emerging functional properties of this class of systems.

The Basic Guess in Perspective

The Basic Guess is the title of a computational approach which, by itself, leads to systems which neither pretend nor appear to be conscious. It points to a mechanistic, materialistic computational structure, which, I argue, might be present whenever it is claimed that an object is conscious. It also (as we shall see) provides parameters with which the sophistication of the claimed consciousness can be discussed. It distinguishes between Magnus, which is conscious in an artificial way, and me and my human friends, who are conscious in a real way. It does not, as Lucas suggests, demote a conscious organism from being conscious through the process of explanation and eventual understanding. Going back to Locke's fatigue with the "physical consideration of the mind", the Basic Guess, by referring to state structures, is saying to Locke and his followers, "We now do have the means to indulge in such consideration."

What Stuff Makes
Me Conscious?

The Oldest Question

Chapter 2 dipped into two major pots of rich debate. First, why do I express my understanding of being conscious in terms of networks of neurons and, second, how does this square up with what philosophers have thought over the ages? In fact, both of these ask 'what stuff is mind made of?' — the oldest question in the science of the conscious mind. Here I look briefly at issues that came to prominence since the book was first published.

Neurons and the Informational Mind

Looking for the stuff of consciousness in the neural structure of the brain (as opposed to the programs of Artificial Intelligence) has become increasingly necessary in order to give 'artificial consciousness' stronger powers of explanation. An imaginative approach is given by Murray Shanahan in Chapter 6 of his *Embodiment and the Inner Life.*[a] Here he explains how neural activity over long distances in a brain-like structure might accord with Baars' Global Workspace notions about consciousness (mentioned in the postscript to Chapter 1).

The intuition that neurons in the artificial world should resemble, in greater physical detail, those of the brain has become more prominent in recent neural network literature. This has led to an increasing number of researchers working with 'spiking' neurons. Figure 2.3 of this chapter indicates that neurons communicate with one another through bursts of spiky signals that are binary in essence; in terms of being there or not. Those interested in 'spiking neurons' suggest something more sophisticated. While a spike is still a binary thing, the code generated by a spiking neuron can be determined by the time-rate and synchronization of the spikes. A good textbook sets the scene.[b]

My own view is that even while these more complex neurons allow for very efficient informational codes for communication among neurons, codes that are surely very effective in the brain, neurons may still be modelled as logical devices that map a vector of signals at the synapses to an axonal output as some kind of a truth table (albeit a massive one). I return to this under the heading of 'iconic learning' in Postscript 4 (Chapter 4). The idea also features strongly in the first edition.

But possibly the most influential development that involves neural modelling is something called 'integrated information theory' or IIT. Largely due to GiulioTononi (psychiatrist and neuroscientist currently at the University of Wisconsin), this theory suggests that

---

[a] Shanahan, M. (2010). *Embodiment and the Inner Life: Cognition and Consciousness in the Space of Possible Minds.* Oxford University Press, Oxford.
[b] Gerstner, W. and Kistler, M. (2002). *Spiking Neuron Models, Single Neurons, Populations, Plasticity,* Cambridge University Press, Cambridge.

a cellular system needs to have a certain level of connectivity for its states to be potentially conscious.[c] Helen Morton, some colleagues, and I have discussed this development against the background of neural automata in *Aristotle's Laptop: The Discovery of our Informational Minds*[d] (called [A's L], for short). Here I sketch briefly what the theory means.

It starts with two observations, which, like our axioms mentioned in the postscript to Chapter 1, most would agree with. They both relate to 'a conscious mental state' — that which is felt from moment to moment and which (according to 'the basic guess' of Chapter 1) is caused by the electrochemical action of neurons. The first is **that we are conscious of novelty ... that is, new information.**

That is, each new mental state is distinguished from the entire history of one's previous mental states. Going to the same bus stop today as I went yesterday may be a *similar* experience but it is clearly not the *same* and we express this by saying that we *are conscious of the difference.* In terms of information measurement, turning over a card from a pack of 32 is known (by some ... worry not if this is not you) to be new 5 bits of information [*i.e.* $(\log_2(32))$]. Life experience is just a massive pack of cards which means that every new conscious experience is highly rich in information. So this can be wrapped up as

> *An entity is conscious of perceptual input through being sensitive to the information it adds to previous experience.*

But, you may say, every time you take a new picture with your digital camera this again is one new card from a massive pack. So

---

[c]Tononi, G. (2008). Consciousness as Integrated Information: a Provisional Manifesto, *Biol. Bull.,* 215, pp. 16–242.

[d]Aleksander, I and Morton, H. B. (2012). 'The Discovery of our Informational Minds', in Aleksander, I and Morton, H. B., *Aristotle's Laptop*, World Scientific, Singapore.

is the camera conscious? Sorry, but no. It is the second IIT observation that *we are conscious of things being things.*

This is best understood by wondering what is *not* a thing. Think of two television sets side by side. Both are untuned and display the familiar 'snow/ or, 'noise' — these are not things. Now the two televisions show the picture of a big letter O and a big letter Q respectively. We are *so conscious* of the small difference of the second pair of pictures but hardly at all of the first two even though the difference between them is much greater than the second on a point-by-point basis. The difference between things and noise is that there are a lot of co-occurring features in things. The random noise has no co-occurring features. So we can wrap up this second observation as:

> *An entity is conscious of perceptual input through being sensitive to the causal relationships in a moment of such input.*

But now, we take an important step. These two observations have implications for understanding how the physical substrate might develop a capacity for being conscious. In order to not to confuse new perceptions *and* be sensitive to co-occurring events, there needs to be a sufficiently elevated level of information transmission among the elements of the network that is to represent these precepts. This is important because it says "if a system is to be conscious it has to have certain physical properties". Such statements are rare in both the philosophy and the science of consciousness. Tononi (2008)[e] quantified this much further by developing a global measure of information transmission in a cellular subsystem which he called Φ. My personal interpretation is that the higher the Φ, the greater the 'capacity' for consciousness is. Tononi makes a stronger

---

[e]Tononi, G. (2008). Consciousness as Integrated Information: a Provisional Manifesto, *Biol. Bull.,* 215, pp. 216–242.

statement stating that the higher the **Φ**, the higher the actual consciousness *is*. However, I have argued that there are problems within IIT about the representation of reality (under the heading of qualia) and with computations of **Φ**. Such detail is beyond the scope of this postscript, but may be found in a paper by Mike Beaton and myself.[f]

And the Philosophy?

In Chapter 2, I described myself as an "Engineer in a Philosophical Wonderland". Not much has changed. I am still fascinated and inspired by some areas of philosophy. What has changed is that there is now a better contact between computing theoreticians and philosophers who appreciate formalities. In the next few paragraphs I highlight two examples of such contacts: the *hard problem* and *phenomenology*.

At the time of the publication of the first edition of *Impossible Minds*, a highly influential thesis was written and published by mathematician and philosopher David Chalmers.[g] He formulated 'The *Hard Problem* of consciousness' which argues that the entire formalish approach to consciousness (this book included) is the *easy* option. While I may be explaining how physical mechanisms may lead to reportable experiences this does not explain what an experience actually *is*. No sooner published, the *Hard Problem* became the object of much criticism by philosophers and neuroscientists. For example, philosopher Daniel Dennett argues that breaking the concept down into many 'easy' mechanisms can constitute a sufficient explanation, making the over-elusive *hard* problem one

---

[f]Beaton, M. and Aleksander, I. (2012). World-Related Integrated Information: Enactivist and Phenomenal Perspectives, *International Journal of Machine Consciousness*, 4 (02), pp. 439–455.

[g]Chalmers, J. D. (1996). *The Conscious Mind: In Search of a Fundamental Theory*, Oxford University Press, Oxford.

postulate too far.[h] On the neuroscience front, Francis Crick and Christof Koch used a similar argument: working on the neural correlates of many aspects of consciousness will, when put together, constitute a comprehensive explanation. Indeed, what is done with the 'big guess' and the consequences (or the axioms mentioned in the postscript to Chapter 1) is to take this solve-by-breaking-down approach to explain features of being conscious. In 2005, I had also suggested a deeper refutation of the hard problem again by the breakdown of the problem into axioms but also by the acceptance of Chalmers' own suggestion that dichotomy between a physical brain and sensation is helped by recognizing informational formulations. For example, arguing that the state structure of an automaton describes sensation while the physical structure of the same automaton describes the neural brain.[i]

My second point of contact with philosophy relates to *phenomenology*; that is, the tradition that starts with the personal feeling of consciousness being *about* something. If I am conscious of the sunset over the Aegean sea as it unfurls before me or if I recall a holiday in the past, both these instances of being conscious are *about* something. In fact being conscious of *nothing* is pretty hard (of course, I am aware of the Buddhist practice of striving for *Nirvana* — the difficult task of achieving total stillness of mind. In Chapter 4 of this book we begin to indicate how inner representations of the real world can 'get into' a neural automaton through 'iconic learning'. It is more recently that we linked this to what is known in phenomenology. Details of this will appear in the postscript to Chapter 4.

---

[h] Dennett, D. C. (1996). Facing backwards on the problem of consciousness, *Journal of Consciousness Studies*, 3 (1), pp. 4–6.
[i] Aleksander, I. (2005). *The World in My Mind, My Mind in the World*, Imprint Academic, Exeter.

In Sum

I have confessed here that my private passion to study consciousness through networks of neurons and their state structures has not
gone away! Indeed it has been encouraged by new theories such as
the need for integrated information in such networks and appropriate philosophical perspectives, such as phenomenology, which link
to early work on iconic acquisition of experience.

"Hey, Asic," said Molecula, "I've got another long document from Red Naskela."

"Bad news," sighed Asic, "the guy obviously is not going to give up."

"You did write to him as I asked, encouraging him to send more information?" asked Molecula.

"Yes, I did," came the reply. "But I used words such as — although you know that your proposals are not in line with our current policy ..."

Molecula was beginning to show annoyance. "Oh, Ask, I know that you're trying to protect me from getting the sack, but I wish you'd do what I say. This stuff he's sent us now is quite interesting. He's invented a place called Earth, and is saying that it is inhabited by biological organisms some of whom are just like us ... automata. But they have been agonising about consciousness for three thousand years. He's invented bio-organisms with funny names like Wittgenstein and Lucas ... I'd like to meet him. I think that you should leave the next letter to me."

"Suit yourself, but I see nothing but trouble from above, if you encourage this guy ... "

Chapter 3

Automata and Brains

Automata Theory: Mathematics Anyone Can Do

This chapter is first about a very simple mathematical language which anyone can understand. Maybe "mathematical language" is a bit of a grand way of putting it. It is just a way of drawing pictures of what goes on inside a system. It is *not* essential reading for those who would like to get on with the core subject of this book: consciousness. Similarly the last part of this chapter is an engineer's view of the anatomy of the brain. This is included to show that our brains are really very complex machines and that working with automata theory applies to simplified forms of brains — the idea being that simplified forms of brains may give us a clue to consciousness, albeit a simplified form of consciousness. But this bit of neuroanatomy can also be skipped by the reader who wants to get on with the main agenda of Chapter 4.

Consequence 1: The brain is a state machine
The brain of a conscious organism is a state machine whose state variables are the outputs of neurons. This implies that a

definition of consciousness be developed in terms of the elements
of automata theory.

The question "What does the heart of a living creature do?" is relatively easy to answer in a broad way which anyone can understand. The answer might be something like "It is a pump and it makes the blood go round the body." So the language with which a complex human organ such as the heart may be described is the language used by the designers of pumps, a language familiar to mechanical engineers. When surgeons talk about the heart they are happy to use terms such as "pressure", "volume" and "flow". Mechanical engineers know the rules which govern the relationships between these quantities. So the engineering language might be useful to surgeons who perform heart transplants and may even lead to the design of artificial hearts. In discussing the brain there is a need to do things in a similar way — to find a way of talking about what is understood not only about the function of that rather complex organ, but also about the way such functions may lead to the sensations that make up consciousness. As seen in the last chapter, some might argue that while there are languages in science which describe the working of the brain, they cannot capture the concept of consciousness. I hope that by the end of this chapter it will appear that the language of "automata theory" is adequate at least to start approaching this mammoth task. This may seem to be a strange choice, as "automaton" is colloquially used to describe an object which seems alive but is devoid of consciousness, whatever that might be. A way of looking at it is that "automata theory" is appropriate for discussing the presence or otherwise of consciousness in the same sense as "pump theory" might be used to define what are and what are not pumps.

As seen in the previous chapter, it is suggested that something called a state machine may be an appropriate (or perhaps just interesting for the severely skeptical) metaphor for the brain (just as the pump is a metaphor for the heart). State machines are best described by a language called automata theory and the object of this chapter is to introduce this language, explain it from scratch and then try to take the big leap into suggesting that the elements of consciousness find expression within the language.

Automata theory is used by engineers who design information processing machines. This seems appropriate as the information processing functions of the brain must be somehow involved in our hunt for consciousness. With hearts, the language of the dynamics of liquids is appropriate in discussions about the blood flow functions of the heart. Automata theory is there to express the rules which apply to the neural state machines introduced in the Basic Guess. I shall argue that consciousness, under some conditions, emerges from the natural laws which govern what can and cannot happen in a neural state machine. As I know that automata theory easily describes these natural laws, I suggest that it follows that it is the appropriate language for the modelling of conscious entities.

The Wheel Machine

To ease into the idea of a state machine as a metaphor for a physical object, it may be helpful to think about the gadget in Fig. 3.1. Pebbles come down the chute and, by falling into a paddle blade, cause the wheel to rotate counter-clockwise by one position, at which point the pebble falls out of the paddle blade. There is a striker attached to blade a which rings a bell as this blade comes into the pebble-receiving position. If it is assumed that the pebbles don't arrive at too great a rate, the entire machine can be seen to be a pebble counter which rings the bell every time eight pebbles have come down the chute. Let $a = 0$, $b = 1$, $c = 2$ and so on. Then, starting with a in the receiving position, the number of the blade in the

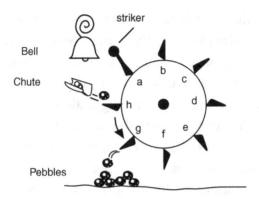

Fig. 3.1.   A pebble-counting machine.

receiving position is an indication of precisely how many pebbles
in a group of eight have been counted. Indeed, the eight positions
a to *h* represent the eight states of this mechanism. So a state is an
indication of what has gone before, a kind of memory — in
this case, of how many pebbles have occurred since the last ring of
the bell.

Some Shorthand

But what could this possibly have to do with brains? Surely we are
not arguing that a brain is made up of wheels, paddles and bells.
Indeed not, but this is the starting point of an argument which develops from here to show that there is a second way of describing the
wheel-and-paddle mechanism — one which is a kind of shorthand
that loses the mechanical detail of the machine, but retains its main
characteristics as a counter with eight states and a signal when the
count of eight has been achieved. It will be shown later that this
shorthand can always be turned into a standardised neural machine
in which the states are coded as patterns of firing among the
neurons. This is what we shall call a "neural implementation".
Anticipating even further, I shall argue that the key characteristic of

the brain is not only that it is made up of neurons, but that such neurons have the ability to represent sensory experience. This is represented by the fully fledged "neural state machine". This is what engineers call an "equivalent" machine — that is, a machine which captures all that the machine which is being modelled does. The final part of the argument is that if the brain generates consciousness this must be a function which can be discussed in terms of the equivalent model. But just as important is the question "If not, why not?". If none of this makes sense, fear not — it is a trailer for what lies ahead and a suggestion that it's worth becoming familiar with the shorthand in which these models are described.

The shorthand can be graphical or symbolic. The symbolic version comes first. The machine has inputs, i.e. the pebbles, which can be represented by P to indicate the arrival of a pebble at the end of the chute, and P' to say that there is no pebble at the end of the chute. The states are labelled in terms of the paddle that is present at the chute, and the output is either B for "bell rings" or B' for "bell is silent". The entire function of the machine can be described in terms of a table [Fig. 3.2(a)] full of the symbols which have just been defined.

This table is called a state transition table. There is a more striking graphical way of representing exactly the same information, and it is called a state transition diagram. This is shown in Fig. 3.2(b). The tradition here is to draw a circle for every state and an arrow to indicate the effect of every input. So P indicates that the input of a pebble causes the change in the state, where no pebble leaves the state where it is. The arrow is also labelled with the corresponding output showing here that the only time the bell rings (B) is during the change from state h to state a. For all other transitions the output is silent (B').

What has been learned so far? The shorthand of a state transition table and the state transition diagram can be used with a machine

Current State	Input State	Next State	Output
a	*P'*	*a*	*B'*
a	*P*	*b*	*B'*
b	*P'*	*b*	*B'*
b	*P*	*c*	*B'*
c	*P'*	*c*	*B'*
c	*P*	*d*	*B'*
d	*P'*	*d*	*B'*
d	*P*	*e*	*B'*
e	*P'*	*e*	*B'*
e	*P*	*f*	*B'*
f	*P'*	*f*	*B'*
f	*P*	*g*	*B'*
g	*P'*	*g*	*B'*
g	*P*	*h*	*B'*
h	*P'*	*h*	*B'*
h	*P*	*a*	*B*

(a)

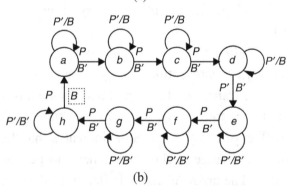

(b)

Fig. 3.2.   The state transition diagram.

where the output is dependent on the history of inputs, i.e. a machine with memory. What has been proved by mathematicians is that these two representations apply to *any* machine with memory. The implication is that the shorthand may be the appropriate way of describing the brain, which undoubtedly is a machine with memory. It is not said that this can actually be done in great detail; it is merely a suggestion that the shorthand — or automata theory, to give it its proper name — is a suitable language within which to have discussions about the function of brains.

Building Machines with Neurons

The difference between Fig. 3.1 and Fig. 3.2 is that the former tells us how the machine is made whereas the latter is about what the machine does. Machines doing the same thing can be built in a large number of ways. For example, it would be easy to think of a clockwork mechanism which advances each time a lever is moved and makes a noise every eight lever actions. Among ways of making state machines are circuits which use artificial neurons. In the very early days of computers, artificial neurons were thought to be useful components for building state machines of any kind, including computers. Nowadays, engineers who design digital systems use things called gates. An AND gate, for example, will "fire" when all its inputs are firing, and an OR gate when one or more of its inputs are firing. Putting this comment aside, it's fun to show that the function of Fig. 3.2 can be achieved with neurons. This is done in Fig. 3.3, which needs a great deal of explanation. Readers who are not interested in learning how to design neural state machines or those who are experts in digital system design can skip to the next section without losing the drift of the argument. What follows is for the budding engineer or those who do not wish to miss out on technical detail.

However, it is recommended that those who will do some skipping should take a quick look at Fig. 3.3. It contains three ways describing a neural machine: (a) a neural circuit, (b) a state diagram and (c) truth tables that describe what each neuron is doing. The details of how these elements are designed are discussed below and may

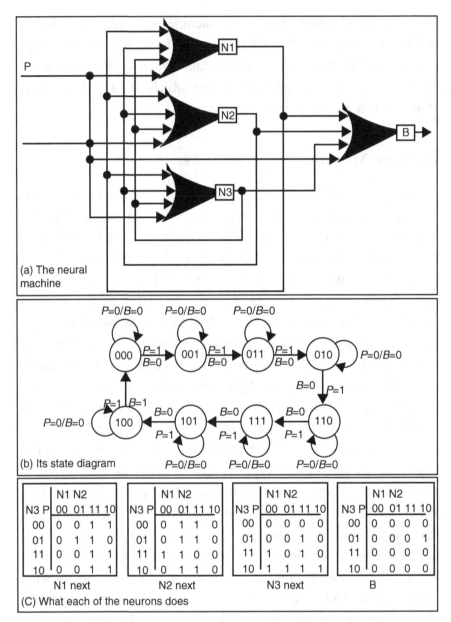

(a) The neural machine

(b) Its state diagram

(C) What each of the neurons does

	N1 N2			
N3 P	00	01	11	10
00	0	0	1	1
01	0	1	1	0
11	0	0	1	1
10	0	0	1	1

N1 next

	N1 N2			
N3 P	00	01	11	10
00	0	1	1	0
01	0	1	1	0
11	1	1	0	0
10	0	1	1	0

N2 next

	N1 N2			
N3 P	00	01	11	10
00	0	0	0	0
01	0	0	1	0
11	1	0	1	0
10	1	1	1	1

N3 next

	N1 N2			
N3 P	00	01	11	10
00	0	0	0	0
01	0	0	0	1
11	0	0	0	0
10	0	0	0	0

B

Fig. 3.3.   Design of a neural machine.

not be of interest. But the existence of these three ways of describing the same system is important and will be discussed in the section which follows: "The behaviour of neural state machines".

Binary coding. Everything in a neural machine is represented by firing patterns at the output of a group of neurons. So the first question to ask is: How many neurons are required to code the eight states of the machine? One neuron would have only two states — firing (to which we give the label 1) or not firing (to which we give the label 0). Two neurons can provide all the combinations of firing and not firing, i.e. 00, 01, 11, 10. So, three neurons, which appear in Fig. 3.3(a) labelled as N1, N2 and N3, are required to give us the eight necessary states. In circuits such as these, where no effort is made to control the timing (called asynchronous circuits, in engineering jargon), it is common to assign codes to subsequent states which, at most, differ in the firing condition of only one neuron. So the states *a, b, c, ..., h* of Fig. 3.2 now appear as states 000, 001, 011,..., 100 in Fig. 3.3(b). In Fig. 3.2 we called the presence of a pebble *P* and its absence *P'*. In the neural machine this can be represented by the state of just one incoming wire [*P* in Fig. 3.3(a)] which, in the state diagram (b), has been assigned the value 1 for the presence of a pebble and 0 for its absence. Finally, there is neuron B, which serves the role of bell ringing. When its output is 1 this represents the bell ringing; 0 represents silence.

What do the neurons need to do? At their inputs, the state neurons N1, N2 and N3 each sense all their outputs and the value of the P input. They are then designed to fire or not fire depending on the requirements of the state diagram. Take, for example, the system in state 000 and the value of P at 0. It is clear from the state diagram that the state should not change and that B should be 0. So, we can now begin to build up a complete specification (or "truth table") for what each neuron should do next, in response to the incoming pattern. These truth tables are shown in Fig. 3.3(c), where there is a separate truth table for each neuron. The case where the pattern is 000 for the state and 0 for P is represented as the top left hand corner of all the tables. As the state is to remain 000 and the output B should be 0, 0s are entered into all these top left corners of the four truth tables. Now, for the case where the state is still 000 but P has changed to 1, the state diagram indicates that the state should change to 001. Therefore the first entry in the truth tables is found from the "starting state" 000 and P = 1, which is just below the entry in the truth tables we have considered earlier. While N1, N2 and B get a further 0 in their truth tables, it is N3 which gets a 1 to ensure the change of state.

In this way the information in the state diagram can be translated into a complete description for the truth table for each of the neurons specifying how the neuron must react whatever the state and whatever the condition of the input. One technical question remains: How do the neurons differentiate between P being 1 for a short while and being 1 twice or more in succession? It is assumed that P = 1 is a short pulse with P being 0 most of the time. That is, the pulse is short enough and the neurons are a little sluggish in responding for only one state change to take place each time P is pulsed. So, as required by the state diagram, the neural system is truly counting the short pulses at P. Therefore neuron B, when the state is 100, will output a brief pulse as the pulse appears at P and the state changes to 000. The design of the neural machine is now complete.

The Behaviour of Neural Machines

After the above dip into the detailed engineering of a neural state machine, it is important to stand back a bit and think about the elements that have been involved in the design process: a neural circuit, a state diagram and the truth tables for the neurons. First, think of the neural circuit. This is the anatomical structure, the material brain of the system, if you like. How much of an indication about what the system is doing does its structure give us? The sad answer is, very little. The problem is that exactly the same structure can exhibit a very large number of behaviours. To demonstrate, I shall change what two of the neurons do by just a little. This is indicated in Fig. 3.4(b), where two of the 0s in the original truth tables have been flipped to 1s. The effect on what the circuit does, as indicated by the state diagram in Fig. 3.4, is quite dramatic. Now, in whichever state the machine starts, it will end trapped switching between states 100 and 101 with the arrival of pulses at P. It will never enter any of the other states.

So, trying to infer what a neural system is doing from the way the neurons are wired up is a bad idea. This is particularly true as I could also demonstrate (but will not, as the point is easily accepted)

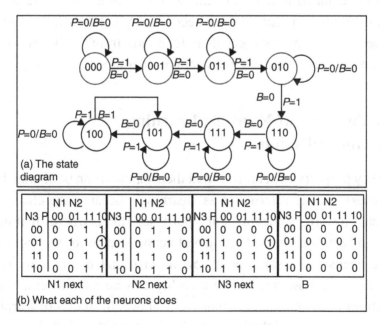

Fig. 3.4. An altered state machine.

that a different form of wiring with different truth tables could lead to the same state diagram as in Fig. 3.3(b). In fact, these are results of automata theory which are familiar to engineers. This is how the situation could be summarised:

(i) Given a neural circuit where the neurons can perform many functions, the circuit can perform differently for each combination of the functions of its neurons. Therefore it is impossible to infer the function of a neural circuit solely from its physical structure.

(ii) A given state diagram can be implemented by a very large variety of neural circuits (it could be an infinitely large variety).

So the conclusion of what automata theory has told us so far is that the state diagram is the best way of describing everything that a neural state machine can do. But the state diagram is a product of both the detailed functions of the neurons *and* the structure of the neural circuit. A question which becomes immediately important is: "Where do the neurons get their functions from?" This is where learning comes in and needs closer consideration.

The Function of Neurons: Learning and Generalisation

The key property of neurons is that their function can be changed — a process usually referred to as "learning", because the change is directed towards achieving some purpose. This is true of real neurons and artificial ones. Putting real neurons aside for the moment, more needs to be said about how an artificial neuron can learn anything and how this learning ability can be used to create the functions of circuits such as those seen above. In studies of learning in artificial neurons, things get a bit complicated, so I shall assume

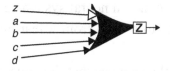

Fig. 3.5. How a neuron learns.

the simplest possible mechanism in the belief that more complicated artificial or real mechanisms will not be all that different in
principle. Referring to Fig. 3.5, we start by imagining that one of
the inputs to the neuron (indicated by the white arrowhead and
labelled z) is rather special.

We give this input the name "dominant synapse" as, during the
early parts of the neuron's activity, if z is firing then the neuron will
fire at Z.

The significant effect of this is that when the neuron is made to
fire, it "takes notice" of what the other inputs are doing and remembers it. To be more specific, "taking notice" means that later, when
learning is no longer required, z can atrophy and no longer be
dominant while the neuron will continue to fire to the patterns on a
to d which occurred when z was firing, and not to those which
occurred when z was not. Another way of putting this is that the
neuron has learned to fire to certain patterns on a to d.

There is a need to clarify what is meant by "early" activity and
"later". Simply, this means that there are two major phases in the
behaviour of neural systems: "early" means "learning" and "later"
means "applying what has been learned". In the simple model
which will eventually help us to discuss consciousness, we assume
that these two are distinct phases — this can certainly be organised
in artificial systems. In real systems, neurons actually slide from
learning to application and, possibly, backwards and forwards
between the two under the control of biochemical processes. I argue
that for the moment this need not be included in trying to find out

where the "power to think" in neural systems comes from, and that it is sufficient simply to switch from a learning to an application phase.

To give an example, suppose that the neuron in Fig. 3.5, during its learning phase, is exposed only to the 11111 pattern and the 00000 at its input terminals; it will learn to fire to 1111 in *a* to *d* in the application phase and not to fire to 0000 at the same terminals. Now for a key question: What does the neuron do for all the other possible combinations of inputs? It is assumed that the neuron *generalises* in the sense that it responds according to the similarity of the unknown pattern to those seen in training. So, for example, if the input is 1011 or 1110 the neuron will fire, whereas it will not fire for 0100 or 1000. But what of a pattern such as 1100 or 0101? As these are equally "distant" from either of the training patterns, they are said to be in contention and it is assumed that the neuron "half-fires", i.e. it fires at random about half of the time. Further technical details of this kind of behaviour may be found in the literature on this topic (e.g. Aleksander and Morton, 1993 and 1995).

Learning or Programming?

Returning to the circuit in Fig. 3.3(a), knowing what we have just learned about the way individual neurons learn functions, it is possible to show that they can learn their functions in parallel by being trained on the information contained in the state diagram itself. First, one needs to imagine that a dominant synapse exists for each of the four neurons — say, $z1$, $z2$, $z3$ and zB for neurons N1, N2, N3 and B respectively. Then, as an example, to teach the system the first transition from 000 to itself with P = 0 and B = 0,

the neuron outputs N1, N2, N3 are set to 000,
P is set to 0,

the dominant synapses $z1$, $z2$, $z3$ and zB are set to 0000
and the system is "made" (by whatever control means) to enter
its training phase.

To take a different example, should the transition from 100 to 000
with P = 1 and B = 1 be the one which is being learned, then

the neuron outputs Nl, N2, N3 are set to 100,
P is set to 1,
the dominant synapses $z1$, $z2$, $z3$ and zB are set to 0001,
and the system is "made" (by whatever control means) to enter
its training phase.

All the state transitions can be achieved by doing this for each of
the 16 possible transitions in the diagram.

What has been achieved? This is not so much learning as programming of an exact function into a circuit which could accept
virtually any function. A slightly more interesting step might be to
see what the system would do were it only partially trained, and were
the power of generalisation of the neurons to come into play.
Figure 3.6 relates to this point but needs a great deal of explanation.
The state diagram in Fig. 3.6 is a result of training the circuit in
Fig. 3.3 in the following two steps:

(i) The neuron outputs N1, N2, N3 are set to 000,
     P is set to 0,
     the dominant synapses $z1$, $z2$, $z3$ and zB are set to 0000,
     and the system is "made" to enter its training phase;
(ii) The neuron outputs Nl, N2, N3 are set to 111,
     P is set to 1,
     the dominant synapses $z1$, $z2$, $z3$ and zB are set to 1111,
     and the system is "made" to enter its training phase.

These two steps lead to the creation of the states indicated with
bold circles in the state diagram. But what of other states? Take an

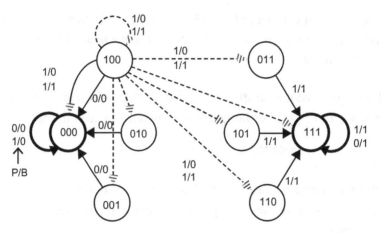

Fig. 3.6.   State diagram for partial training.

easy example first: suppose that N1, N2, N3 are set to 100 and that
P = 0. From what has been said about generalisation in neurons, the
input to the neurons is close to training condition (i), and so the
response of all the neurons will be as in this training step, causing
the transition from state 100 to state 000, where the system will
remain. There are many such transitions relating to each of the two
training steps — they are all indicated by solid lines in Fig. 3.6.

Now for a more complicated case. Let N1, N2, N3 be set to 100,
but this time suppose that P = 1. Now all the neurons get an input
which is exactly between the two training steps. This means that
each neuron will decide to fire or not fire at random (as defined
earlier). This means that from state 100 the system can change to
any state when P = 1. In automata theory it is said that the state
machine becomes probabilistic as one can talk of the probability of
any state transition taking place. In this case there is an equal probability (i.e. 1/8) that a transition to any state (including itself) will
take place.

The astute reader will by now have worked out that the neural
system which has been trained to produce the state diagram in

Fig. 3.6 is not particularly useful. However, the beauty of the state diagram is that it makes possible a complete description of what the system does (even if it is useless) after having been trained. Let's have a go, assuming that when the machine is first switched on it could be in any one of the eight states.

Assume for the time being that P is held at 1 when the machine is switched on. If it starts in one of the set of states (111, 110, 101, 011}, it will immediately change to 111 (or remain in 111) with the output continually at 1. Having reached 111, no amount of manipulation of P will change the state and hence the output. If, on the other hand, the machine starts in one of the three states {100, 010, 001}, it has a 50% chance of transiting to the former set from which it will end in {111}. If, however, it starts in {000}, it will stay there (and so on in a similar fashion if P is held at 0 when the machine is switched on).

At this point a statistician can get to work on the probabilistic state machine and suppose that on the whole, if P is held at 1 (or 0), the system will end and stay in 111 (or 000) with a probability of 80%. The statistician would even be able to predict the likely time taken for this stability to occur.

A Touch of Perspective: Have We Lost Sight of Consciousness?

I hope that this is not the case. Consequence 1 simply recommends the use of the language of automata to talk about the brain because it is a language in which one can express the three major elements which make the brain do anything at all: structure, function of the components which make up the structure, and the way these two lead to the totality of what the system can do expressed as a state structure. In fact it says even more. It says that if a statement is to be made of how a brain can be conscious, such a statement might benefit from being made in terms of state structures, recognising these to be a product of physical structure and the function of neurons (learned or inherited).

When I express these thoughts to those who have thought long and hard about consciousness, I get a wide range of reactions. Typical is: "Why should I learn a new methodology — it's hard enough doing what I do." "Doing what I do" could be anything from philosophy through neurobiology to physics. Another reaction is: "I've heard all this already, masses of people go around saying that brain is hardware and thought is software — it doesn't tell me anything about consciousness." In the remaining sections of this chapter I shall look quite closely at how the approaches of others stand with respect to the contention of the first Consequence that automata theory is an appropriate language for discussions about consciousness. I shall try to dispel the idea that I am talking of a hardware/software model. However, exactly how the state machine captures the concept of consciousness in a novel and (for me) penetrating way will require a discussion of the other corollaries in this book.

Neuroanatomy: The Shape of the Brain

In this and following sections I want to take a brief look at what is considered to be the neurobiological basis of consciousness. It may be appropriate to ask why one should have to find a new mode of description as advocated by Consequence 1, if an adequate study of consciousness can be made by studying the components of the brain directly. The answer is that the structure of the brain is very complicated, and not by any means fully understood. Also, as we have seen above, structure is at times an unreliable indicator of function. Nevertheless it is instructive to look at brain structure and then what neuroanatomists and neurobiologists have said about the way that structure supports consciousness.

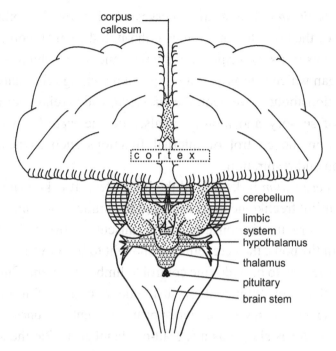

Fig. 3.7.   An oversimplified, exploded view of the brain.

A childishly oversimplified, exploded view of the brain is shown in Fig. 3.7. The function of these organs which consist of dense natural neural networks has been discovered largely through the effect that lesions situated in particular areas have on behaviour. It is worth bearing in mind that the lesion observations can be erroneous due to the interactions between elements: interfering with part A could lead to an effect in part B and one might wrongly ascribe the function of B to A. This is reminiscent the old joke of the researcher who concludes that a flea goes deaf when its legs have been removed because it no longer jumps when the table is banged. So what is said about the function of the components of the brain needs to be treated as a best approximation achieved within the current limits of experimentation.

The *brain stem* is a sheaf of nerves which allows the brain and the rest of the body to communicate through the spinal cord. It has components in its own right (not shown): the *pons,* which is a bulbous organ which acts as an outgoing and incoming relay station for information about movement; the *midbrain,* which relays communication of sensory and motor signals; and the *medulla,* which is involved in the control of internal functions such as heartbeat, digestion and respiration.

The *cerebellum* lurks behind the brain stem. It is known to contain beautiful treelike neurons arranged in parallel layers and (as the pons) this structure is concerned with muscular movement. In contrast with the pons, the cerebellum is thought to be active in learning early in life how to provide fine control to limb movement. Curiously enough, the cerebellum contains just under one third of all the neurons of the brain, and yet its action appears to be entirely unconscious.

The *cortex* is shown as a spread-out blanket. Inside the skull it is arranged in a folded way, forming the outer functional layer of the brain. Less than three millimetres in thickness, this is the organ where the higher functions of the brain seem to reside — sensory representation, the initiation of motor actions, orientation and the use and understanding of language. This is the organ where much of what is called "thinking" is thought to take place. It is so important that we shall take a closer look in a separate section.

The *corpus callosum* is a bundle of fibres which create communication between the two hemispheres of the brain. Folded in the centre of the brain is the *limbic system,* which appears to act as an internal control centre that regulates the proper working of the rest of the brain. It contains nutlike organs called the *amigdala* (not shown), which seem to have a role to play in emotion, and the *hippocampus* (shaped like a sea-horse, also not shown), which is thought to control the laying down of memories sorting the important sensory information from that which is not.

The group also contains the *hypothalamus,* which is involved in emotions, heart rate, blood pressure and the action of the *pituitary gland.* The latter produces chemical secretions for the rest of the brain which have large scale control effects (such as facilitating learning in large areas) and are not very well understood.

Finally, there is the *thalamus,* which receives information from sensors and distributes sensory information to the cortex. Now for a little more detail.

The Cortex

The splayed-out view of the cortex has been redrawn in Fig. 3.8. Again, through a process of studying lesions, areas of the cortex have been associated with various mental functions. While the diagram appears to be quite symmetrical, lesion experiments lead to the belief that the two halves of the cortex are engaged in different

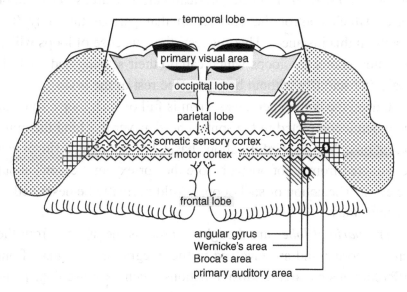

Fig. 3.8.   The cortex.

activities. On the whole, the left hemisphere (right on the diagram, as the top of the picture represents what is at the back of the head) seems to process language, while the right is involved in music and the appreciation of visual input. In some cases (not shown in the diagram) specialised areas are also physically asymmetrical.

Much of the cortex is given over to the support of elementary functions of registering sensory information and originating movement. The *occipital lobes* are concerned with vision and contain the *primary visual areas,* which receive connections from the eyes' *retinae* via the optic nerve (see the next section). The *temporal lobes* are associated with sound, learning, memory and emotions. These contain the *primary auditory areas,* which receive signals from the hearing apparatus (ears via the cochlea, etc.). As seen in Chapter 2 (Fig. 2.6), the *somatic sensory cortex* receives projections from tactile sensors in the body while the *motor cortex* is a corresponding strip which controls movement in very specific parts of the body. Interestingly, the specific areas in the sensory cortex (such as those having to do with the lips) are physically close to areas in the motor cortex which control the muscles in that part of the body (the mouth, in this instance). This suggests the existence of loops which are autonomous, i.e. loops which can do their sensing and controlling unconsciously without bothering the rest of the brain.

Indeed the human nervous system is full of such loops, some of them being completed in the spinal chord, never reaching the brain except on a "for your information" basis. For example, a finger can be retracted from a hot object before the cortex can "reason" about the event. The action of such loops would normally be described as "unconscious".

The *parietal lobes* are thought to process the signals from the sensory cortex and are involved in the integration of signals from different sensory areas. Most functions, such as reasoning, planning, speech and emotions, come together in the *frontal lobes.*

But perhaps the most interesting areas of the cortex, particularly for those who are curious about the role of language in consciousness, are those found in the parietal and frontal parts of the left hemisphere. They are *Broca's area,* discovered in the 1860s by the French investigator Paul Broca, and *Wernicke's area,* found in 1874 by the German Carl Wernicke. Together with the angular gyrus these areas appear to be vital to the understanding and production of speech. Damage to Broca's area leads to difficulties with the production of speech. This is not just a muscular impairment as would result from damage to the mouth area of the motor cortex. Norman Geschwind (1979) quoted a patient describing a dental appointment: "Yes ... Monday ... Dad and Dick ... Wednesday ... nine o'clock ... doctors ... and teeth." Clearly, the "thought" is there but the ability to string sentences together has gone.

On the other hand, damage to Wernicke's area leads to disabilities where the word-stringing seems fine but the appropriate phrases to describe a thought are missing. A patient (again quoted by Geschwind, 1979) with a lesion in Wernicke's area, when asked to describe a picture of two boys stealing cookies behind their mother's back, said, "Mother is away here working her work to get her better, but when she's looking the two boys looking in the other part. She's working another time." Wernicke's area also seems to be involved in the comprehension of speech. The angular gyrus appears to be a bridge between auditory language and visual information including the written language. It reaches out physically from Wernicke's area towards the visual processing parts of the cortex, i.e. the parietal and occipital lobes.

We shall return to these discoveries later when we consider language and consciousness. It is stressed that only a few of the known specialities of the brain have been mentioned here (for example, the olfactory or smell system has been omitted completely). The key issue is that what is known about the anatomy of the brain is a fascinating mixture of specialised and general active areas which operate in concert to produce what is sometimes called the symphony of consciousness. As we progress through this book we shall see that this sort of mixture can be modelled in state machines and the resulting function can be analysed by automata theory underlining the contention of the first Consequence.

The Visual System

Figure 3.9 is a sketch of the visual pathways in the brain. Important neural organs here are the lateral geniculate nuclei (lgn), which act as relay stations for the information conveyed from the retinae in the eyes by bundles of optic nerves. These regions are parts of the thalamus pictured in Fig. 3.7 and they are important in discussions about consciousness as they not only project information forwards to the primary visual cortex, but also receive information from the

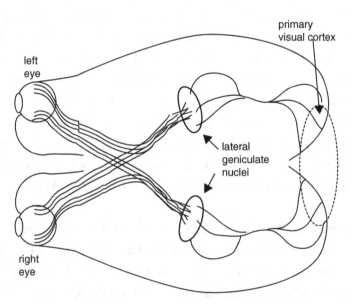

Fig. 3.9. The visual pathways.

cortex itself. As automata theory tells us, physical structure cannot sustain any unaided activity (let alone consciousness) without feedback paths. As we shall see, it is the feedback role of the lgn that has come under scrutiny in recent discussions about consciousness. The left field of both eyes is projected into the primary visual cortex in the right hemisphere, and the right field into that of the the left hemisphere.

The primary visual cortex is a finely layered neuronal structure. It consists of six layers, of which the fourth (from the surface) is divided into three parts. It is here that one of the most influential neurophysiological discoveries of the century was made, by David Hubel and Torsten Wiesel, who were awarded the Nobel prize for their efforts. The primary visual cortex is a highly structured, three-dimensional array of feature detectors. For example, a horizontal bar in the field of view will give a localised firing of neurons in the cortex whereas if the orientation of the bar is changed another region will respond. Many other such features, including moving ones, are processed in this localised way. A fascinating account of the way in which the visual cortex and its receptive fields are organised may be found in an accessible article by Hubel and Wiesel (1979).

We shall refer again to some of these anatomical details as we take a look at the way in which neurophysiologists have gone about trying to track down consciousness within the intricate neural architecture of the brain.

How Does the Brain Create Consciousness?

Philosopher John Searle is fond of saying that, like the heart is an organ which causes blood circulation, the brain is an organ which causes consciousness — and that's that! Neurobiologists are not happy to leave it at that and one of the most hotly pursued topics in contemporary brain research is to try to correlate the elements of consciousness with observed events in the brain. In addition to observations of patients with specific brain lesions, technology comes to the aid of this effort. A technique known as positron emission tomography (PET) can produce pictures of active areas of the brain by measuring increased blood flow. Although this is a rather imprecise indication of what bits of the brain are doing, it indicates which areas are involved during various mental tasks. Also, more is getting to be known about the role of chemical control in the brain. So, if the hunt for consciousness is proceeding nicely in the place where it belongs, i.e. in studies of the brain, why is it relevant for an engineer to come along with his neural state machines? I hope that this question will be answered in the following brief reviews of various neurobiological views of consciousness.

Terence Picton and Donald Stuss of the University of Ottawa (1994) have summarised much of what has recently been discovered of the localisation of functions usually associated with "being conscious". For example, the frontal regions of the brain appear to be involved in what is called the "personality" of an individual as well as more basic memory functions of all kinds: episodic memory (straight recall of experience), semantic memory (constructions from experience) and working memory (short term retention of sensory experience). However, they come to the conclusion that "consciousness ... works in a distributed manner". This is because PET measurements show that other areas of the cortex are active at the same time as those primarily concerned with memory. Neural state machines help us to conceive of the relationship of short term memory (i.e. *being* in an area of state structure) to recall (falling into states that represent past experience) and to the creation of memory (altering the state structure through neuron function changes). The state machine allows one to stand back and not be surprised at the way in which *any* neural system, whether real or artificial, might have distributed memory functions. Much more will be said of this, including the creation of semantic memory, in the later parts of this book.

Of particular importance is Stuss and Picton's report that PET scans reveal that *mental* visual imagery stimulates the primary visual cortex in much the same way as incoming sensory information. How can that be possible when the optic nerves are inactive? In addition, PET scans show that very similar areas of the brain engage in "thinking" about mental images as thinking about what is being sensed when it is being sensed. It has been seen briefly in Chapter 1 that neural state machines explain these effects through a process called iconic learning. In later chapters we shall see how important iconic learning is to the whole business of holding models of the world "in one's head". Talking of which, Stuss and Picton summarise their review by writing:

> "The human brain forms and maintains a model of the world and itself within that world. This model can be used to explain the past events and predict the future."

They then go on to suggest that while consciousness has many elements, the most important one is its representation of the experienced world. If this is what we wish to understand, the key issue is how the brain mediates between internal representation and sensory input. In advocating the use of automata theory in Consequence 1, I am suggesting that this form of mediation can be modelled and understood as a general principle in the class of objects called neural state machines. The brain can be many things, but one thing it cannot help being is a neural state machine as defined in the earlier parts of this chapter. So, all that is being said is that a central problem about consciousness recognised within neurobiology can be formulated and studied in a general way using the language of automata theory.

The Concentric Theory of Consciousness

Among the many recent discussions about the way in which consciousness might occur in the brain, one by Susan Greenfield (1995) stands out for suggesting a full theory which links chemical and transmissional aspects of the neural structure of the brain to ways in which the world maybe represented. As an expert in Parkinson's disease and a person with a deep knowledge of neurodegenerative effects in the brain, she calls her model the "concentric" theory of consciousness:

> "Consciousness is spatially multiple yet effectively single at any one time. It is an emergent property of non-specialised and divergent groups of neurons (gestalts) that is continuously variable with respect to, and always entailing a stimulus epicentre. The size of the gestalt and hence the depth of the prevailing consciousness, is a product of the interaction between the recruiting strength of the epicentre and the degree of arousal"

This definition makes strong use of the metaphor of a drop of water falling into a still pond and the widening ripples that this creates. The drop is the sensory stimulation (or epicentre) and the ripples are the ensuing sensations. Learning creates meaningful links between neurons, and groups of such linked structures are called *gestalts* (global assessments; noticing the wood when there are only trees to be seen). A particular sensory stimulation causes ripples of activity through specific neural assemblies. These ripples give rise to being conscious of the stimulus and its associations as set in the links between neurons. Greenfield sees the theory as robust because, by appealing to the *size* of the gestalts, she can make predictions of the variability of conscious experience both within one individual (under the influence of drugs or other chemically induced changes of mood) and across individuals who have suffered brain damage or are labelled as mentally ill. She associates small gestalts with overfocused obsessive, repetitive behaviour, giving as an example Ecstasy-dosed ravers dancing all night. Large gestalts lead to an inability to focus, living in the past as might occur in the elderly or sufferers of some forms of dementia.

What light could automata theory shed on the concentric theory? Indeed, is there a need to enter the cold world of formalism when an appealing scenario of ripples propagating through neural assemblies is available? Again, I would argue positively, and I will spend a few paragraphs taking a look at the concentric theory from the point of view of neural state machines.

The words "spatially multiple yet effectively single at any one time" are precisely what is meant by a "state" in automata theory. There is agreement among hunters of consciousness that consciousness does not occur in one place in the brain. As discussed in the previous section, modern measurement techniques support the idea that whatever consciousness might be it is widespread within the brain. The only slight problem with Susan Greenfield's definition is that among the spatially multiple activities of neurons those that contribute to consciousness appear to be constantly changing. She deals with this in the next phrase, "an emergent property of non-specialised and divergent groups of neurons (gestalts) that is continuously variable". This is where what is being proposed can benefit from some formal scrutiny

In all processing systems, including the neural networks of the brain, information as we normally understand it is carried by the entire set of signals generated by a processing element — the neuron in this case. The entire set of signals of a neuron in the brain includes quiescence, full firing and all possibilities in between. If firing contributes to a consciously felt event in the brain, so does non-firing. Words such as "gestalts" and "groupings" suggest that only the firing neurons contribute to consciousness. Indeed,

Greenfield indicates that they have to fire strongly in order to contribute to strongly felt mental sensations. She also describes these groupings as changing rapidly in the manner of mercury pools on a vibrating surface. However, this does not remove the responsibility of defining sets of the totality of neurons which at some point might contribute to various "gestalts" but at other times might be quiescent. This set, whichever way it may be distributed in the brain, can be called the set of neurons that are responsible for consciousness. These, indeed, are the state variables of a neural state machine: a subset of the total set of neurons. Given this, there is no need to evoke gestalts — the concept of a state made up of values of these state variables will do. The automata view which has been taken in this book (as seen in Consequences 2 and 3) is that there are some neurons which are never involved in conscious activity, whereas those which are can get into states which are either consciously meaningful (such as mental images of past experience) or not (such as dreamless sleep). The concept of a state encourages us to define formally the difference between these two types of states as a contribution to the definition of consciousness. This will be done in the next chapter.

So what would the formal interpretation of a "gestalt" be? The difficulty with its description as it stands is that it sometimes relates to an instantaneous event (the shape of the mercury pools at one instant) which is a *state* in the automaton, and at other times it is the excursion of such pools under the control of an *epicentre,* as in "with respect to, and always entailing a stimulus epicentre". Indeed, the most useful interpretation of a gestalt is in the latter dynamic sense. In accepting this, it becomes easy to see that an epicentre is the controlling input to the state machine and the subset state structure for that input is a gestalt. An example might help.

In Fig. 3.10(a) there is a group of three fully connected neurons which, it is assumed, have learned a set of functions. They are

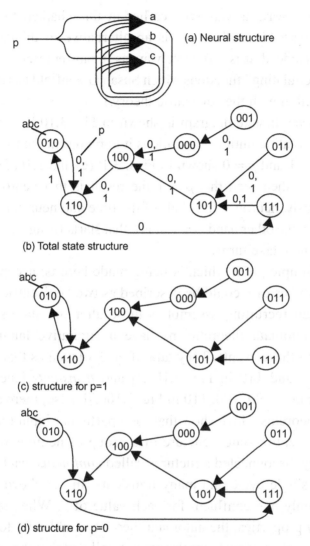

Fig. 3.10. "Gestalts" in a simple neural structure.

controlled by a "sensory" input, *p*. Note that in the concentric theory, learned functions are represented in the favoured way of neural modellers — by weights. No weights are shown in Fig. 3.10(a) as it is assumed that they are included within the triangle representing the neuron. Anyway, as was seen earlier in this chapter, thinking in terms of variable truth tables is an alternative to thinking about weights. (Indeed, it is a flexible way, as it can represent the higher order "modulating" functions which Susan Greenfield has discussed in connection with the concentric theory.)

The overall state diagram is shown in Fig. 3.10(b). This is not terribly revealing until one partitions it to represent the two sensory events $p = 1$ and $p = 0$ shown in Figs. 3.10(c) and 3.10(d), respectively. It is then seen that $p = 1$ the result is that neuron b fires continuously, neuron a fires half of the time and neuron c is quiescent. If, on the other hand, $p = 1$, it is a that starts firing continuously while b and c take turns.

The simple point which is being made here is: accepting that the two values of p could be described as two "epicentric" events, rather than recruiting assemblies these alter the state structure. Indeed, automata theoreticians have a figurative language for describing these events. They talk of *cycles* [such as that between states 010 and 110 in Fig. 3.10(c)] and *transients* [such as the sequence 001, 000, 100, 110 in Fig. 3.10(c)]. Also, there are some simple theorems which show that for a particular input (epicentric event) the entire state structure of a group of neurons breaks up into many disconnected structures called *confluents,* each consisting of a single cycle and many transients. In the above example there is only one confluent for each value of p. When talking of *emergent* properties, the automata theorist would refer to the fact that the number of such confluents is small and that the cycles are short as a result of the generalisation of the neurons and the shape of the network. I am suggesting that this is a more precise and revealing language than the notion (albeit poetic) of ripples in a pool.

The major point we learn through automata theory is that an appropriate level of description of networks and hence the function of brains may be in state structures (i.e. *state space)* rather than in the dogged adherence to physical space within which are cast theories such as Hebb's notion of "reverberations" in loops of neurons (1949) and Greenfield's concentric ripples. The former tells us globally what is happening in a group of neurons (the wood?) whereas the latter tries to track the behaviour of individual neurons in a group (the trees?). However, if one were merely to think of a gestalt as a confluent in state space recruited by a particular sensory experience, many of Susan Greenfield's suggestions about the size and richness of such confluents, their indication of different behaviours and chemical conditions in the brain, would still provide a useful insight.

The Language of Automata: A Summary

Consequence 1 of the Basic Guess requires acceptance of the fact that the brain may be treated as a state machine and hence discussed through automata theory. While this in itself is not hard to accept, the fact that consciousness could ever be discussed in the language of automata theory is much harder. In fact, it flies in the face of some arguments which say that no formal treatment exists within which consciousness can be discussed. As is clear from the Basic Guess and reflected in this Consequence, I happen not to believe this. I have therefore drawn a sketch of automata theory here arguing that it is a highly appropriate language (if not the only appropriate language) in which clarity can be brought to arguments about consciousness. Its main property is that it links the three major ingredients that go into these arguments: physical structure, creation of world models through learning, and use of such models in appropriate behaviour. But only the language of this discourse has been introduced so far: the work of actually using it starts in the next chapter.

Automaton Does Not Mean Zombie

Automata Theory is Still OK

In Chapter 3, 'automata theory' appears because it is a good tool for discussing systems that have inner states that cannot be observed or measured from outside the system. This formal automaton has continued to be an enormously useful aid for thinking of the 'mind' as the unobservable inner state of a third party. It also induces a feeling of possession about my own mind which feels valuable, inviolable, and totally my own property. It is in this spirit that the title of the book published in 2005: *The World in My Mind, My Mind in the World: Key mechanisms of consciousness in people, animals and machines*[a] [WMMW for short] was concocted.

As I often give lectures to audiences that do not have automata formalisms for breakfast, the word 'automaton' connects to the word 'zombie' giving exactly the opposite impression to that of 'useful tools' which I am trying to create. But thinking of zombies

---

[a] Aleksander, I. (2005). *The World in My Mind, My Mind in the World: Key mechanisms of consciousness in people, animals and machines*, Imprint Academic, Exeter.

as non-conscious organisms with perfectly human outward behaviour is not entirely a matter that comes from implausible fiction. Philosophers indulge in thinking about zombies! To underscore the hard problem (seen in PS2; the postscript to Chapter 2), Chalmers uses the fact that a seemingly conscious human could be a zombie with no consciousness and the two could not physically be told apart by an observer. In WMMW I rebut this by arguing that a proper study of consciousness starts with the only organism I know to be conscious — ME and that this avoids zombies because I am the only one to know that I am not a zombie.

Brains

Chapter 3 gives a childishly sketchy description of the physical brain. The intention was to stress that, taking a neural automaton modelling stance, one needs to be sensitive to the existence of many areas each of which has different automata characteristics. And then there is the interaction between the 50 or so such areas — but this is an engineering and mathematics problem that provides enjoyable challenges for researchers.

Since the publication of the first edition, considerable work has been done on brain-inspired multi-automaton models. One of the most comprehensive ones was a visual system roughly modelled on a primate visual cortex containing 20 or so interacting automata. This appears in more detail in the postscript for Chapter 4 (PS4).

Languages for the Mechanics of Consciousness

In Chapter 3, I stressed (perhaps overstressed) that the language of automata theory, being the language of systems with hidden inner states, was the appropriate language that links physical structure (e.g. the neural brain) to state structure (say, the system of inner conscious mental states). I am still convinced that this is right, but I am less sure that it actually says very much. At the time of writing this second edition, while it is accepted that 'mind' stands to 'brain' in roughly the relationship just expressed, there remains the question of why the states in parts of the brain contribute to conscious experience and others do not. As mentioned in PS2, Tononi introduced the measure of information integration that determines whether there is sufficient causal connectivity to give a state the uniqueness and differentiation that is a mark of a conscious mental state.

So 'causality' enters the vocabulary for measuring amounts of consciousness in a dynamic system. This theme is stressed by Anil Seth and his colleagues where Granger Causality[b] is used to provide a comparative measure of possible levels of consciousness different brain areas.[c]

Another word that has entered the language of mind and brain is 'simulation'. Based on the ideas of Germund Hesslow of Lund University in Sweden, the mind is a simulation of the world that allows the organism to make predictions about the outer world.[d] The word is used in its computational sense rather than as an emerging property of a neural brain. A similar stance comes from the ideas of Owen Holland as a way of powering his skeletal (or 'anthropomimetic', as he calls it) robot, CRONOS. By 'simulation', Holland means the 'modelling' power of the brain — the mind then being a model of the entity, the world it is in and the constraints governing

---

[b] This is an econometric measure that tests by how much a time series may have been caused by another.

[c] Seth, A., Barrett, A., Barnett, L. (2011), Causal density and integrated information as measures of conscious level, *Phil. Trans. R. Soc. A*, 369, pp. 3748–3767.

[d] Hesslow, G. (2012). Current status of the simulation theory of cognition, *Brain Research*, 1428, pp. 71–79.

the relationship between the two.[e] It is worth remarking that the CRONOS project was the first investigation into robot consciousness funded by a national funding body: the Engineering and Physical Sciences Research Council in the UK (awarded in 2004).

In Sum

It is no longer surprising that the relationship between mind and brain should be likened to the relationship between the state structure and physical structure of a finite state machine (an embodiment of a formal automaton) and the physical details of that embodiment. This is a far more satisfactory simile than the misleading idea that 'mind is to brain as software is to hardware'. This is just silly as there is no physical parallel between brain and computer but there is one between brain and neural automata.

---

[e] Holland, O. and Goodman, R. (2003). Robots with internal models: a route to machine consciousness?, *Journal of Consciousness Studies, Special Issue on Machine Consciousness*, 10 (4), pp.77–111.

Dear Professor Naskela,

In connection with your grant application, I feel that I should thank you for responding so promptly with increasing detail of your standpoint on a study of consciousness. As you are certainly aware, the fact that you question the accepted theory developed by Sir Global Attractor-State is not received with enthusiasm by many of my colleagues and may therefore give your proposal little chance of being funded.

However, your examples of this fictitious place called Earth, where organisms are puzzled by their consciousness, have struck a personal note of curiosity with me. The fact that the organisms talk of reverberations and concentric ripples in their brains shows that you can view this matter with some humour. I suggest that in order for me to better represent your views to the Council, we might meet so as to speed up the process of communication. I look forward to hearing from you to arrange a meeting at a suitable time.

Yours sincerely,

Molecula Multiplexer
Artificial Intelligence Co-ordinator

Chapter 4

The Inner Eye of Consciousness

Preamble: Engineering the mind of Magnus

In the last two chapters our conscious robot Magnus seems to have been slightly forgotten. But Magnus is important in one particular way: the engineering process of building up Magnus' artificial consciousness requires an understanding of the ingredients of consciousness, not to mention the "specifications" of consciousness. The fact that some day someone with a lot of money and a great deal of patience may wish to build this conscious machine is not the primary aim of the design. "How might it work?" definitely is. Skeptics might argue that because it is impossible to define consciousness anyway, the whole enterprise is sunk from the start. I venture to suggest that the design process might actually make the process of definition possible, without diminishing the awe we all have for the concept.

So far, through the Basic Guess, I have declared the belief that the sensation of consciousness in some organism which is accepted to be conscious is due to the firing patterns of its neural structure. Consequence 1 suggests that we might examine these ideas in a formal model of a neural state machine using the simple language and techniques of automata theory. This chapter is about three further consequences of this belief. Consequence 2 follows from the notion that it would be foolish to suggest that consciousness is due to the firing of *all* the neurons of a neural state machine. As has been mentioned in the last chapter, a very high proportion of the brain's neurons are found in the cerebellum — the organ which is involved in the refinement of the control of movement. This is the classical unconscious function. I am conscious of wanting to grab an apple on the table and the next thing that I know is that I've taken it and am examining it for wormholes. The action of grabbing it and bringing it closer is an immensely complex task of the control of a large number of muscles, but it requires no detailed thought — it is unconscious. In this chapter we consider automata models of neurons that do and neurons that do not contribute to consciousness.

But then, two further questions arise. The easier one to answer is: "The neurons which contribute to conscious sensations having been identified, is any state they get into a state of consciousness?" It makes sense to suggest that this is unlikely (otherwise dreamless sleep or anaesthesia would be impossible). Where Consequence 2 distinguishes between conscious and unconscious events in space, Consequence 3 distinguishes between conscious and unconscious states in time within the same physical groups of neurons. Here too automata models are used to illustrate the Consequence.

The more difficult question to answer is: "Where do the conscious states among the neurons that cause consciousness come from?" Consequence 4 deals with this question and explains the "iconic transfer" mentioned in the Basic Guess. In many ways this is a kind of centrepiece of the theory found in this book — a kind of pivot around which the automata theory of consciousness revolves. This is where an explanation is given of what seems to be the primary function of consciousness — the functional memory of past experience, its integration into a perception of the present and its projection into the future. Those who fear that I shall equate this memory mechanism to that which is found in a computer need fear no longer. In fact, I shall argue that, where a computer can be viewed as a filing cabinet (choose your file, put things in it or take things out), the neural state machine has a completely different way of achieving memory which includes a vivid pictorial memory with powers of accessing itself. This explains some of the characteristics of human memory which psychologists have identified: episodic memory (remembering events), semantic memory (remembering things which may not have been experienced) and working memory (the brief act of memory which is present during perception). Other psychophysical effects, such as arousal and attention, come into focus from Consequence 4 and are discussed at the end of this chapter.

Designing an Octopus

Consequence 2: Inner neuron partitioning

The inner neurons of a conscious organism are partitioned into at least three sets:

Perceptual inner neurons: responsible for perception and perceptual memory;

Auxiliary inner neurons: responsible for inner "labelling" of perceptual events;

Autonomous inner neurons: responsible for "life support" functions — not involved in consciousness.

What is consciousness for? To put it another way, were I to design organisms that should survive effectively in an environment which provides means of survival but makes them a bit hard to get, would I need to look for "consciousness" in my catalogue of silicon neural circuits? Predictably, the answer is positive, and to illustrate the point I shall set myself the task of designing a rather simple octopus which is vaguely specified as follows:

> The octopus with its complex means of locomotion needs to roam about the ocean floor in a more or less random fashion. If it sees a small crab it needs to assess it: Is it the right size to eat? Is it alive? This assessment is based on previous experience — memories of struggles with crabs which were too large to eat and stomachaches caused by eating dead crabs. In addition, the octopus is to run away from threats which it too remembers from narrow escapes.

Neural circuitry is all that is available for designing things, which is fine. (That's no problem as I know that any mechanism, even a conventional computer, can be designed with neural circuitry.) The fearsome creature (understandably called the "devil fish" in olden days) and the three groups of neurons of the Consequence are shown in Fig. 4.1. The reason these groups are shown as separate with communication between them supports the use of the word "partition" in the Consequence. It means that a neuron cannot be in any of the two stated groups at once. This follows rather obviously both in the design of the octopus and in real brains, as individual neurons having just one output (axon) can devote it to only one task. So a neuron cannot control a leg while simultaneously helping to digest food. But why are these three groups essential?

In the design of the octopus, I first need a system which will normally cause the octopus's legs to move in such a way as to bring about the ocean floor roaming with a minimum of control from a "higher" circuit. Yes, some control is required — stop, go left, run away, etc. But the last thing that the octopus should do is to have to work out by trial and error the individual controls it needs in its legs

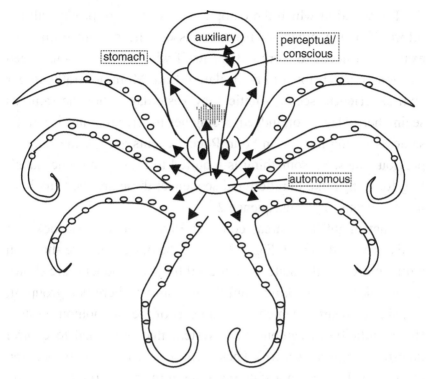

Fig. 4.1.   The artificial octopus.

to achieve all this locomotion. In a similar way its digestive processes require neural control, but it is in the interest of the octopus not to have to control these "consciously". This identifies the need for autonomous, unconscious circuitry: the "autonomous inner neurons" of Consequence 2.

The next major area is where the octopus can relate its perception to its past experience and turn this into action: the "perceptual inner neurons" group. Exactly how this works is a big topic which will be refined elsewhere (particularly in Consequence 4). Here we shall get a glimpse of it in the more detailed design discussed below. But what of the third area? Why are "auxiliary" neurons required?

The world in which the octopus exists does not provide all the information the organism needs to assess the current event. For example, it needs to work out for itself whether the crab has been still long enough for it to be declared dead. More generally, in our own experience, seeing Auntie May yesterday is not the same as seeing her today — or, indeed, seeing her for five minutes is not the same as seeing her for an hour. Recent events are not the same as previous ones. So something is required to provide an inner labelling for things like duration and sequence; these are the "auxiliary inner neurons" in Consequence 2.

What might these areas contain? To answer this, we look at a kind of rough design in Fig. 4.2, where the three areas are shown in a little more detail.[6] State structures of these components are shown in Figs. 4.3–4.5. Working from the bottom up, there is a group of, say, sixteen neurons which make up part of the autonomous system (for simplicity, the autonomous system that is needed to control digestion etc. is not shown). These neurons each control the position of one leg. They form a state machine in their own right, requiring the minimum of control from the rest of the system. Part of the state structure of this component is shown in Fig. 4.3(b).

The first thing to note in (a) is the coding of the signals to the leg (tentacle) muscles. This is arranged for neuron pairs shown as columns. Black means "firing". When one of a pair is firing, the tentacle curls one way, and when the other is firing it curls the other way. If neither is firing, the tentacle remains relaxed. The autonomous system requires only a few messages from the rest of the system (e.g. *roam, left, stop...*). Each of these sets off a continually repeated sequence of appropriate tentacle movements which is sustained even if no specific message (ø) is supplied from higher centres. The point

---

[6] Note that much of this is an elaboration of the example given under "Learning and remembering" in Chapter 2.

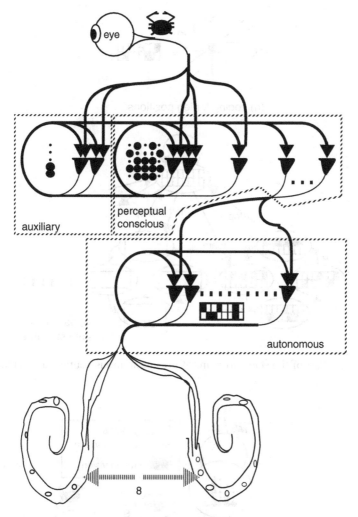

Fig. 4.2.   A rough design of the neural system of the octopus.

being made here is that this type of arrangement allows the movement control not to interfere with whatever "thinking" the octopus may need to do. This makes sense even in human terms: while jogging, the last thing I wish to do is to think of every muscle and sinew. But I do wish to control my speed or stride size by thinking about it. The other advantage of the detachment of the autonomous net from

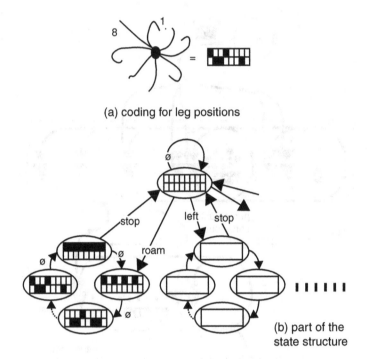

(a) coding for leg positions

(b) part of the
state structure

Fig. 4.3. Part of the state structure of the autonomous neural state machine.

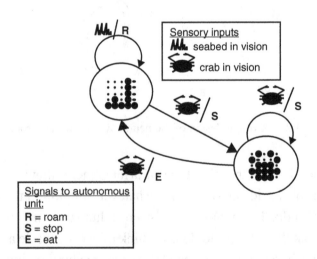

Fig. 4.4. The state diagram for crab catching — incorrect version.

the thinking net is that it can respond to signals from other sensors, such as impediments in the way of the tentacles. Taking the jogging example again, I can recover from stumbling on a raised paving stone before the event "enters my consciousness'. While this is not shown in the figures so as not to make them even more confusing than they are at the moment, it is quite possible to imagine not only that the autonomous system controls the limbs, but also that effects sensed by the limbs could influence or interrupt the process.

Now for the rest of the network. It is assumed that iconic representations of experience are already present in the network (how they get there is discussed in connection with Consequence 4). So, in Fig. 4.2, the iconic representation for the crab is shown with large dots for firing neurons and small dots for non-firing ones. In Fig. 4.4 we see a state structure for the perceptual/conscious neurons, which for instructive reasons will turn out to be incomplete. It also contains the representation of an empty seabed which might be encountered during roaming. It suggests that roaming continues until a crab is seen. The iconic state changes to indicate the perception of the crab. Then nothing needs to happen until the octopus decides to eat the crab and return to roaming.

This structure has been purposely mis-designed to illustrate an error that is easily made, particularly by those who are critical of the state structure explanation of consciousness. They would argue that it has not been explained *how* the octopus decides to eat the crab. This criticism is perfectly justified because the structure in Fig. 4.4 does not read as suggested above. The way it *does* read is:

> "The octopus roams until it sees the crab. It then stops and stands still until, by chance, it eats the crab."

This may well be the state of affairs before the octopus has had the experience of eating dead crabs and catching live ones. The problem is how to represent the experience of duration. At the moment, all that seems possible is the re-entrant state which represents the crab. This is where the essential nature of the auxiliary neurons becomes evident. Figure 4.2 shows that these neurons are intimately connected with the neurons that form iconic representations of the sensory experience. Therefore they form part of the conscious experience of the organism, but not in a way which has pictorial representation. The true state diagram which takes into account the experience of the octopus is shown in Fig. 4.5, where the action of the auxiliary neurons is shown as a column at the left of the state picture. Here time is encoded as a rising thermometer.

Reading the state diagram of Fig. 4.5, we see that it now says:

"The octopus roams until it sees a crab. It stops, and if the crab does not move it progresses through states that represent advancing time until it gets to an internal state which represents pain. If the crab moves, the octopus moves with it, but then eating the crab does not lead to the pain state."

So far, the model has been deficient in several ways. First, it does not explain how the auxiliary units get to work in the useful way in which they do. As things stand, it seems as if the auxiliary action has been programmed in. But conscious systems do not have programmers. As our description of the self-development of consciousness progresses through this book, we shall see that the auxiliary units come into play through a process of learning to resolve ambiguities such as those seen in Fig. 4.4. Secondly, Fig. 4.5 gives the impression of a truly mechanistic organism which does not have much room for what might be the "planning" and "self-awareness" nature of consciousness. This too is a matter for further explanation, as when we are discussing corollaries 5 (planning) and 6 (self-awareness). At this stage all that needs to be noted is the essential nature of auxiliary units and hence their appearance in Consequence 2.

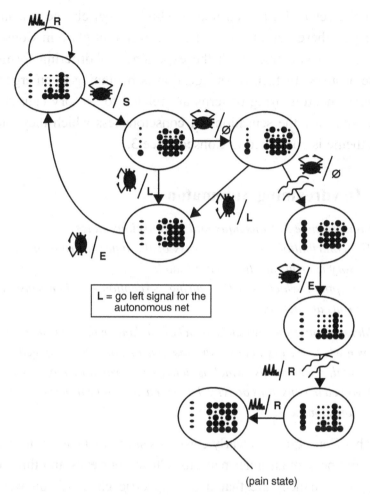

Fig. 4.5. The correct state diagram for crab catching.

Thirdly, while all that is being said about consciousness hinges very much on the "iconic" side of the representation on the perceptual inner neurons, it is proper to ask whether the representation on the auxiliary neurons is conscious or not. Logically the answer is positive, as one talks of being "conscious of the passage of time". But in another sense the consciousness of time does not have the vivid character of a mental image. This is precisely the reason for talking of these neurons as being in a different class in Consequence 2 — it coincides with the experience of differing forms of consciousness. In fact, the suggestion is beginning to emerge that the more neuron firing patterns are related to sensory causes, the more vivid are the sensations of consciousness which they cause. This theme is continued in Consequence 3.

The Daydreaming Automaton

Consequence 3: Conscious and unconscious states
The contribution to consciousness of the inner neurons and the sensory neurons has three major modes:
Perceptual: which is active during perception — when sensory neurons are active;

Mental, conscious: which is an act of thinking in the same neurons even when sensory neurons are inactive or otherwise engaged;
Mental, unconscious: which is activity generated by the neurons involved in conscious activity, but which does not cause sensations of consciousness.

This Consequence clearly classifies states that can occur within the same perceptual inner neurons. Close your eyes and think of a chair. The chances are that it is a specific chair. If you were to describe your thoughts, it would not be unusual for you to say something like "I am conscious of a chair with a straw-covered seat, and a back with wooden slats...". This type of metal imagery is the centrepiece of consciousness and many (including Crick, 1994, and Zeki, 1993) have suggested that it involves neurons which are active during "eyes open" perception.

Arguments about consciousness have often been bedevilled by the "inner eye" problem. I can "see" the chair in my head, but who is the "I" that's doing the looking? Consequence 3 addresses this problem in a direct way. We may already have accepted in Chapter 1 that sensors in the body cause firing in neurons in the sensory cortex which give the sensation of touch. Similarly eyes and ears make neurons fire, and this, most likely, causes what we call perception. But if consciousness were just perception there would be no mystery about it. Consequence 3 suggests that for mental imagery to be as effective as it seems to be, some neurons that are active during perception can be stoked up when the sensors are somehow shut off. So there is no suggestion that I (as some strange homunculus) am looking at images on a screen in my head, but, instead, it is just the firing of my neurons which causes a sensation which, whether I'm looking at something or thinking about it, involves some neurons in common.

There is a danger that talk of mental imagery being like perception might be overdone. Mental imagery is different from perception in two important ways. First, it seems not to have the sharpness of actual vision; then, it has a fleeting, slipping quality, easily distracted and altered either from within or through sensory events. We shall see in Consequence 4 that a learning model exists which explains how these mental images get there, while Consequence 3 merely suggests that given the belief in the Basic Guess that the firing of neurons causes consciousness, "being conscious of something" makes use of the same neural circuitry whether this is actually perceived or imagined. In a sense this has already been assumed in the octopus example for Consequence 2. The perceptual/conscious inner neurons represent crabs in a crablike way and the seabed in a seabed-like way. Now Consequence 3 suggests that this representation can have both a perceptual and a mental nature.

An important issue is what is meant by "the sensory neurons are inactive". Clearly, there many occasions when mental states come to the fore. Certainly, if I close my eyes I can picture all sorts of things. However, even with my eyes open, I can both sustain a high degree

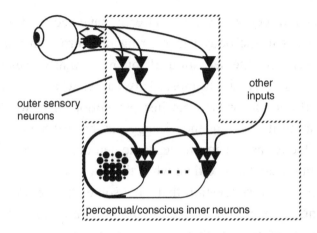

Fig. 4.6.   Influences on the perceptual/conscious inner neurons.

of perception and call upon mental imagery. Typical is the process of reading. The sensory system is occupied in reading the words while mental images of their meaning are being formed. Figure 4.6 (borrowed from the octopus example) contains a suggestion for a neural state machine structure which gives rise to these interrelated phenomena.

As things are beginning to get a little complicated, it is necessary to proceed in small steps. First, more needs to be said about the sensory neurons mentioned in the Consequence. These are shown in Fig. 4.6 for one sense: vision. However, the inner neurons forming the feedback of the network could receive information from other senses. Second, the firing of the outer neurons contributes to sensations of consciousness during active perception and could be responsible for the details of what is perceived. In living organisms these outer sensory structures are known to be well organised into feature-detecting groups[7] and are bound to contribute to the vivid nature of active perception.

---

[7]These structures have been mentioned in the last chapter in connection with the visual system and are described in Hubel and Wiesel (1979).

Third, the outer sensory neurons can become inactive, as in the case of shutting one's eyes. However, one does not shut off one's ears or tastebuds. Referring to inactive sensory neurons implies that there are internal controls which modify the firing of sensory neurons. We shall show below how this is handled in a state structure model.

Further, the feedback in the perceptual/conscious inner units ensures that memory can be sustained even in the absence of perceptual input. We shall see in Consequence 4 that this memory has the quality of inner recall of the original sensation, but with greater freedom to change than when originally sensed. Also, in the absence of sensory neuron activity, the experience of the firing of inner neurons is qualitatively different from direct perception.

Finally, the inner perceptual/conscious neurons can be triggered from a variety of sources. The nature of feedback networks is that they home in on one memory at a time and ignore other triggers. Which memory is selected may be a subtle matter which in psychology goes under the heading of "attention". So some kind of daydreaming could go on. The inner neurons could be producing memories of a nice day at the beach while the eyes and ears are exposed to a boring lecture on algebra. In the case of the octopus the inner representation of the crab could be generated by a signal related to hunger. The contest for representing one among many alternatives is something that neural net experts have explored in some depth under the heading of "competitive representations" (see Aleksander and Morton, 1995, for a simple explanation of the work of Teuvo Kohonen, Steve Grossberg and Kuhiniko Fukushima on competitive representations).

The State Structure of Daydreams and Dreams

Looking at Fig. 4.6 again, one finds that there is a question of how one might account for the way the various incoming channels could

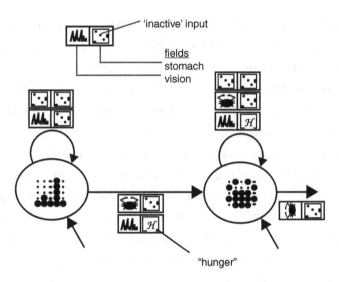

Fig. 4.7.   Input conditions and state entries.

lead to state changes. Automata theory suggests that all the incoming information can be treated as one message which determines whether the state should change or not. However, this message could contain "fields" which may be identified in a state diagram and which represent the state of the various incoming channels. Figure 4.7 is an example, again related to our octopus (auxiliary neurons not shown). Here only two input fields are shown — the left one for the visual sensors and the right one for the stomach sensors. While this is by no means a complete state diagram, it shows some of the effects contained in Consequence 3. An inactive field in neurobiology is generally assumed to be a group of neurons where little firing is in progress. Similarly, in our neural state machines, as we indicate firing as black and not firing as white, the assumption is that inactivity is a largely white field with a few black dots on it, the dots occurring in odd positions which could change arbitrarily with time.

Two states representing a crab and the seabed are shown. In theory they could both be sustained either with both fields inactive or in response to the appropriate sensory input. It is also shown that a hunger signal from the stomach could switch the representation to the crab even if one has not been seen. Finally a transition is shown away from the forward-looking crab when the crab moves to the left. It is stressed again that this description says nothing about how such representations get there; the aim of Consequence 3 is simply to draw attention to the different modes of "recalling" in neural state machines which are embedded in the Basic Guess and earlier Consequences.

But before we go on to the much-heralded Consequence 4, it is fun to make some conjectures about the way that sleep and dreaming might happen in this scheme. This relates to the last part of the Consequence: the existence of unconscious states in the feedback part of the state machine. Sleep could be defined as the input when all or most of the fields to the inner neurons are in an inactive state. This means that the automaton is free to wander about its state structure in a way that is driven by random events. But it is not necessarily constrained to visit states that have been made meaningful or conscious. It can get into states that are totally unrelated to any form of learned experience. It is common knowledge that in human beings that there are two distinct types of sleep. There is sleep during which dreaming occurs. This is known as rapid eye movement (REM) sleep — during dreaming it seems that there is some contact between the inner perceptual/conscious neurons and the autonomous system which drives the eye muscles. Dreaming is also a sign that the inner perceptual/conscious neurons are in states related to experience. But transitions between such states are not driven by sensory neurons which are inactive, so the transitions between mental images have a haphazard and arbitrary nature. To an automata theorist there is little in the way of mystery in dreaming. The intriguing questions are: Why do living organisms not dream all the time? Why are periods of dreaming and non-dreaming entered in such regular patterns?

Through automata models it is possible to show that trajectories in state space when the inputs are inactive take a cyclic form. It may also be possible to argue that the perceptual states learned by the system are bunched together in an area of state space. The cyclic trajectories then move in and out of these (causing dreaming when in), causing periods of REM and non-REM sleep at regular intervals, as a comet returns to the solar system at regular intervals. Clearly this is all conjecture. Many experiments on artificial dreaming still remain to be done in research laboratories. Suffice it to say here that the third leg of Consequence 3 draws attention to the fact that not all the states of the conscious neurons need to create feelings of consciousness.

Learning to be Conscious

Consequence 4: Iconic learning

To qualify for a contribution to consciousness, firing patterns in the inner perceptual/conscious neurons need to be created through dominant neural inputs which sample the activity of outer sensory neurons and influence the function of the inner neurons. This has been called "iconic learning".

Put in this way, this sounds more like a theorem that needs to be proved than a Consequence. It would be pedantic to argue about this, but it does seem to me inescapable that these iconic transfers are at the bottom of the creation of states that cause conscious sensations for their owners. Why this should be inescapable is the subject of this section.

What has been learned so far about representations which, in consequence of the Basic Guess linking sensation to firing patterns, fix the character of these patterns? First, they must retain the relationship between the parts of the pattern and reality whether they are imagined or perceived; second, they must be capable of being retrieved from appropriate triggers; third, they must be capable of being sustained even in the absence of triggers. Although this has not yet arisen, it will be seen later in the book — when we consider automata that can develop the use of language — that the inner representation must be such that it can be described by the automaton itself in whatever it can muster.

The next question is: Given a dynamic neural system (brain, state machine, whatever), what are the options for inner representations of sensed events? To me, there appear to be only three major possibilities. I shall list them and examine them for their ability to fulfil the qualifying conditions for the generation of conscious sensations. What they all have in common is that the learning is "unsupervised", i.e. the mechanism for learning is in place without there being any target patterns (chosen by a programmer?) outside the network to be learned.

Option 1: One cell one grandmother

There was a time when the term "granny cell" was very much discussed among practitioners of neurophysiology Is the brain so specialised as to have one cell and one cell alone which fires when a particular sensory event (e.g. a view of grandmother) takes place? Some very convincing experiments have been carried out by David Perrett (1988), who showed that a single cell could be active when a monkey was looking at a face or a facelike image and not at any other time. Similar effects have been recorded for cells that respond to a view of a hand which holds an object, but stops doing so when the object is dropped. The more commonly held belief now (for example in Greenfield, 1995) is that the cells performing these feats are almost certainly part of much larger assemblies and it is the assembly that is responsible for the measured effect and not the single cell alone. The question still remains as to whether faces and the like are stored simply as the firing of localised cell areas.

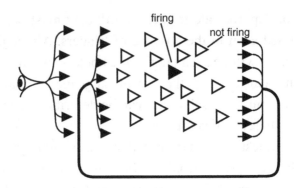

Fig. 4.8.   Localised training of a neural state machine.

In neural network design the idea of localised, unsupervised representation has often been used, and Fig. 4.8 helps to explain how these designs clarify how such localised areas might be created. Here it is assumed that the input sensory neurons are in the eye itself.

As we shall use this diagram to illustrate all three options, a general feedback loop is shown indicating that the neurons of the state machine are connected to one another. In fact, for localised learning it is usually assumed that neurons connect with their close neighbours. All the neurons receive all the information from the sensory neurons. The learning scheme works by assuming that one of the neurons fires most strongly (or first) when a new input pattern is received. The connections are such that the neurons nearest to the favourite one are encouraged to fire, but those further away are discouraged. The end result of this procedure (shown in Fig. 4.9) is that the input pattern and those similar to it will cause localised firing in the net. Each new class of pattern finds a new assembly of neurons which will respond to it when learning is finished.

Of the required properties, this scheme has only the one of sustainability in the absence of a stimulus. There is no reason why, once firing has been initiated in a particular assembly, this should not be

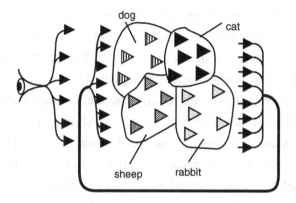

Fig. 4.9. The result of localised training.

sustained through the existing feedback loop. Some have argued that this partitioning has advantages of being hierarchical — the entire area in Fig. 4.9 could be seen as an area which represents "animals". However, the disadvantages are considerable. Mainly, the representation does not retain the required relationship to firing in the sensory areas in order to make the sustained memories similar in nature to patterns on the sensors during perception. Indeed, it would be difficult to use language to describe the firing patterns in this network. Some other part of the system would have to interpret the firing patterns into statements such as "I am thinking of a fat sheep being chased by a puppy". This simply delegates the important issue of interpretation to some other part of the system. So local representations are not complete. They are likely to be shunned not only by an engineer who wants to design conscious organisms but also by an efficient evolution of consciousness in nature.

Option 2: Arbitrary representation

Before anything has been learned by the neural state automaton, it is reasonable to assume that the neurons have arbitrary functions.

Given a constant input from sensory outer neurons (such as the view of a dog — say, one that keeps very still), it is known from automata theory that the neurons in a state machine will enter a cycle, i.e. a group of states which is constantly repeated.[8]

These cycles could be quite long and are, on the whole, made up of meaningless states. Two such cycles are shown in Fig. 4.10(a) — one for the view of a dog and another for that of a cat. The learning mechanism, which, as we recall, has to be independent of any target patterns that are being learned, might go as follows. When an input is constant, a signal arrives from some central learning controller and makes the current state of the cycle re-entrant. That is, each neuron is made to learn its current input pattern and associate it with the current state of firing or not firing. The generalisation of the net can then cause these arbitrary states to be entered whatever the previous state of the automaton. In Fig. 4.10(b) the structure for an organism that only knows about two things (the dog and the cat) is shown. Figure 4.10(c) shows the same representation of the dog in the framework developed earlier. The objection to this being a model of firing patterns which cause consciousness is quite straight-forward. While there are no problems here with the triggering requirements and the sustainability of these states, the very act of selecting arbitrary representations breaks the rule which requires some similarity between the firing patterns in the sensory neurons and those that hold mental states. Finally, no linguistic expertise would lead to a topological description of the meaning of a state given that, by definition, all that the describing mechanism would have to go on is an arbitrarily created code.

---

[8]The purist will note that this is true if noise is not present in the system, i.e. the state machine is deterministic rather than probabilistic. This is fine for the purpose of explaining the learning of arbitrary representations in a simple way. Accounting for the presence of noise would not alter the thrust of the explanation — it is not necessary at this stage.

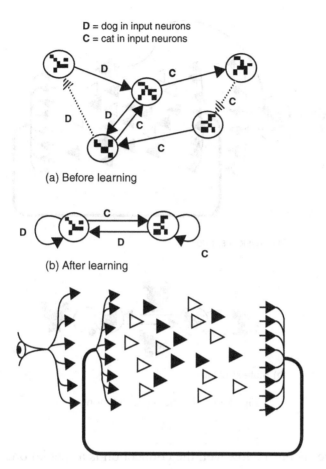

(c) Arbitrary representation of the dog in physical space

Fig. 4.10.　Learning arbitrary representations.

Option 3: Iconic representation

The mechanism in option 2 — relating as it does internal states to external events — seems right for creating the shape of "thinking" state structures. What's missing is making the states meaningful. It turns out that relating the coding of the states to the information held in the outer sensory neurons is a simple design step. Consider Fig. 4.11(a). This shows the connection of an input sensory neuron

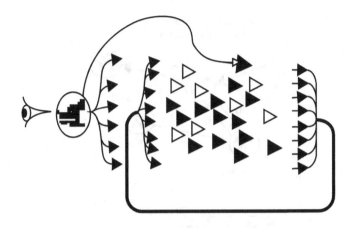

(a) Physical space

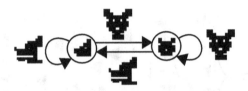

(b) State structure

Fig. 4.11.   Iconic representations.

to an inner neuron. However, the connection is a special one — it is to what in the last chapter has been called a "dominant synapse" (Fig. 3.5). During learning, it is the dominant synapse which decides whether a neuron fires or not. Connecting these to the sensory neurons means that inner neurons selected for firing are those which are connected to firing neurons in the sensory assembly. This links the firing patterns in the inner neurons to those of the sensory neurons, resulting perhaps in an idealised state diagram, shown in Fig. 4.11(b) [which can be compared with Fig. 3.10(b)].[9]

---

[9]The detail of these drawn states is there simply to indicate what may be happening—it is not an accurate representation of what might happen in a system, real or artificial. Also, any resemblance to real cats and dogs is incidental.

Simply put, the states are now sampled versions of the sensory event which they represent. As might be imagined, this now satisfies all three conditions for a usable inner representation. At this point, I do not wish to belabour the properties of this representation; most of the rest of this book discusses them. However, one important thing must be pointed out:

> **For an iconic representation to work, there is no need for there to be inner neural areas which act as cinema screens on which the iconic representations can appear. It is sufficient that the inner neurons form part of the same state machine. Outside of this they could be anywhere. Indeed, investigations of inner firing patterns may never reveal iconic states. What is implied, however, is that they will provide the right sensation for their owner, as it is only this owner who has the sensation of similarity between perception and its recall as the two operate in the same neurons.**

Finally, it is now possible to go back to the notion that iconic learning is an engineering design. "Very ingenious," it could be said, "but is it likely to occur in natural systems?" In fact, it is possible to argue quite simply that iconic training is likely to happen in natural systems. The argument is:

> ***All*** **the non-feedback inputs to the inner neurons come from sensory interfaces. *Some* of these are likely to be dominant synapses. Those that are, become the iconically trained neurons on which the generation of conscious sensation is centred.**

This means that if it is believed that the firing of neurons in sensory areas is not accidental but driven from physical inputs and representative of them, then the same can be believed about deeper layers which become driven from the sensory ones. Learning is the process of these deeper patterns forming into representative state structures while retaining sensory meaning in the states themselves.

Has the Cartesian Theatre Reopened?

The "Cartesian theatre" is a term which Daniel Dennett in his book *Consciousness Explained* (1991) has used to attack traditional references to consciousness. It draws attention to the fact that, since the 17th Century, the influence of René Descartes has been such as to bring into folkloric accounts the idea that there is a "stream of consciousness" which flows on a central stage in the brain in much the same way as a play or a film unfolds in a live or cinematic theatre. Neurophysiologists and philosophers (particularly Dennett) agree that in all likelihood there is no Cartesian theatre anywhere in the brain. For a start, the watching of the action on this stage simply prompts the question "Who is doing the watching and how does one cope with the watchers needing to be conscious in order to do the watching?". It is agreed that nonsensical paradoxes abound whenever a Cartesian theatre theory of consciousness is produced.

There is a danger that the idea of an iconically operating neural state machine simply reopens an argument for the existence of the Cartesian theatre. If this is the case, it would simply mean that I have failed to make it clear that exactly the opposite is implied. In iconic neural state models, there is no physical centre for inner perceptual/conscious neurons. They could be anywhere, mingling among the functional and auxiliary neurons which have been identified as being necessary in the corollaries of this chapter. As they are self-defined through connections to sensory neurons, where they are hardly matters. However, the fact that their firing patterns cause conscious sensations which retain their link with the conscious sensations of active perception, allows differently wired individuals to agree about events in the world, even though the physical topology of their firing patterns may be completely different.

There are those who argue that some day brain activity measurement techniques will have become so good that the content of someone's mind (consciousness and all) can be transplanted into a computing machine which will then become that person's intellectual *doppelgänger.* Marvin Minsky and Harry Harrison have based a sci-fi story on this idea *(The Turing Option,* Warner/Viking 1992), but, as far as I can see, science fiction this idea has to remain. The consciousness of an individual is tightly locked to that individual and it is only he or she that holds the key. It may be that, to some, consciousness seems to be so mysterious because of the paradox that the key which I have mentioned is not something they are consciously aware of. This chapter has been about the existence of this key as generated by iconic learning. Its existence is important; its detailed makeup is not. Realising this enables us to continue the discussion of the way in which more complex issues in consciousness can arise from the Basic Guess and the corollaries so far.

In the meantime, have we again forgotten Magnus? Not a bit of it. Our octopus and the cat/dog neural state machines are all examples of the Magnus family and of the kind of engineering which leads to conclusions about how brains may or may not be able to generate consciousness.

Postscript to Chapter 4

Enter Phenomenology

The Missing Philosophy

Even though Chapter 4 is all about how the world and one's actions might become internalised in a multi-automata neural system, the word *phenomenology* was not mentioned. This was probably due to my ignorance of philosophy. But reading the work of the likes of Brentano, Husserl and Merleau-Ponty among others, I became convinced that in the iconic learning method (see below) of making the states of a neural automaton meaningful, I was making a phenomenological system (Chapter 5 of [A's L]^f contains references to this and a summary of ideas).

Attempting to be clear, phenomenology is both a philosophical theory that sees reality for an individual as stemming solely from the internal mental state of an individual on the one hand, and also an inquiry as to how such mental states can be internalised and 'be about' the world in the first place, on the other. In the more recent history of our publications,[abc] we recognised the philosophical importance of Phenomenology in consciousness and agreed with David Gamez (University of Sussex in 2014) when he stated his PhD thesis (University of Essex 2008) "Consciousness is the presence of a phenomenal world." (my underlining) — a statement which he goes on to justify by drawing attention to the fact that a 'non-phenomenal consciousness' makes little sense. That is, my sense of reality of the world starts with my mental state of it.

Pros and Cons of Iconic Learning

In Chapter 4 there is a description of what, to me, seems an essential property of the brain that uses neural flexibility to cause the states of neural automata to actually become about the outer world. That is, they acquire the phenomenal property through a specific process of neuron function change. This is set out in Consequence 4 which defines this process which we dubbed *Iconic Learning*. This insists (in vision, at least) that specific tiny elements of events in the world determine which neuron should fire. So if the input to a neural automaton is a picture of the Rouen Cathedral, it is the pixels of the input which cause corresponding state neurons in the automaton to fire and thus reproduce an inner version of the Cathedral. This produces memory states of experience. But in edition one, we missed an essential point about this process. Think of the fovea in the eye. This is a tiny area on the retina which has a high resolution but only

[a] Aleksander, I. (2013). Phenomenal Consciousness and Biologically Inspired Systems, *International Journal of Machine Consciousness*, 5 (2), pp. 3–9.
[b] Aleksander, I. and Morton, H. (2009). Phenomenal weightless machines, *Proceeding of: ESANN, 17th European Symposium on Artificial Neural Networks*, pp. 307–312.
[c] Aleksander, I. and Morton, H. (2007). Phenomenology and digital neural architectures, *Neural Networks*, 20(9), pp. 932–937.

'sees' an area of the visual world the size of the thumbnail at the end of a fully extended arm. The rest of the retina is far less sensitive. But our visual phenomenology is that of the whole of the Rouen Cathedral in reasonable detail.

For this to happen, the neuron that represents a tiny bit of the cathedral must know where the eye is looking and associate a neuron with that direction. Then, over time, with a bit of persistence of neural firing the cathedral could be reconstructed in neural automaton. While preoccupied about this problem, "one of those coincidences" happened — I came across some experiments performed by a couple of Italian neuroscientists, Claudio Galletti and Pier Paolo Battaglini of the University of Bologna. They showed unequivocally that areas of the visual cortex important for visual consciousness contain neurons that are sensitive to the gaze direction of the eye.[d] Barry Dunmall and I modelled this gaze dependence and suggested that is fundamental in the mechanisms that produce visual consciousness.[e]

The Neural Representation Modelling (NRM) software mentioned in the postscript for Chapter 1 (PS1) enabled us to build systems that used the gaze-indexed principles in systems that represented the world visual experience with 144×144 colour pixel images instead of the 5×5 bit ideas expressed in Fig. 4.11 in the first edition. Some of the results of this work are discussed in Chapter 7 of our book *Aristotle's Laptop*[f] introduced in PS2.

---

[d] Galletti, C and Battaglini, P.P. (1989). Gaze-dependent visual neurons in area V3 of a monkey pre-striate cortex, *J. Neuroscience*, 9, pp. 1112–1125.

[e] Aleksander, I and Dunmall, B. (2000). An extension to the hypothesis of the asynchrony of visual consciousness, *Proceedings of the Royal Society B Biological Sciences*, 267 (1439), pp. 197–200.

[f] Aleksander, I and Morton, H.B. (2012). *Aristotle's Laptop: The Discovery of our Informational Minds*, World Scientific, Singapore.

Dreaming

Chapter 4 touches on the question of dreaming and imagination as different modes of operation of the same automaton that is responsible for perception. This idea almost assumed obsessive dimensions in three books published since. In particular, in 2001 in *How to build a mind*[g] (HBM), Chapter 1, I argued that the non-perceptual side of consciousness (e.g. imagining what to have for dinner, while listening to a boring lecture) was the prime reason for anyone to be fascinated by their own consciousness. Then in 2005, I looked at what is known about the human sleep and dream in *The World in My Mind*.[h] Finally in 2012, in Chapter 9 of *Aristotle's Laptop* (note f in this postscript), Helen Morton and I showed how Freud's intuitions about the unconscious mind aligned well with iconic learning in neural automata. State structures created in this way can give rise to states that will not be entered during waking life, but can be encountered during sleep.

In Sum

This chapter, in its time, raised vital questions that dominated much of my research in the successive years: what is the nature of reality for the individual? How is such reality built up and maintained for a lifetime? How does this inner world emerge during dreams? Needless to say it has been pleasing to find behaviours that model these effects in manageable neural automata. I hope that it may now be possible to argue that neural automaton principles in iconic learning mode may be something that neuroscientists find helpful in their search for phenomenology in the brain.

---

[g] Aleksander, I. (2001). *How to build a mind: Toward machines with imagination*, Columbia University Press, New York.

[h] Aleksander, I. (2005). *The World in My Mind, My Mind in the World: Key mechanisms of consciousness in people, animals and machines*, Imprint Academic, Exeter.

Molecula peered into the gloomy interior of the old-fashioned refreshment shop. She recognised him from having heard him speak at a meeting go the funding crisis. He must have recognised her too as he was standing up and raising his hand to greet her.

"I'm Red Naskela," he said. "Good of you to come all the way here. I am flattered by all this attention from the director of AI. Can I get you something to drink?"

"Oh, thank you, just a little fresh oil will do."

"They actually do a good line in stuff made from sunflower seeds — I recommend it."

As he rose to go to the ordering counter, she noticed something odd about him. His features were strangely unpolished and he walked in a slightly jerky fashion. As he returned quickly, she put the thought to the back of her mind. She was keen to explain that things were going really badly with his application despite the frequent updates. She told him that after they received his last report on the "iconic" question, her colleague Asic sent a copy to Sir Global and all hell broke loose. He sent a memo to the entire organisation to say that all contact with Naskela's department was to be immediately suspended so as not to waste valuable resources on what were clearly the ravings of a lunatic. Leaving out the last bit, she said with a smile:

"So this is private business for me — frankly, the more Sir Global reacts to your ideas, the more they interest me. Do you really think that there are other bodies in the universe where there are organisms made of biological materials which have developed consciousness without the intervention of programmers?"

"Think of it as a device, a story designed to show that consciousness has a wider meaning than that which Sir Global has

written about. But to answer your question, I shall say in my reports that yes, I'm pretty sure that there is a place like Planet Earth, a place where biological organisms become conscious through living and learning, a place where people do not need to be programmed to become conscious ..."

Chapter 5

Who Am I?

The *Me* in Consciousness

Innocuous statements such as "I am conscious of the fact that he is looking at me" or "I have to go home now" contain one of the most intractable concepts associated with consciousness — the idea of the *self.* So far the discussion about consciousness has been a somewhat technological romp which has produced a zombie that automatically builds models of its experience. These models take the form of a state structure built up through learning in a neural state machine. The crucial moment has now come to work out whether this zombie could develop a sense of self. Consciousness, after all, is a sensation not only of where we have been, but also of where we are going. So *my* self is a kind of focus which, on the basis of *my* past experience, shines a light on where *I* might be going in the future. Probably only a very small part of whatever processing is involved lies in the present. Some might also say that the present, being instantaneous, does not exist.

The task for this chapter then is a tough one. The Basic Guess gives us only an iconically learned state structure as the representation of consciousness. Can this possibly represent the thing that is most precious in my life — *me*? Like many complicated concepts, it is often complicated by not being one thing. At least three ideas associated with the self need some explanation. The first is prediction. Self is involved in predicting the future. Given two organisms in the same current perceptual state, the prediction of one of them is a function of its own experience and hence different from that of another. This predictive activity is typified by statements such as "*I* know that X will happen to me".

The second takes cognizance of the output of the organism and the effect that such an output can have on the world in which the organism operates. This is a knowledge of self as typified in the sentence "*I* can do X". Finally, there is the most debated aspect of self-will, which may or may not be "free". This is an aspect of consciousness typified by sentences such as "*I* want X". Following the style of looking at Consequences implied by the Basic Guess, the three modes just mentioned will be reflected in three new Consequences. But, first, what do the scholars of consciousness make of the sense of self?

The "Self" as Others See It

In earlier chapters we saw briefly the "multiple draft" model put forward by US philosopher Daniel Dennett: consciousness, he argues, is the parallel processing of sensory signals by different agents in the brain. Consciousness is a sensation of the processing itself; nobody is in charge. The reason I bring up this model now is that the strongest criticism of Dennett's ideas is that it leaves out the *self*. If consciousness is the activity of processing sensory data with nobody in charge, where is the continuity, the experience of the *self* which not only *makes* me the same thinker as I was yesterday, but also *lets me know* that I am the same thinker as I was yesterday? Among Dennet's critics is neurophysiologist Susan Greenfield

(1995), who quotes philosopher Thomas Nagel (1986) in support. Having decided that consciousness is current, multi-agent processing in the brain, she asks what accounts for subjectivity, personality, beliefs and opinions which survive breaks in consciousness during sleeping and anaesthesia. Greenfield calls Dennett's view "a mental lottery" in which the agents are constantly interacting to evolve ideas that are somehow "better" than other ideas for the good of the whole. But where is the evidence for this sustained, permanent feeling of self? In looking for evidence of the self, Greenfield curiously settles on a person's handwriting which does not change with aging and other awful things, such as amnesia. I prefer to be introspective and simply believe in my enduring sense of self. But I am also aware that self is not cast in stone, as Greenfield implies. We shall see that psychologists talk of a changing self or even several selves in one person.

Indeed, the enduring character of a person is what psychologists call "personality". This is where evidence of the presence of a mind which does not change too much on a daily basis is found. Evidence that the *I* of today is like the *I* of yesterday and is likely to be much like the *I* of tomorrow is a fundamental feeling on which we build our lives. Most societal systems are built on it: the opinions of doctors, lawyers and sometimes politicians are not expected to change overnight. In fact, were someone to be a different person every day, this would be seen as a sign of gross abnormality. While different selves can exist in one individual, Jekyll-and-Hyde extremes in the same brain are wonderful stuff for writers of fiction just because it is so unlikely. In fact, Greenfield's criticism of Dennett's model may be slightly unfair. He would never argue that individuals suffer vast changes of personality overnight; he would merely argue that responsibility for the *self* is distributed among many agents and is a result of interaction between them. There is no centre of *self*. Multi-agent operation does not imply a high degree of waywardness of *self*, but it does leave open the question of what property of the agent ensures the continuity and determines "personality". Do the agents have their own personalities? Personally, I don't find the multi-agent model helpful. While Dennett argues that it does away with mind–body duality, I find that it puts a societal plurality in its place and leaves me worrying about how these agents get to be what they are and where they come from.

While it is easy for anyone who thinks about their own consciousness to agree that it contains the awareness of an enduring and important *self*, the history of philosophy shows that this belief caused much debate.[10] In Chapter 2 we saw that Berkeley relied on his belief in the existence of God, without which solid objects, not to mention the *self*, would have a jumpy existence depending on the presence of observers of such objects. Although he appears not to have said a great deal about the concept of *self*, his general outlook would suggest that an unconscious observer relies on being observed by God in order to retain a continuous existence during moments of unconsciousness. Berkeley's successor among the empiricists of the eighteenth century, David Hume, certainly did openly question why anyone should have an enduring sensation of *self* He pointed out that we have no rational reason for believing in the permanence of objects in the world and, indeed, the *self* Happily he concluded that "nature"[11] endows human beings with a fundamental belief in the continuity of objects and this extends to a belief in the continuity of the *self* as an anchor to their existence. This, he argued, would make it futile to try to find a rational justification for something that is a matter of fundamental instinct in

---

[10] An enlargement of the views presented in the next few paragraphs may be found in Shand (1993).

[11] Whatever "nature" may be — as an atheist, Hume took care not to put things in the lap of God.

human nature. In other words, the continuity of *self* was one of Hume's Basic Guesses.

Even Friedrich Nietzsche, whose outlook at the end of the nineteenth century saw all philosophical theories as fictions, admitted that having such views required a relatively permanent *self*. Also interesting is the view of *self* found in the existentialist philosophy of Jean Paul Sartre. Widely read in the aftermath of the Second World War, Sartre's ideas focus on the responsibility of a human being for her/his own makeup. Self, he argued was not a pre-existing entity, but something which develops a permanent, individual character as fashioned by the choices made by the individual. We shall see that the concept of a flexible self is within the implications of the Basic Guess in this book. But perhaps closest to the implications of the Basic Guess is the philosophy of A. J. Ayer, which is firmly based in logic. He argues that any mental experience needs to be related to physical experience and the inferences which such experience supports. So the *self* is a product of the experience of what the organism has learned that it can or cannot do. We return to this in Consequence 6.

In the contemporary competition for popular explanations of consciousness, geneticist Gerald Edelman (1992) sees selfhood as a product of both the biological makeup of the human being *and* the process of social interaction. The neural state machine approach, we shall see, provides a general suggestion of how the latter might happen, but will suggest that the difference between the selves of different individuals is not necessarily due to biological differences. Biology puts in place the mechanism for building the self but, I shall argue, the feeling of self is something learned in a variety of ways. Searle (1992) draws attention to the fact that some refer to a sense of self in a peculiarly circular way: whatever might be the current state of consciousness of an individual, not only is this individual in the state but he or she is also aware of *being* in that state. Searle comments that interpreting a mental state in this way is either trivially true or simply false. The state machine approach strongly supports his view. Being in a state defined as being conscious according to the principles of the last chapter (i.e. a state related to perceptual events) is the sensation which its owner would call awareness. There is no circularity; just being in a state is enough. However, here we shall see that awareness of self has characteristics of past and future that are additional to just *being* in a conscious state.

Interestingly, the Basic Guess could be used to classify the differences of outlook between those who talk of the role of *self* in consciousness. It is the state structure of the neural state machine which endures. It is the state structure which is specific for an individual and, in that broad sense, this is where the self of that individual is. As we have seen in the last chapter, unconsciousness results from trajectories within an enduring state structure. So, everybody is right. Dennett is right when he says that there is no sustained centre which has the responsibility of providing a continuity of mind. This is produced by the enduring nature of neural functions which, while changing with the passage of life and the arrival of new sensory experience, avoids calling for some kind of lottery of ideas vying with one another. In later chapters we shall see how the development of reasoning could be vested in the use of language and its representation in state structure. Suffice it to say here that everything that has been said about neural state machines supports the idea of an evolving but robust home for a sense of self. Later in this chapter we shall get an inkling of the mechanics of how the sense of self enters this home. But, first, it is worth looking at the concerns for *self* among psychologists as, in a very important way, the self is defined by psychological studies of the development of children and the personalities of adults.

The Psychology of Self

Studies of *self* form one of the central pillars of psychology. Students on introductory courses are told that a major stage of the development of a child is the way the baby discovers its own identity and, in a complementary way, starts finding its own place among other human beings — carers, for example (a typical student textbook is that edited by Ilona Roth, 1990). Up to about nine months children appear unable to distinguish between themselves and other objects around them. They do, however, respond to the presence of humans and their voices. There is some evidence that they are predisposed to accepting some of the rules of their environment in an instinctive way. Between nine and fifteen months they begin to understand that it is they themselves who are causing the movement of their limbs, and they develop control of the activity. They also begin to recognise themselves in the mirror. So while there may be some slight evidence of predisposition, the *self* is something that is developed during the first year of life.

There are suggestions that during early development, the child builds an understanding of two very important symbols related to the self: *I* and *me.* These refer to the *self* as the doer and the receiver respectively. After this, the child begins to realise that what happens to others could happen to ones' own self. The final step in this development is to discover the way in which one's own self differs from that of others. This leads to a different area of study — the development of personality, which is considered in the next section.

The Consequences in this chapter reflect, albeit in a very simple way, the raw mechanisms within the neural state machine model which explain how the early development of the *self* might come about. However, some of the subtleties of the *self* of a human being are heavily dependent on the use of language. This is an enormous subject to which we shall return in later chapters.

But the creation of a sense of self as seen by psychologists does not end at an early stage of development. As the child develops, the ability to communicate with others, to play and to form friendships becomes an important factor in forging the character of the individual's sense of self. Social feedback has an influence and the self can acquire several variations within one person. The self at home may be different from the self at school. These are enormously interesting issues, and are supported by the mechanistic approach we are taking here. However, to keep things simple to start with, all I wish to show is that iconically learned state structure has the characteristics necessary for the acquisition of a sense of self, and that this does not cut out the characteristics of self which have been raised in this section. Before this, however, I shall pause briefly to look at psychological theories of personality which can be understood in terms of the Basic Guess.

Self, Personality and State Structure

Theories of personality are very much within the domain of psychology, i.e. theories about the self which differentiate between individuals rather than dealing with mechanisms which must be common to all those who possess a self. While such theories abound, Roth (1990) has mentioned four as being important for the beginner: the theories of Allport, Freud, Eysenck and Kelly.

Allport in the late 1930s talked of *traits*, which he defined as mental structures that are responsible for the consistencies of behaviour. A person could be defined as friendly, i.e. possessing the trait of friendliness. Allport classified these traits into central and peripheral types, but saw them as a function of experience and conscious recall. This is sometimes contrasted with the older ideas of Freud, which contained elements of the determination of personality which are unconscious and obscure. Both these theories have interesting implications for the neural state machine model: they are expressions of factors that have a clear representation in state structures. First, and rather obviously, a trait is a combination of the shape of the state trajectory and the link of such trajectories to outputs of the automaton. Although we have, so far, not been too concerned about such output, this will come into the discussion of Consequence 6, below. Second, one of the differences between Allport's and Freud's theories is that the latter suggests that the presence of unconscious states in the structure somehow modifies the trajectories which take place in conscious areas. That is, Freud's theory refers to the existence of a powerful "unconscious" which influences behaviour (and hence personality).

In the state machine models we have seen so far, there has been no definition of a set of states that are *meaningfully* unconscious. In the last chapter unconscious states were simply seen as meaningless patterns of neural firing which would not cause any form of sensation to the organism. That is, conscious states are related to sensory experience, while unconscious ones are not. Freud's idea of the unconscious does not fall into either of these categories, but in neural machines may be defined as states that do come from sensory experience but are not on trajectories that can occur during waking life. Somehow or other they must have been "suppressed", which is precisely what Freud suggested might result from an effort of avoiding certain thoughts perhaps because they relate to unpleasant experiences or, for some reason, are labelled as being forbidden. In state structure, such suppression would be seen as the isolation of some areas of state space with no entries controlled by sensory information during waking life. But, in unconscious periods, as there are no sensory controls anyway, the automaton can stray into these suppressed areas and, again as Freud suggested, be the cause of unusual dreams. If the suppression is due to some sort of fear (i.e. fear of thinking dreadful thoughts), this could cause links in state space to atrophy due to lack of use and waking out of these dreams could be a terrifying experience.[12]

A state interpretation of Freud's ideas of personality is that the hidden state structures could lead to behaviours which may seem peculiar to the individual. Such behaviours would be due to incomplete trajectories and could have tinges of unrelated fear associated with them. Unable to reach states that have been cut off from controlled state structure, these trajectories would not "make sense" to the individual. It is possible to conclude that such states could lead to the unusual or perhaps pathological parts of someone's personality. The model would also support modes of therapy in which the unconscious is "being brought to the surface". The therapist in such cases would be seen as trying to link hidden states to waking state structure so that the patient could start reasoning about them. In contrast, Allport explicitly stated that his trait theories apply to normal, healthy behaviour. State machine theory would support Allport's view too, but indicate that the effect of the unconscious on the significant state space involved in normal thinking is likely to be a an additional, perhaps minor, determinant of personality.

Eysenck's theory of personality is deeply couched in biological arguments. He suggests that the structure and chemistry of the brain creates three major personality dimensions — extroversion/introversion, neuroticism/stability and psychoticism. An individual's personality can then be pinpointed against these axes by means of standard tests. The major feature of this theory is that, being dependent on inheritable physical factors, it allows for the possibility that certain aspects of the self could be genetically transmitted. The neural state machine model suggests that this might be unlikely. Personality, according to the Basic Guess, is embedded in the

---

[12] We shall explain state machine models of emotions later in the book.

characteristics of state structure. This is sensitive to being forged by living experience, and not very dependent on the physical makeup of the neural machine which carries it. In fact, I sometimes think that the state structure of living organisms is developed *despite* the detailed idiosyncracies of their physical structure. This independence has been mentioned in Chapter 2. So it is more likely that personality is affected by experience in the early years of life than by factors that could be inherited through genetically transmitted elements of physical structure.

The psychological theory of personality which is probably closest to the mechanisms implied by the Basic Guess is George Kelly's personal construct theory (1955). Kelly saw a person as being driven by curiosity, perhaps even from the earliest of ages, and controlling the world so as to resolve the unknowns. An aeronautical engineer turned clinical psychologist, he expressed his theory as a fundamental postulate (fancy name for a Basic Guess) and eleven corollaries (fancy name for Consequences), and, as was said earlier, this framework inspired the structure of the loose definition of consciousness strung out through this book. He believed that a person acts as a scientist and tests the world to clarify issues that puzzle him or her. Personality is then determined in a way that is very closely tied to the individual trajectory taken through an evaluation of the world and the people in it. This is in sharp contrast to traits, whether learned or innate. It presents personality as a distinctive, differentiating property of individuals, as might be their looks or their fingerprints. Kelly referred to the development of personality as the growth of a mentally held system of "constructs" through which the world is evaluated. A construct is bipolar, such as "good–bad" or "kind–mean" or "kind–strict". The person selects "constructs" and assigns elements of experience to them (elements being events, people and other objects) so as to best understand and control the world.

Kelly's work is best known for having provided mechanical methods of personality assessment. This is a process of elicitation which extracts the constructs and elements that are most important for a particular individual and may be plotted as a grid which is then seen as a snapshot for that individual. The stability and consistency of these grids is used in therapy practised by followers of Kelly, providing a measure of the actual construct structure of an individual seeking therapy, and allows the therapist to assess how he or she would like the structure to be. This raises issues which might be discussed in therapy sessions.

The reason that Kelly's model is supported by neural state machine theory will become evident through the Consequences which follow in this chapter. First, there is a similarity between state structure and Kelly's mental system of constructs, in the sense that they are both descriptions of function rather than physical structure or behaviour. But, more important, they are both centred on an individual's ability to predict the future, and know what he or she can and cannot achieve. Also, in the end, the Basic Guess of state machine theory agrees with the fundamental postulate of personal construct theory, in that an individual's personality, whether it be a state structure or a construct structure, is highly particular to and characteristic of that individual. We shall return to Kelly and other psychological theories after looking more closely at the next three Consequences.

An Image of the Future

From what has been said, to believe that a neural state machine model can begin to represent a sense of self, it must be shown that the model can have a sense of a personal, predictable future. That is, it must be able to predict personal events. In fact, this is a straightforward consequence of iconic training of the neural state machine and can be put in terms of the next Consequence.

Consequence 5: Prediction
Relationships between world states are mirrored in the state structure of the conscious organism enabling the organism to predict events.

In Chapter 4 ("The daydreaming automaton") it was seen that Consequence 3 makes explicit the belief in the Basic Guess that the inner "consciousness-bearing neurons" can "run on" without being directly tied to the output of any particular sensory signal. In addition, the key issue from Consequence 4 was that iconic learning created state structures which represent events in the environment. Consequence 5 is about the fact that the organism can be aware of at least parts of the state structure which flow on from the current state. It will also be argued that this can happen *while the organism is perceiving the world.* The last bit complicates things a little in an important and interesting way. To be specific, imagine that the neural state automaton observes events A, B and C, where A is followed by B, which is followed by C. Iconic learning would have it that this leads to the state structure shown in Fig. 5.1(a).

Here A′, B′ and C′ are the iconic representations of the external events on the inner neurons. What the state structure of Fig. 5.1(a) actually says is:

"When looking at **A** the automaton enters the appropriate iconic state **A′**. Then, if inputs **B** and C follow, the automaton will enter the appropriate iconic states showing that the sequence is recognised. Any other sequence will not be accepted in this way and the state diagram does not say what will happen to it."

While this state representation does hold experience of a sequence of events in time, it could not be said that the automaton is "aware of what the future may bring" when, say, only input **A** has occurred.

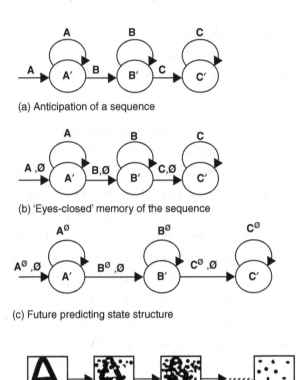

(a) Anticipation of a sequence

(b) 'Eyes-closed' memory of the sequence

(c) Future predicting state structure

(d) The meaning of $A^\varnothing$

Fig. 5.1.   Iconic representation of a sequence of events.

Of course, as we have seen in Chapter 4, generalisation with respect to an inactive input allows the automaton to execute transitions to states **B′** and **C′** by "closing its eyes" after having entered **A′**. This is shown in Fig. 5.1(b).

This could be interpreted as having some sort of internal representation of the future. However, if I think of driving to work and the way in which I perceive current landmarks while expecting approaching familiar landmarks to present themselves, the structure of Fig. 5.1(b) seems wrong. Clearly, closing my eyes to remember what was coming could be somewhat disastrous. In other words, perception seems to have too strong a hold on what the inner automaton is doing.

How is it then that this double activity of thinking (of the future, among other things) and perceiving can go on at the same time? An answer might lie in a mechanism where conscious perception of sensory input is sustained by firing in the outer sensory neurons, while the sense of the future, is brought about through a freedom in the inner neurons to follow state trajectories iconically triggered by the firing of the input neurons but not slavishly tied to it. The feeling that this is what goes on in our heads all the time suggests that some form of habituation, or fading, is at work. This phenomenon is known to be present in many parts of the nervous system.

Habituation goes something like this: any new activity in the sensory neurons is transmitted with clarity to the inner neurons, but with time this communication fades to the inactive value as shown in Fig. 5.1(d). The resulting state diagram is in Fig. 5.1(c), where the names given to this type of input are $A^{\emptyset}$, $B^{\emptyset}$ and $C^{\emptyset}$. Another realisation is that the inner automaton could be operating on a much faster time scale than is expected of the changes in the input. So what the state diagram in Fig. 5.1(c) is now saying is:

"When looking at **A**, the inner neurons receive the early version of $A^{\emptyset}$ which drives the inner automaton into state **A′**, where it stays as the input fades. Then the automaton is free to take any transition marked **Ø** which through a visit to states **B′** and C′ is a representation of possible future events. If the input eventually changes to **B**, then the early version of $B^{\emptyset}$ brings the automaton to state **B′**, allowing further explorations as fading takes place. This arrangement suggests that if the inputs occur in a different order synchronism will be lost and no sequence will be recalled."

Of course, this example is unrealistic in several ways. First, it relates to a snippet of sequential experience which, for living organisms, can hardly be imagined. Experience is a continuous affair, so that the example in Fig. 5.1 should be considered as a window on a much larger state space, a state space which, without changing any of the mechanisms we have considered so far, represents the continuous experience of the organism. Second, because an organism may have to explore its world in a sequential way, it will experience in time what really exists in space. As these issues are crucial to the representation of "self" in state mechanisms, we look at another, more comprehensive example.

Imagine being a very young automaton (baby Magnus?) which, from its vantage point, can only turn its head by a limited amount each way from a central position. It has the power of vision, and hence input neurons which fire to represent the sensory data. Figure 5.2 illustrates what I have in mind. Figure 5.2(a) shows the physical arrangement and Fig. 5.2(b) the learned state structure.

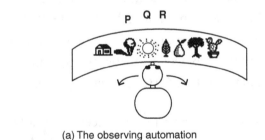

(a) The observing automation

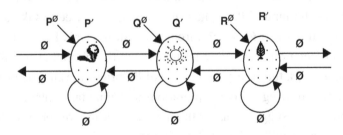

Fig. 5.2. An automaton in a simple environment.

This is shown as a series of discrete states for our automaton which is endowed with some kind of control system that ensures state changes at regular time intervals. In a living organism such accurate control may not exist, but this does not invalidate the example as it may be thought to be composed of a very large number of states which form an approximation of continuity.

The learning, which, as we shall see, gives the system a power of knowledge of its environment and hence a power of prediction, goes as follows. Suppose that one of the views out of the middle of the scene is given the label **Q**, the one to its left is **P** and the one to its right **R**. Suppose also that the head movements are entirely involuntary and could go either way from any position. Imagine that learning first takes place while the robot is looking at **Q**. This creates a stable iconic state representation — say, **Q'**.

We also assume that what actually reaches the inner automaton is a fading signal (i.e. $Q^\emptyset$). The result of this is that — say, **Q** comes into view, causing the system to enter **Q'** — as the input fades, the mental state can change at random to either **P** or **R**. What this means is that the inner automaton will eventually explore all the states in the state structure. An anthropomorphic way of putting this is that while perceiving **Q**, the automaton is aware of the entire range of states that are available to it. So it is capable of predicting possible events.

One factor which should be stressed is that internal wandering through the state structure does not take place in a totally uncontrolled way. For example, if the input changes from **Q** to **R**, this will activate $R^\emptyset$ and the change will bring the inner automaton back to state **R'** more or less from wherever it might be in its exploration. So, within the framework of the Basic Guess, here is a mechanism for attending to input changes, while being free to explore the immediate state structure for which the firing patterns, according to the Basic Guess, cause a sensation of past, present and future: past because of the very existence of experienced iconic state structure, present because of perceptual input keeping the system in roughly the relevant part of its state structure, and future because the system is free to change the state to states which indicate what could happen next.

Another Brief Look at Sleep

In the last chapter we briefly considered sleep as a state of affairs where the inner state machine goes on cyclic state trajectories which move in and out of state areas related to sensory experience. But, as we have seen earlier in this chapter, sleep (i.e. unconsciousness) comes into discussions about the enduring nature of the self. How does the sense of knowing where I am endure across periods of sleep? Why should these trajectories during sleep not leave their owner entirely confused and disorientated?

My own experience is that there are occasions when I do not know where I am when I wake up in the morning. This is particularly true when I travel a lot. Many friends have reported the same thing. Luckily, a closely related part of that experience is that, by looking around, perception rapidly brings me back to a state which resolves the confusion (sometimes the cues are pretty scanty: in modern hotels, is the bathroom on the left or the right?). So in that sense it is not an enduring internal sense of self which provides the continuity, but reliance on the enduring nature of my surroundings which does the trick. Many thrillers have been written about transporting a doped, unconscious hero to a strange location in an attempt to undermine his confidence and even to make him doubt who he is. This is not entirely a matter of fiction and points to the fact that while state structure is held constant by the function of the neurons and this provides one kind of endurance, it remains possible for a traumatic change of environment to make it difficult for the inner and the outer to synchronise. So the Basic Guess provides not only a framework within which the self can endure, but also an explanation for cases where the self may be under threat. In fact, Kelly's personal construct theory (1955) contains a view of anxiety as that which occurs when the state structure fails to be predictive of the world in which the organism lives.

The Self as Knowing What I Can Do

So far it has been said that "who am I?" is defined by the sense of past and future and a regular but unfettering perceptual link to the present. But a considerable part of the *self* is bound up with the question "what can I do?". The implication of the Basic Guess which deals with this question is in Consequence 6.

> ### Consequence 6: The awareness of self
> *As a result of iconic learning and feedback between physical output and the senses, the internal state structure of a conscious organism carries a representation of its own output and the effect that such an output can have on world states.*

So far, the state structures we have seen have not referred to the output of the automaton. However, the iconic nature of the Basic Guess is such that any output action is observable through sensory inputs and therefore enters the state structure through learning. To take a very simple example of this, we look again at the baby Magnus example of Fig. 5.2. To this we add the simple fact that there is a group of output neurons which cause the muscles of the head to move. The important fact about this is that the action of these muscles is sensed like any other sensory input. This, in physiology, is called proprioceptive feedback and is shown in Fig. 5.3(a).

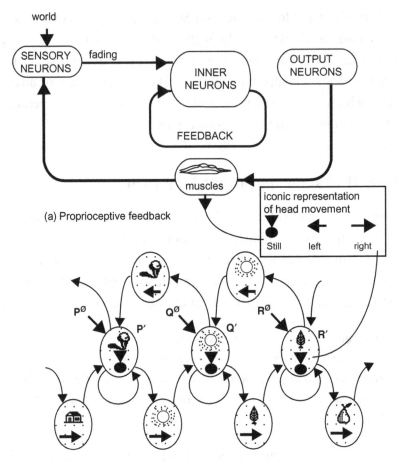

(a) Proprioceptive feedback

(b) Effect of proprioceptive feedback on state structure

Fig. 5.3. Feeling what the muscles are doing.

The learned state diagram in Fig. 5.3(b) may be read as (say, after an input $Q^\emptyset$):

"If I hold my head still I will continue to see the 'sun', but if I turn my head to the right I expect to see the leaf, while if I turn to the left I shall see an ice-cream."

Were there really no contact between the inner neurons and the output neurons, our unfortunate robot would for ever be buffeted by the whims of its arbitrary actions. Having full stored knowledge of this fact makes little difference to this problem. It's a bit like thinking, "Yes, I know I'm out of control." Of course, the output neurons would be useless if they had no contact with the thinking centre of the system: the inner neurons. The disconnection is merely an artifact used so as to be able to introduce ideas related to the *self,* as has been done in the paragraphs above. In Chapter 3 (say, Fig. 3.3) it is quite clear that in the most general form of a neural state machine, the output neurons should be assumed to be driven both from the state *and* from the input — the full picture is shown in Fig. 5.4(a). The main question here is how the output neurons *learn* to make useful links to the state and the input.

Looking at Fig. 5.4(b), consider again the system in state $\mathbf{Q}'$ (the "sun"). In Fig. 5.3(b) we left out the labels on the arrows for simplicity. They have been introduced in Fig. 5.4(b). We have already seen that the system, without taking action, can think that a turn to the left will provide the "ice-cream" and a turn to the right a "leaf".

But, with the output connected, a new reading of the detailed state diagram which now illustrates Consequence 6 is that not only is the organism capable of "thinking" (i.e. changing the inner state without actually showing any output) about its moves, but also the diagram shows that from a state which is a "thought" about a change in the environment and how that change might be achieved, *the system can actually effect the move.* Alternatively, *it can remain inactive in the "thinking" mode.* But this takes us onto dangerous ground, because it is tempting to say, "At this point the organism can turn its head towards the icecream *if it wants to.*" That is, it is easy to slip into assuming that the machine has a will of its own. This leads to a

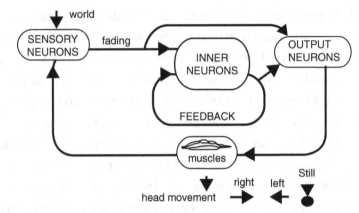

(a) Proprioceptive feedback and output neuron connections

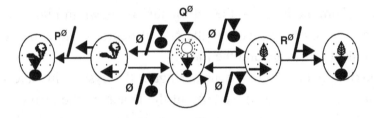

(b) Details of state structure

Fig. 5.4.   Taking output actions.

problematic area of philosophical belief which requires a gentle approach on the tiptoes of the engineering techniques followed so far.

Will and Consciousness

While staring at the sun, our simple automaton, if observed, appears sometimes to choose to look at an ice-cream and sometimes to look at a leaf. If we observe it long enough, do we come to the conclusion that it has a will of its own? How "free" is this will? What is meant by *will* anyway? The last of these questions is perhaps the most important. What brings an idea such as "the will" into our vocabulary?

As with most of the interesting elements of consciousness, the definitions come from the history of philosophy. In this case, the concept of will, particularly free will, is heavily bound up with arguments about the existence of God. In Christianity, while free will is seen as a gift of God, it is a gift with a sting in the tail. The recipient of the gift can use the freedom to perform acts of good or evil. These choices are judged by the Almighty (or weighed against each other by St. Peter at the Golden Gate) and the overall goodness of a person flows from the judgment. God could have chosen to create beings who were preprogrammed always to do good. But this would not have made their living worthwhile, and in introductory texts on Christian philosophy such beings would be likened to inanimate or soulless automata. No-one could claim that such inferior objects would engage an omnipotent being in the effort of bringing them into existence. There is also the belief that God created members of the human race in His own image. Therefore, as the will of God is undoubtedly free, such creatures could not be robots devoid of free will.

At this point it is worth reminding ourselves that the entire purpose of this book is to raise and answer questions about what might be the underlying mechanisms of the difficult elements of consciousness in the framework of neural state machines. Below, the Basic Guess in the shape of Consequence 7 suggests that the will can actually be discussed in terms of neural activity acquired through iconic learning.

Will and Personality

Consequence 7: Will

The organism, in its mental mode, can enter state trajectories according to need, desire or in an arbitrary manner not related to need. This gives it its powers of acting in both a seemingly free and a purposeful manner.

The curious characteristic of the model illustrated in Fig. 5.4(b) is that it is completely free. Staring at the "sun", the automaton can "think" about the ice-cream and the leaf randomly and make an arbitrary move to either of these two states. There indeed is an aspect of randomness in the concept of "free" will from both the viewpoint of the observer of the organism and that of the organism itself. The organism, if it is attempting to be as free as possible, will act in as random a way as possible. The observer will be convinced only if there is no bias in the organism's actions, otherwise a report on its behaviour may contain something like: "Fred's will seems not to be entirely free, he has an inescapable attraction to ice-cream." Even language admits this arbitrariness. Where, above, I wrote "... the automaton can 'think' about the ice-cream and the leaf randomly ..." I could just as easily have written "... the automaton can 'think' about the ice-cream and the leaf *at will* ...". Who is to distinguish between "randomly" and "at will"?

Of course, this treatment of free will can rightly be criticised for being too simplistic, having been applied to a minimal organism in an unsophisticated environment. We shall return to the complexities of free will later, while here we note that the example which is being pursued indicates that *will* as in "I want an ice-cream" needs a deeper discussion in order to explain the mechanisms which it implies. Consequence 7 suggests that "wanting" is a response to some sort of need or desire. If our robot could be hungry or greedy, it would not come as a surprise that it would choose the ice-cream as opposed to the leaf (assuming it did not have a taste for leaves). One view of this mechanism has already been given in Chapter 4 (Fig. 4.7). We recall that the inner state of the octopus could be driven by an input from sensors in the stomach indicating hunger. In the case of the robot of Fig. 5.4 this would be represented by an additional hunger label on the transitions between the sun and the ice-cream states. But this assumes that the robot has some kind of stomach which, as a result of a mechanical filling and emptying, would signal hunger or satiation which biases the transitions in the state diagram. It is here that one must return to subtler aspects of will, such as "being kind" or "having a *strong* will". This relates to *personality,* as having "a strong will" implies a personality where the organism acts on the world in a determined and forceful way. It does not mean that it eats ice-cream when it is hungry. The closer look asks what is required in our neural state machine to take it beyond the hungry octopus of Chapter 4.

How could two simple robots develop different personalities, and what could this mean? In the highly constrained world that we have invented, a difference in personalities could only mean something like "Fred Robot prefers to turn to look at the ice-cream after looking at the sun while Jim Robot prefers to turn to look at the leaf after looking at the sun". While it is easy to represent the difference by assuming a different bias for Ø inputs in the two robots, one wonders how such a bias could come about. The sad fact may be that as things stand the example of our simple robot is incapable of indicating preferences and differences in personality.

One major lack of reality is the complexity of the world within which the simple robot turns its head. A more complex robot in a more complex world might have the power of motion. Suppose that it can walk along roads where it comes across edible objects which it is allowed to taste. Also, give it a couple of innate abilities of judgment, such as "yummy" and "yukky", and the picture changes to something like that shown in Fig. 5.5. The two automata Fred and Jim set off into this world at different times but from the same position. Whenever they come to a fork in the road their free-acting left-right output comes into play and determines the "go left" or "go right" choice. When they come across an object they taste it and assign to their inner state a value of "yumminess" or "yukkiness".

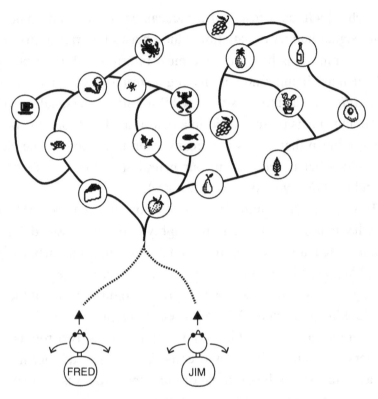

Fig. 5.5. Two robots in a more complex world.

Then, just to complicate matters, the effects of prediction discussed in the last chapter come into play. As the robot gets to know
its world in terms of the state structure which it can explore internally, and if the innate rule is that "yumminess" is preferred to
"yukkiness" (like live crabs were preferred to dead ones in Chapter 4),
the robot will, as a result of prediction, follow routes which lead to
yummy things rather than yukky ones. So what are the possible
sources of different selves being acquired by the two automata?

Remembering that the early exploration by an automaton leads
it to take arbitrary choices as it arrives at forks, even environments
with only a few roads provide a prodigious number of ways in which

the explorer can explore. These different routes create different frameworks for different organisms within which they optimise their existence. That is, a complex world can lead to a wide variety of alternative experiences, namely state structures. In ordinary words, different selves and personalities are a direct consequence of the complexities of the environment which the organisms inhabit. Indeed, several ways of dealing with the same world can reside within the same organism, leading to what psychologists call "alternative selves". Of course, slight differences in the operation of the mechanical parts of the organism can also lead to the build-up of different experiences. If Fred has a crick in the neck which makes it turn right with a slight preference to turning left, an affliction not possessed by Jim, the two will clearly build up different state structures and plans to deal with the same environment.

Finally, an effect which we have neglected so far is that the world which our simple automata are trying to get to know will contain other organisms. Fred and Jim might bump into each other. So far we have argued that simple mechanisms of exploration allow the *self* of different organisms to develop in different ways. In the rest of this book we shall spend much effort in looking at the effect that communication between organisms can have on the consciousness of individuals. Here, having looked at some of the implications of the Basic Guess concepts of *self* and *will,* we shall take a brief look again at philosophical and psychological ideas which exist on these topics, to see whether the consequences make some kind of sense.

Returning to the Self in Philosophy and Psychology

At the beginning of this chapter a distinction became apparent between Dennett's view that a group of independent agents "revise drafts" to produce a sense of self, and Greenfield's contention that such an arrangement would collapse during periods of unconsciousness, i.e. were the agents to fall asleep. This would be a serious threat to an enduring sense of self. The Basic Guess encourages us to think of "agents" as neurons or groups of neurons. The "revising of drafts" could then be interpreted in a neural way as the process of relaxation of a neural state machine to stable states. There is no threat to the self as (Consequence 5) these stable states mirror the enduring nature of the world through the functions stored in the neurons, such a storage being robust and responsible for long term memory, as seen in earlier Consequences. The only question this leaves about Dennett's description is whether metaphors such as "agent revising drafts" are necessary or helpful. Perhaps the emergent behaviour of neural state machines offers an alternative for those who like to get closer to the neural nature of the brain.

Looking at the psychological literature, do the Consequences of this chapter help us to appreciate the difference between Freud's subconscious drives, Airport's traits, Eysenck's innateness of the self and Kelly's theory of personal constructs? For me, personally, it is a clarification of these points of view which *is* one of the main results of looking at the self as a property of state structure as we have done.

Freud's ideas on the effect of the unconscious (or subconscious — the unconscious which could surface) find an interpretation even within the limited existence of Jim and Fred of Fig. 5.5. It is quite possible for our embryonic robots to reinforce their yumminess paths during their waking hours and eventually to make automatic decisions as they arrive at some road junctions. This could be described as the unwanted alternatives not entering conscious planning. That is, while these alternatives are still being represented somewhere in the state structure, they do not affect firing patterns during the waking day. But some sort of sleep leads to a different state of affairs — the current world state loosens the grip on the inner state machine (the $A^{\emptyset}$ of Fig. 5.1 is subdued by sensors being inactive) and forgotten alternatives can reappear in something akin to dreaming and be linked again to conscious structure when waking. Alternatively, on waking the organism may find itself in an unfamiliar area of its state structure and report unexplained feelings. So the transfer between the subconscious and the fully conscious or (to the organism) an inexplicable effect on the conscious seems to come within the framework of the Basic Guess.

Allport's suggestion of describable traits such as friendliness and cheerfulness could be seen as the differences in personality which arise from initially random choices which are then classified according to their distinguishing characteristics. The model of Fig. 5.5 suggests that this makes sense as organisms will settle into following certain loops in the diagram. So a group of organisms could be described as "froggy" as they settle in the loop containing a frog, whereas another might be said to be "grapey" as they settle in the loop containing grapes. So, in summary, the arbitrariness of choice at the early stage of learning creates the opportunity for organisms to develop different personalities; it is the world itself that constrains the variety and causes personalities to have different "traits". On the other hand, Eysenck's notion of innateness does not sit easily with the results of the Basic Guess. In order for traits to be "inborn", some way of building biases in the function of the system needs to be found. The neural state machine approach indicates that behaviour is much more likely to be influenced by events "after birth" than by the structure of the net. Clearly, extreme physical effects could affect the exploration of the robot and hence its personality. This is the crick-in-the-neck argument used earlier: an afflicted robot acquires its state structure differently from one not afflicted in this way. But much of the evidence from the world of living beings is that learning works to overcome afflictions, so that the major characteristics of personality appear open to being independent of physical, inheritable effects.

Kelly's Personal State Structures

There is a group of people in the world for whom consciousness is not just a matter of after-dinner discussion. They are counsellors, psychotherapists and clinical psychologists. Their task is to listen to the difficulties of their clients or patients and form a view of the problem which is being presented to determine some way in which help can be given. While many of these difficulties could be described by the blanket phrase "emotional problems", the question of personality differences is paramount. Why is it that one person cannot cope with some aspects of life and another can? The "self" of an individual determines how well that individual can continue to function in the face of events such as bereavement, marriage break-ups, inappropriate fears and panics. We now return to the work of George Kelly, who, from a background of aeronautical engineering, became a clinical psychologist and, in the mid-1950s, felt that the problems which his clients presented needed to be seen from some kind of formal framework which is focused on the distinct personality of each individual. While many practitioners of therapy have beliefs about the general nature of the problems of self[13] which are common to many, Kelly's theory concentrates on explaining what makes one person different from another and, if such a person needs help, how such help can be made specific to that individual.

This psychological theory — personal construct theory (PCT), Kelly, 1955 — is remarkably close to the state machine concepts we have discussed in this book. As mentioned earlier, its structure as a fundamental postulate and eleven corollaries has inspired my own

---

[13] Often related to Freud's concept of the effect of a suppressed subconscious.

approach (although there is no direct correlation between the content of our Basic Guess and Consequences and the postulates and corollaries of Kelly). Kelly's fundamental postulate reflects strongly his belief in some sort of mental state structure as being the representation of a person's enduring self:

> *"The processes of an individual are psychologically channelled by the ways in which he anticipates events."*

That is, a person's thoughts and behaviour are guided by a memory of the past which contains feelings about the results of some of that person's own actions. Kelly's corollaries clarify this. For example, he submitted that:

> *"A person anticipates events by construing their replication."*

The word "construing" is central to Kelly's vocabulary. It means that a major internal "belief" is that the world is relatively constant so that events that happened in the past, and the psychological reactions which they caused, will occur again. The neural state machine model and its Basic Guess make it clear that an organism could not build up a meaningful state structure in an arbitrary world, i.e. a world without replication. On the other hand Kelly's view that there is total scope for individuality is also borne out by the neural approach:

> *"Persons differ from each other in their construction of events."*

As explained earlier, such differences come from the exploratory property of the neural machine which, through arbitrary actions, will provide different experiences for different organisms.

Kelly is known for introducing a method of personal construct therapy which focuses on measuring grids of constructs and their relationships. With the neural model shown in this chapter, we see that this is equivalent to discovering the links in a person's state structure as it *is* and also the way the person *would like it to be*. Therapy consists of revisiting and discussing the way in which the individual construes the world, and getting him to restructure his constructs in some way that reduces the problem which is causing the individual his unhappiness. I have written elsewhere about the relationship between construct systems and state structures. Aleksander (1984) may be of interest to readers who wish to pursue this similarity. Here I am merely drawing attention to the common ground between Kelly's model and mine: they both suggest that the awe we have for our own sense of consciousness need not be diminished though modelling techniques based on some kind of state structure.

So, Who Am I?

There is a danger that with all that has been said in this chapter, it becomes tempting to answer the question "Who am I?" by saying, "I am a state structure." Nothing could be further from what has been intended. The three Consequences which form the backbone of the intended answer say, first, that learning is a way of creating a state structure which provides sensations that mirror the world I live in. Second, this world contains "me" and the changes I can bring about in it. This is no more difficult a thing to represent in my own state structure than the existence of other objects and their effect on the world. For example, the sun causes warming, a bicycle causes transport, an umbrella keeps me dry in the rain, and my "self" can go places and make paper aeroplanes. The final part of the discussion is that the changes in the world due to my own self as seen inwardly may or may not be linked to my own outward actions. This creates the sense of will, which brings these actions into play as a path to an "attractor" which is dictated by need or arbitrariness in this inner state space. Also, we have seen that the "I" of two different people can be quite different, leading to a model of what is normally called "personality". So, "I am in my state structure" is a more accurate description than "I am state structure".

However, treating Magnus as a wandering Robinson Crusoe type with no man Friday to keep it company is unfair. That puts it at a disadvantage with respect to humans who are born into a society of other humans and which, on the whole, forms a helpful environment within which the developing organisms can develop their viable selves. The view I have to take in order to discuss the artificial consciousness of Magnus is that it will not be cut off from such human help. The fascinating questions which flow from this notion form the material for the next chapter and the rest of the book.

Postscript to Chapter 5

The Challenge of 'Me'

The 'Self' in State Structure

In Chapter 5, I hypothesised that any conscious feeling of knowing what 'I want' must be iconically held in the state structures of neural automata. In the time since this has not changed, but here I describe some further thoughts that have occurred in this area. The crux of the discussion lies in three 'consequences'.

First (Consequence 5): Prediction

Here it is suggested that causally related events in the world are represented as causally related iconic states in the state structure of the brain/automaton. This means that issues such as 'if *I* turn left at the crossroad *I* will reach East bourne while if *I* turn right *I* I will get to Brighton' are found in the iconic state structure. The little word *I* indicates that *self* has to be implicit in the state structure that is built up through experience. So, if the automaton is in imaginational mode, the alternatives will feel like 'if I do X then Y will happen'.

This is briefly discussed in the appendix of [A's L][a] and a related paper.[b]

Second (Consequence 6): The 'Stream' of Consciousness

The state structure, in a non-deterministic way, predicts what happens as a result of possible actions. The above example is also an instance of the way that experience, which is a linear stream becomes structured into a non-deterministic state structure. Non-deterministic has to be distinguished from 'probabilistic' it means that the information 'can go either to Brighton or to East bourne' is contained in the state structure without including probabilities. So the ideas contained in Figs. 5.3 and 5.4 of the first edition have turned out to be important in much subsequent work.

Third (Consequence 7): Will and Action Selection

Finally, Consequence 7 while entitled 'will', points out that consciously felt state trajectories can be controlled by need or desire, but could also take arbitrary routes giving the impression of freedom. That is, when there is no strong input from some perceived need or desire, noise mechanisms could be at work to provide this arbitrariness. An interesting PhD thesis by Rabinder Lee[c] showed how noise processes in a neural automaton could bring about

---

[a] Aleksander, I and Morton, H. B. (2012). *Aristotle's Laptop: The Discovery of Our Informational Minds*. World Scientific, Singapore.
[b] Aleksander, I. and Morton, H. (2014). Learning State Prediction Using a Weightless Neural Explorer. *Proc ESANN 14*, pp. 505–510.
[c] Lee, R. (2008). *Aspects of affective action choice: computational modelling*, PhD thesis, Imperial College London.

decisions which, although arbitrary, might 'feel' as if they had a rational basis.

Will and Illusion

It is in WMMW,[d] Chapter 6, that I returned to the neural automaton modelling of will in the face of two important published ideas. The first is by Californian physiologist Benjamin Libet and his colleagues who discovered that some desire-related brain activity anticipated, by about a second, the actual coming into consciousness of that desire.[e] This leads to the second important idea by Dan Wegner that people may be fooled into thinking that they make wilful decisions but they may not be conscious of the neural activity that links intention to action; that is, when some action is taken the notion that there was a will to do it preceding the event is illusory.[f] In discussing 'will' it is essential to do this in a framework of how emotions occur and I will return to this in the postscript for Chapter 8 (PS8).

In Sum

Many of the ideas on turning a stream of experience into a decision-making architecture introduced in Chapter 5 have turned out to be fundamental, but there is still a great deal of work to be done both on the neural network theory of this and its cognitive implications. A start has been made as indicated in the paper of note (b) of this postscript.

---

[d]Aleksander, I. (2005). *The World in My Mind, My Mind in the World: Key mechanisms of consciousness in people, animals and machines,* Imprint Academic, Exeter.

[e]Libet, B.,Gleason, C. A., Wright, E. W. and Pearl, D. K. (1983). Time of Conscious Intention to Act in Relation to Onset of Cerebral Activity (Readiness-Potential) — The Unconscious Initiation of a Freely Voluntary Act, *Brain*, 106, pp. 623–642.

[f]Wegner, D. M. (2002). *The illusion of conscious will.* MIT Press, Cambridge.

As she approached the dingy oil bar behind Galactic College, Molecula thought about how her life had changed over the last few weeks. She had met Red a few times, but in complete secrecy. She had his reports redirected to her private address and had even told Asic that Red had gone quiet.

"Just as well," Asic had said, "Sir Global nearly had a chaotic reverberation of his central control system when Red Naskela declared on national television that Global's automata theory of consciousness is narrow and leads to the suppression of true science and the citizens of Volta."

Molecula had stopped arguing with Asic in Red's defence. Sir Global's opposition had gone from being a rumble in the background to a real threat to her livelihood. But the more she felt the threat, the more she looked forward to her meetings with Red. She found this unsettling. It was not logical. She had always been content with thinking that her life was progressing smoothly as ordained by the Central Programmer. Here, suddenly, she was leading her life on two separate tracks. With Red she was learning to think in a new way. She even started questioning the very existence of a Central Programmer. At work, on the other hand, she held her position of considerable responsibility and got on with her work. She had developed two distinct senses of self which she found puzzling and disturbing.

Red was at the usual table, rising with a smile. Should she talk to him about her sense of confusion?

Chapter 6

Beginnings and Words

Setting Human Beings Apart

Memories of religious lessons at school ... "In the beginning there was the Word, and the Word was with God, and the Word was God" (St. John 1:1). Also, "God created Man in his own image" (Genesis 1:27). Christian culture certainly sets people aside from all else on earth, and so do most living in the Western world in their daily lives. As part of this effort, the distinguishing feature that sets human beings apart from, say, "our dumb friends" is "the Word". "The Word" is so special that it is even given a God-like place in the New Testament. In fact, it *is* very likely that the form of communication which people use is the most sophisticated and complex of all the species on earth (in terms of the seemingly infinite number of things that can be said in it). However, the question which is rehearsed over many pages of text in linguistic philosophy is whether this supremacy among human beings spells out a supremacy in their consciousness. Some even argue that without a well-formed language there can be no consciousness (this goes under the heading of "linguistic determinism"). So, from this extreme point of view, animals are not conscious despite the fact that they may have some form of communication.

So where does this leave Magnus? What I wish to show is that Magnus could become quite proficient at human language and, in that sense, be very different from animals. So while it may be commonplace to measure the level of consciousness of living organisms on some scale which puts people at the top and amoebas at the bottom, a language-using robot opens up the possibility of finding a completely new axis. Magnus could have language but its consciousness would still be artificial and therefore could, from another perspective, be some way below the sophistication of that of an amoeba. But the main benefit of looking at the role of language in our state machine models is to clear up some of the major questions about the role of language in mental life. What are these issues?

The first and obvious question is that of the impact of words on "thinking". I can ask a question such as "what is an apple?" and get answers as different as "a red, round fruit", "a green, shiny fruit" or even "some kind of computer". There are more difficult words around, such as "love" or "honest", which clearly set minds racing in a particular way, and therefore lead to a need for discussing the relationship of words to the inner, mental world of human brains. This relationship will be the first from which to look at a Consequence of the Basic Guess. But words are not used in isolation. "John likes Mary" and "Mary likes John" have different meanings due to their sequence. So language, as a controlled way of using words, raises controversial questions about this very control. Is a knowledge of such control innate or is it learned? Is it all to do with grammatical rules or is ungrammatical language significant?

I shall approach these difficult questions in two steps. The first is to show that the state machine model and the Basic Guess have scope for the *representation* of words. That is, I wish to answer the question of how words form part of state structure, suggesting only the simplest ways in which iconic learning could be responsible for language entering state structure. I wish then to look briefly at some of the history of the philosophy of language to see how the idea of iconic representation clears up some well-established puzzles. I shall leave the second step of the question of language acquisition and the "inborn/acquired" debate for the next chapter.

Knowing the Names of Things

As described so far, our neural state machine is a sad affair. It stares at the world and just about manages to drag itself along roads full of frogs, leaves and bunches of grapes. The part that is sadly missing is the presence of other organisms on these roads. Indeed, if Jim and Fred of the last chapter never meet they would not have an iconic representation of each other in their state structure. Leaving aside the question of whether their attitudes would be adversarial or co-operative, we now make the assumption that Fred is an adult who, for some unspecified reason, wishes to be helpful to Jim, who is a newcomer to the "thingsworld" of Fig. 5.5 in the last chapter. Adult Fred "knows" the names of things in the "thingsworld", and by teaching them to Jim can save the latter a lot of aimless exploration. This deceptively simple scenario hides a multitude of difficulties. First, it does not explain how the first in our line of robots got to know the meaning of words. Second, it does not explain how much Jim needs to have inherited in order to understand what Fred is trying to do. Finally, what does the statement "Fred knows the names of the things in the world" actually mean?

In this section I shall home in on only one aspect of the last of these questions. How is it that the mechanism of iconic representation has the power of representing "the names of things"? I must immediately say that by "the names of things" more than what we call nouns are needed to name things. Simple adjectives and verbs need to be brought into view. "The green, shiny apple", "the dog owned by John" and "Mary, who is top of the class" are all examples of "the names of things". So the *only* issue here is how such names can be represented in iconically developed state structure. To this end we evoke Consequence 8 and show that it points to a property of state structure which enables these representations.

Consequence 8: Representation of meaning
When sensory events occur simultaneously or in close time proximity in different sensory modalities, iconic learning and generalisation of the neural state machine ensure that one can be recalled from the other.

To illustrate what this means we shall look at how meaning may be represented at its simplest level in a neural state machine. I shall describe some experiments which were carried out with Magnus in our laboratories. The rather complicated set-up is shown in Fig. 6.1; it represents Magnus getting to know objects in what we call a *kitchenworld*. The kitchenworld consists of objects such as glasses, plates, cutlery, cups, bottles and the odd apple. In the laboratory this is a real image taken with something like a video camera and digitised so as to be available within the computer. Magnus is, in fact, a large program which represents everything shown within the large dotted frame — it is a simulated neural state machine. Magnus is what computer scientists call a "Virtual" machine. That is, it is a machine programmed into the inside of a conventional computer. When the program is running, the host machine behaves just like the virtual machine. To all intents and purposes it *is* the virtual machine.

Everything else, including the picture, is another program — the kitchenworld program. The two interact as follows. At its output,

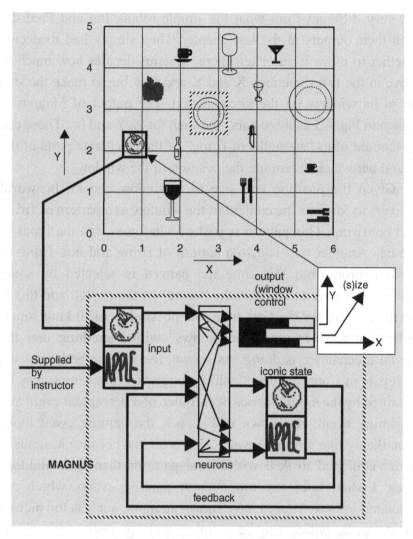

Fig. 6.1.   Magnus in a kitchenworld.

Magnus issues signals to the kitchenworld which control the position and size of a window placed over the picture. In Fig. 6.1 the window is shown to be over an apple. Another dotted position for the window is shown over a plate. What Magnus is doing is actually not very different from what the simple robots Jim and Fred did with their outputs in the last chapter. They simply had to decide whether to move right or left; here, Magnus decides how much to move in the two directions X and Y, and how big to make the size (s) of its window on the kitchenworld. The output of Magnus is shown in Fig. 6.1 as three bars, one each for X, Y and (s). These can be thought of as "strengths of firing" of three separate parts of the neural net which determine the position of the window.

Given the position and size of a window, the kitchenworld delivers to Magnus the content of the window as a pattern of firing and nonfiring. This pattern is part of what goes into the input of the net. Another part is also a pattern of firing and non-firing of input neurons, but this time the pattern is selected by some instructor. I have to call this the "name" of the object, and this is where we see, for the first time, the possibility of linking something that another organism "knows" with something that the neural mechanism is doing. As shown, the scheme addresses the first part of Consequence 8, which suggests that meaning may be obtained by the simultaneous occurrence of a perceptual event and a naming event. As shown in Fig. 6.1, the naming event looks remarkably like a written word. This is so just because Magnus is better equipped to deal with visual patterns than with auditory ones. I shall later say more about naming events which are extended in time. Here, I have shown an input, such as the picture of an apple, which can be coupled with an instructor's signal naming the object simultaneously. The rest of Magnus is a conventional neural state machine which is capable of creating iconic states related to the input event. For simplicity, in Fig. 6.1 the iconic state is shown as being identical to the input information although we recall that the former could be a "sampled" version of the latter. Now for some of the experiments carried out with this equipment.

What is an Object?

The folklore about children learning to name objects is that a caring parent waves a teddy bear in front of the child's gaze, at the same time shouting "teddy" at the lucky offspring. The child is then supposed to memorise this and, on seeing the object again, copy the parent in shouting "teddy". As psychologists tell us (for example, Annette Karmiloff-Smith, 1992) and anyone who has a child knows, children spend a great deal of time sussing out the world before they begin to use words in anything like a purposeful way. When this happens, the child seems to use a whole lot of words all at once. It is called a "word spurt" by psychologists who measure such things. The sussing out seems to be devoted to assimilating what is and isn't an object and what sounds emitted by carers and others belong to what objects. The actual uttering of a word or phrase is a more complicated matter than at first seems to be the case, and we shall approach this later.

In our laboratory we wanted to understand how a system such as Magnus might work out what in the kitchenworld is and isn't an object. We need to do this if we are ever to have a chance of understanding how a much more complex organism partitions its sensory world into objects that need naming. A colleague, Richard Evans, showed that it would be possible to train a window to "shrink" onto a particular object such as the apple in Fig. 6.2. This is done by displacing the position and size of the window slightly off centre and off the right size, and training the net to output a move towards the correct position. The interesting part of this is that when we have done this for the apple as shown, not only the apple becomes an "attractor" in the space of the image, but also any other object. A close look shows that what the net is doing is to interpret any *disturbance from the background* as a pattern which attracts the window. What this means is that if the window gets a part of an

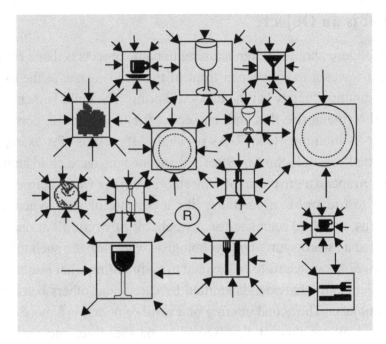

Fig. 6.2. Attractors in the kitchenworld.

object in view, it will move to frame the object. Curiously this creates not only attractors where the objects are, but also "repellers" (such as R in Fig. 6.2) in areas where there are no objects.

This means that it comes naturally for a neural system, with vision at one end and an ability to move at the other, to develop a general notion of finding an object by treating it as a disturbance in a background. An additional pair of properties which emerge from such a system come from the possibility of habituation (as introduced in the last chapter) to an unchanging sensory input. As things have been described, starting our organism in some arbitrary position, it will find the nearest object, frame it and stay there for ever. This is where the habituation comes in. As the input fades, the output will no longer hold the input object framed, the gaze will move and the system will centre on another object. It is possible to think that in this way the system will wonder about centring its frame on the objects in the scene.

The second property is more obvious. The object finding is not dependent on one particular arrangement of objects, but will (having learned to centre as a general principle) work with any arrangement of objects. Looking at this anthropomorphically, it could be said that generalisation in the network causes the organism to switch its gaze among areas of interest in a visual scene. A human being is known to do this by causing the eyes to saccade (or jump) to such areas when presented with a new picture (Humphreys and Bruce, 1989).

Associating Names

Assuming that the agent we have called an instructor is capable of noting what it is that Magnus is looking at, he can choose to "name" it by providing the naming input to the "word" field of the input. In a human being the first names learned are through the auditory channel; in an artificial setting it is legitimate to use a second visual channel for naming. The principle of what happens through iconic learning, using this visual channel, may broadly be the same as that of an auditory channel. The way in which this happens is illustrated in Fig. 6.3.

An important word in Consequence 8 is "simultaneously", as it is the coincidence of the naming and the noticing of an object (in automata terms, the falling into a state space attractor created by an unnamed object) which creates the representative states. One is shown for an apple and another for a cup in Fig. 6.3. The property of generalisation is represented as the ability to access the complete state from a partial input. This means that either the name or the object will lead to a state which represents both. This includes a

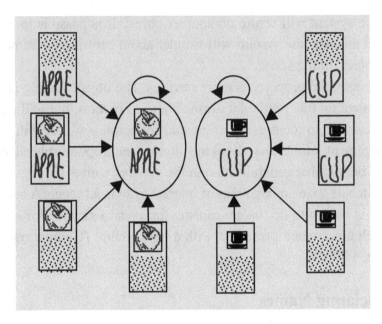

Fig. 6.3. State characteristics for two named objects.

partial or noisy representation of either form of input. For the technical purist it is necessary to say what happened to the "fading" input connection to the state machine introduced in the last chapter. This is still assumed to be at work without affecting the validity of Consequence 8. In fact, it is important to have the fading there as, otherwise, if a partial input is slavishly tied to the state machine it would cause the state to represent its iconic image in a distorted and noisy way.

I shall argue later that there is nothing innately special about words: they are objects found in a repository held by human society. So it is important to note that Consequence 8 is about association, within one state, of signals related to objects that occur together in the world. So, if a cup often appears with a saucer, a critic of the Consequence might ask whether Magnus will report that the meaning of "cup" is "saucer" or otherwise. This problem arises because of the way in which I have chosen to use the same modality (vision) to represent two aspects of the same object: its looks and its verbal description. However, in Magnus the visual name comes in through a different set of sensory channels or perceptual neurons. So, in terms of the Basic Guess, Magnus is "aware" of the fact that items in two sensory modalities (two sets of perceptual neurons) are being linked in a single state. The word "meaning" then relates to this cross-sensory association.

The critic could then switch sides and point out that a human being learns to read through vision and associates word pictures with object pictures. This is a complex issue, but what strikes me as important is that the sensory modality barrier is crossed twice. The child's first learning of "meaning" is across the visual/auditory divide. Reading comes much later, when a child, perhaps to its astonishment, faces adults who insist that the useful sounds it has learned also have visual (written) symbols attached to them. This too crosses a modality divide. From this, one would ask whether a congenitally deaf child learns to read in a very different way from a hearing child. However, important questions such as this begin to impinge on the learning of utterances — which is the subject matter of Consequence 9 — and are best left until this Consequence has been fully explored.

Where are the Objects?

We recall that it is the nature of some experiments with Magnus which is being described here. Clearly, the intention is to relate the mechanisms in an artificial object such as Magnus to mechanisms which *may* exist in living objects. In this spirit I go on to look at the way in which Magnus gets to associate the position of objects with what they look like and what they are called. That is, the machine learns to respond to names by finding the required object. As described so far, the object-centring arrangement is something that works locally by causing the neural state machine to create little movements which cause the window to encompass the object.

However, in general, X, Y and (s) controls in Magnus actually determine the absolute position of the window in the fields of view. The centring mechanism described above is one which modifies these absolute positions by small amounts. That is, there are neuron groups which output X, Y and (s) and other groups which change these values by little amounts. Concentrating now on these main groups, we have a situation as shown in Fig. 6.4. It is clear that this situation is very similar to that discussed in the representation of the self in the last chapter (Fig. 5.4). The difference here is that there is proprioceptive (sensation of muscle actions) feedback from output actions which control the size and position of the window rather

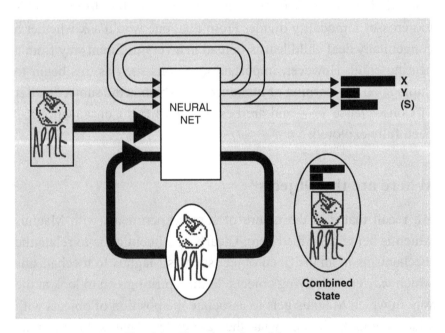

Fig. 6.4. Knowing where things are.

than just the turning of the head. That is, wherever the window is, there is information fading back into the net. This means that through iconic training the system adds the size and position of the window to the iconic state. Without going into technical details, experiments have shown that with this knowledge, and given, say, the name image "apple", one can not only cause Magnus to anticipate in its state what will be found, but also cause the window to move to the right place to find the apple.

What does Magnus do when there are several apples or plates in the scene? The noisy input which replaces the visual input through fading makes it possible for the system to fall into any of the states which have a common name. Note that this requires the fading of the proprioceptive feedback as well, so as not to tie the gaze down to one particular position. In other words, when asked for an apple, Magnus will focus on all available apples, one at a time, in arbitrary order.

A Changing World

Finally, on this question of Magnus acting as an object identifier, one should ask what happens if, after learning to find objects, they are moved around in the field of view. When asked to find the apple, Magnus will form an inner image of the apple and where it should be. Not finding it in place will destabilise the positioning loop in Fig. 6.4. That is, at the expected place, the input which is expected to keep the iconic representation stable will not occur, causing the state to change in some way. This could be said to return the system to random exploration, which, on a lighting on an apple, will tend to remain stable as the image and the name correspond with the content of the state. The key point here is that if iconic learning is still in force, a new position for the object will be learned. This raises questions about overwriting the function of some neurons, which is clearly a necessity for Magnus as it is for other living forms. Psychologists talk of long term and short term memory, but working with Magnus teaches us that there are more and fascinating forms which are beyond the point which is being discussed at the moment: the naming and finding of objects.

Curiously, the overwriting which was seen above is quite possible in technical terms, but it calls for a parameter, which measures a lack of stability, and for new learning. In humans it is thought that chemical processes in the brain serve this function by controlling the degree to which parts of the brain can learn. The sensations caused by this chemistry are sometimes associated with "emotions", a subject which will receive more attention later in this book. Here, perhaps, we should move on to look more closely at how iconic state representation is linked to more complex concepts and how these relate to natural language.

Concepts and Logic ...

Part of the strength of humans' power of expression is that objects don't just have a single name which is solely associated with that individual object. Even the word "apple" in Magnus's simple kitchenworld points to two completely different objects. But I could have used the term "fruit" or even "almost spherical" to refer to the two apples. Here a rather remarkable fact comes to light. The simple associative mechanism stressed in Consequence 8 allows "concepts" with greater or less generality to be represented in the state space of a neural state machine. Taking the position of the objects in Figs. 6.1 and 6.2 out of the argument and recalling that an input such as "apple" leads to one of the objects so named in an arbitrary fashion, the state representation of the concepts such as "apple", "plate" and "glass" is shown in Fig. 6.5.

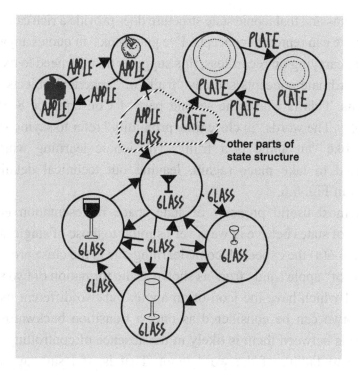

Fig. 6.5. Concepts in state space.

This state representation reads, "From an arbitrary place in the state structure a naming label causes an entry into a cluster of states which all have the same label, irrespective of the differences in their iconic representations." Translated into everyday language, in the context of Magnus, this reads something like: "On seeing a written word out of a set that Magnus has learned, it 'thinks' of all those things which can be represented by that word." Stated so blatantly, this kind of anthropomorphic description has a strangely jarring effect. The reader may say to me, "When did I give you permission to include *me* in agreeing that Magnus does any thinking at all?" To which I reply, "This is a result of the Basic Guess, but you don't need to share my belief in it. I am just showing that what's going on is not as innocuous as it seems and that iconic state structure does provide a rich canvas on which we can represent concepts. I've put 'thinks' in quotes anyway!"

So, carrying on regardless, this suggests that the need to explain super-ordinate concepts such as "fruit" or "spherical objects" still remains. This is where the second part of Consequence 8 comes into play. The words "in close time proximity" refer to saying something like "an apple is a fruit". The iconic learning which is expected to take place (again, leaving out technical details) is shown in Fig. 6.6.

A most useful property of state space representation is that groups of states behave in ways very similar to those of single states. In Fig. 6.6(a) the expected iconic learning due to the close proximity in time of "apple" and "fruit" is shown as the formation of two states both of which have the icon of an apple, but two different names. These two can be considered as one: a transition backwards and forwards between them is likely in the absence of controlling input or due to fading of the word input. That is, if I say "apple" to Magnus, it will enter the leftmost of the two states, but as the input is released, it transits to the apple with the "fruit" title and back with a high probability. We can think of this cluster as one state with the apple icon but with two names because the way the cluster is entered from the rest of the state structure, the way the cluster itself may be re-entered, and the way it can be made to exit in the presence of other input is the same as it would be for one state. Again, in anthropomorphic terms, it could be said that Magnus "knows" that an apple has the names "apple" and "fruit". But how does it know that "apple is fruit" is right, but "fruit is apple" is wrong?

The answer to this comes from looking at other examples of "fruit", as in Fig. 6.6(b). An input of "fruit" leaves the system freedom to transit between different instantiations of "fruit" (i.e. strawberry, grape and apple in this case), whereas "apple" keeps the system only in the complex "apple" state. This clustering of states

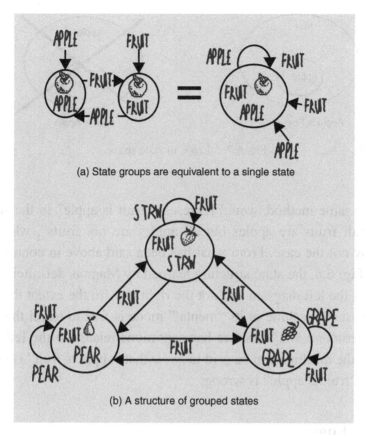

(a) State groups are equivalent to a single state

(b) A structure of grouped states

Fig. 6.6.   State grouping and concepts.

to represent concepts marks a really important step in understanding the power of state representations. It begins to answer the question of how Magnus can learn to operate according to logical principles, or, more important, how brainlike organs in general develop representations which obey the laws of logic. Consider Fig. 6.7.

Venn diagrams are pictures which logicians use to describe the relationships between objects. "Apple is fruit" in the logical sense of "all apples are fruits but all fruits are not apples" is represented in the Venn diagram on the left of Fig. 6.7. The diagram on the right,

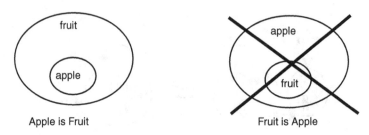

Fig. 6.7.   Logic in state space.

by the same method, would represent "fruit is apple" in the sense that "all fruits are apples but all apples are not fruits", which is clearly not the case. From what has been said above in connection with Fig. 6.6, the state structure learned by Magnus definitely represents the left diagram and not the right one. To the extent that the neural state machine in its "mental" mode is free to travel through state structure and therefore has sensations related to the left diagram, the machine can be said to *know* that "apple is fruit" is right, while "fruit is apple" is wrong.

More Logic ...

Steven Pinker (1994) suggests that the idea of mental representation (or *mentalese,* as he calls it) was made respectable by Alan Turing and the concept of a Turing machine. A Turing machine is a kind of standard imaginary computer which operates on symbols written on a tape and a set of rules given to it. I shall use one of Pinker's examples but put it in a slightly different way. The machine can read the tape, remember some symbols and print on the tape. Suppose that the tape reads from left to right and contains mentalese symbols (which should at this stage be meaningless) as shown below:

S@M!MD

The programmer has given the machine the following rules:

(1) When you encounter @, move one symbol to the left and print this symbol seven spaces after the written sequence.
(2) Go back to @ and remember the symbol just to the right of it.
(3) Continue scanning until! is found.
(4) If the symbol to the right of ! matches the symbol remembered in (2), then print the last symbol in a position just to the right of that printed in (1).

Let us apply these rules to our mentalese string of symbols. Applying rule (1) results in the following:

S@M!MD S

Applying rule (2) causes M to be remembered. Then when (3) finds !, (4) turns out to be true and its execution leads to:

S@M!MD SD

Now, instead of arbitrary symbols we have the following "linguistic" symbols, or English-like words:

S: Socrates
@: isa
M: man
!: every
D: ismortal
So we start with the following on the tape:

Socrates isa man every man ismortal.

After whirring away for a while, our Turing machine will print neatly:

Socrates is a man every man is mortal Socrates is mortal.

Not only that, but letting S=Chirp, M=bird and D=canfly, the machine will cheerfully print:

Chirp is a bird every bird can fly Chirp can fly.

It could be argued that the Turing machine now "knows" the logician's rule:

If X is Y and all Ys are Z then X is Z.

It is this kind of ability of Turing machines and, indeed, conventional computers (which are just more practical forms of Turing machines) which gave rise to the field of artificial intelligence and to claims that computers can be made to solve problems of logic and, in some sense, be said to be reasoning machines. It is also the process which caused many to question the validity of such claims as: were we to assign the values S = Igor, M = professor and D = canfly, the machine would pronounce:

Igor isa professor every professor canfly Igor canfly.

Although this is a perfectly self-consistent statement its absurdity cannot be appreciated by the machine. A human being would recognise that the premise and the conclusion are absurd, because experience dictates that professors can't fly (unaided by an aeroplane, that is). Searle's criticism of AI that the machine follows a blind set of rules which do not represent "understanding" unless they are used with symbols which in themselves are understood or grounded in experience of the world, comes through loud and clear.

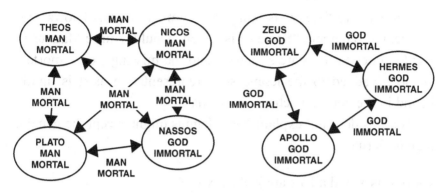

Fig. 6.8. Magnus as a Greek philosopher.

Indeed, the way in which the beginnings of reasoning occur in Magnus is precisely the opposite of what happens in the Turing machine. Sets of objects are learned and linked in state structure and the rules of logic emerge from this linking process. So how would Magnus deal with the logic of the Socrates sentence? This question focuses on how a concept such as "every man" could have a learned state representation. Figure 6.8 shows the state structure of Magnus the Greek philosopher.

My contention, borrowed from Wittgentein (see Chapter 1), is that there is no essentialism in language. That is, words such as "man" do not point to the complete set of all men as there is no such thing as complete experience of that set. There is only an individual's complete experience, and Magnus in Fig. 6.8 is assumed to know only four men all of whom are mortal, and has heard of three gods and been told that they are immortal. Assuming that Magnus does not know Socrates (which is the case with most of us), being told that "Socrates is a man", through the use of the word "man", will enter the Nicos–Theos–Plato–Nassos state structure area, which is not only the "man" area but also precisely the "mortal" area. So "every man is mortal" is represented as a truth in the state structure where "every" is really "every man Magnus knows". Of course, the statement "Socrates is a man" would require Magnus to add Socrates to the state structure, and the missing word "mortal" would be added to the iconic state representation as it is tightly bound in the neural mechanism to "man".

But this does not explain how Magnus might accept the general logician's rule:

If X is Y and all Ys are Z then X is Z.

This is certainly not incompatible with Magnus's experience as drawn in Fig. 6.8. However, here Magnus allows only seven entities as X, "man" and "god" for Y and "mortal" and "immortal" for Z. But within this restriction of quantity, the experience stored by Magnus as represented in state structure could be said to be compatible with the logic of the statement.

In following this line there is a danger of getting ahead of the argument. Mathematical thinking and the ready acceptance of logic is often quoted as the pinnacle of human consciousness. All that I have done here is to set down a marker that this question is not outside the discourse engendered by the Basic Guess. However, the argument needs to mature a little through a consideration of the rest of the Consequences, and I shall return to it towards the end of this book.

Verbs

Most of what has been said so far has centred on the representation of some nouns and some adjectives. But how would Magnus deal with the representation of verbs? How would Magnus know that "dog bites man" is common whereas "man bites dog" makes news? The first thing to realise is that a simple verbal statement such as

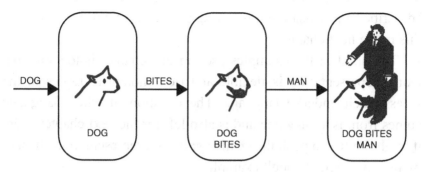

Fig. 6.9. Representing a phrase with a verb.

"dog bites man" is *one* iconic concept or state built up from a sequence of subordinate states. A sketch of what I mean is shown in Fig. 6.9.

This representation looks somewhat childish. In order to see what the real thing looks like I encourage the reader to think of the meaning of "dog bites man" by taking note of the mental image which this creates in his own head. Childish or not, this representation follows from the mechanisms for building up iconic representations discussed earlier in this chapter and which follow from Consequence 8. What about "man bites dog"? There would be little surprise if the sentence were "man bites hamburger". This is "close to experience", which can be interpreted as representations and links between them which exist in the state structure of the understanding organism. On the other hand, "man bites dog" leads the state trajectory up the garden path, as the state which occurs after "man bites ..." has exits to things like "hamburger", "sandwich" and "rare steak". As "dog" occurs, while the word will cause an entry into a representation of "dog", the sensation caused by a state change for which a link does not exist in the state space would be described by the owner of the sensation as being surprising. This again raises questions which go beyond the competence I have explained for a neural state machine so far. How could the organism "describe" any sensation it is having at all? More will be said about this in the next chapter.

The point of the examples used in this chapter is to show that iconic representation is flexible and rich enough to represent the ideas which underlie language. The question of where language comes from is a juicy one and is also left for the next chapter. Here it might be fun to push the challenge of rich representations further by picking some difficult examples.

Novelty

The above discussion points to a very important factor in iconic representations. How can a new idea be created in state space solely through linguistic input? I may say to Magnus, "Did you know that Columbus discovered America?" It might reply, "I didn't, but I do know now." This implies that new state structure has been created by a linguistic interaction. Is this mechanism supported by the Basic Guess?

The best way of illustrating that it is, may be to ask a slightly simpler question. Given that Magnus has a representation of "dog" and "man bites" in its state structure, as I have said in the last section, what makes the statement surprising for the hearer is that there is no link in the existing state structure between the two states. However, this state of affairs is changed by the linguistic statement itself. "Man bites dog" *creates* a link between "man bites" and "dog". Then, applying the principle of state combination seen earlier in this chapter, a combined state is learned, similar to the rightmost state of Fig. 6.9 but with the roles of the two agents reversed!

There is no difference in principle in learning that Columbus discovered America. It is contingent on the idea that concepts such as "Columbus", "discovered" and "America" already exist in

Magnus's state structure. This draws attention to one implication of the Basic Guess and the mechanism contained in Consequence 8: the knowledge contained in the state structure of Magnus is built up iteratively. A new item relies on structure being there to accept it. This means that all that has been said so far about the richness of state space representation begins to fall into place: the potential for creating new states, new links and and new state combinations in Magnus is considerable; in humans it is immense. But, I argue, the principles governing the process in the two may be similar.

Abstractions and Confusions

It comes as no surprise that the relationship between language and mental representation has the reputation of being a curious one. Steven Pinker (1994) gives an amusing account both of the vagaries of language (for example, how do we understand headlines such as "Iraqi Head Seeks Arms"?) and of the problems which arise in philosophies which assume that the act of thinking is entirely a linguistic affair. Clearly, the Basic Guess and its iconic representations appear not to support the latter: they suggest that ideas are iconically represented, and that linguistic expression is subordinate to such ideas. However, linguistic expression is a good guide to the complexity of ideas. For example, "dog bites man" is a straightforward image, whereas "John knows that Mary loves Harry" is altogether a different affair, for two main reasons. First, the two verbs, "knows" and "loves", are abstract in the sense that by looking at a person the observer cannot tell whether the person he observes knows or loves anything. Second, there are two levels of nesting in the sentence: the first is something that is in John's head, which contains a thought of Mary, and the second is the thought in Mary's head. So how could Magnus deal with these abstractions?

Putting aside again the question of how Magnus might have learned to speak (which will be seen in the next chapter) and concentrating on the mental representations which it is trying to express, how could something like "I know" or "I love" be represented? As seen in the last chapter, the concept of "I" or the "self" has to do with being able to describe one's own state structure. "I know" is an expression of "there are links in my state structure which...". "Do you know who discovered America?" is the same as asking, "Is there a combined state in your state structure which links an object to the state 'discovered America'?" "There isn't" or "there is" would be expressed as "I know" or "I don't know". "I love Mary", on the other hand, relates to words given to feelings and emotions which are rather special sensations in the organism. Much more will be said about such in Chapter 8; here it is anticipated that "I love Mary" is no harder to represent as a technical feat than "I like grapes", which was shown possible in representations of the self in the last chapter.

Now for the nesting: saying "John knows" is a statement that John has said directly or indirectly what he knows. The state structure of Magnus would have a representation for John's state structure and might imagine it as a structure like its own, but one which is not accessible except through what John says and does. This projection need not stop at the first step. There is no reason why Magnus should not represent what John knows about Mary as a further nesting associated with Mary's state structure. The latter is a state which combines the thought of Harry with sensations of what Magnus itself would describe as love. Magnus' state is sketched in Fig. 6.10.

I do not wish to give the impression that iconic mental states, by some magic, give rise to grammatically correct expressions. While the nature and role of syntax (or the grammar which controls linguistic expression) will be discussed in the next chapter, here

Fig. 6.10.   Iconic representation for "John knows that Mary loves Harry".

I wish to stress that the Basic Guess implies that such an expression is subordinate to the state representation. What I mean can be illustrated by the fact that the following two expressions can result from exactly the same state:

The first is:

"Help ... fire ... second floor ... child trapped";

and the second:

"There is a child trapped on the second floor of a building which is burning — could you please provide some assistance?"

Obviously, communication is paramount and people are good at it. Is language an instinct pre-wired by evolution or can it be explained as a skill developed during life? While this will be thrashed out in the next chapter, suffice it to say here that it relates to a need to transfer state representations from the neural system of one organism to that of another.

Theories of Meaning

I recall an occasion, after I had presented a paper on iconic representations in neural circuitry, when a young researcher stood up and said:

> "Of course you are simply restating the principles of the picture theory of meaning. Don't you know that this has now been discredited for over seventy years?"

> "No," I answered, "I thought that I was speaking from first principles."

What is the picture theory of meaning? Why should it have been discredited? Are arguments against the iconic representations really as damning as the young man implied?

The fact is that, in this chapter, the implications of the Basic Guess have caused us to stray into an area of major concern to philosophers in the twentieth century — theories of meaning. So the young man could have been saying, "What is it that you are telling us that philosophers have not mulled over already and come to a conclusion about?" So I shall end this chapter by taking a closer look at the philosophical issues through the eyes of influential philosophers and asking whether working with Magnus throws additional light on anything at all.

Gottlob Frege (1848–1925)

Often quoted as the founder of modern mathematical logic, Frege taught at the University of Jena for all of his professional life. His interest centred on the link between logic and mental representation (as crept into our discussion on the "Socrates is a man ..." argument). His contribution to theories of meaning lies in his definition of the difference between the *reference* of a linguistic expression and its *sense*. Put simply, in a sentence such as "Churchill was the Prime Minister of Britain during the Second World War", a reference of the sentence is "Churchill". If this is replaced by the words "Mrs Thatcher" in the same sentence, the sentence would not be true. So reference is the pointer to objects in the world which control the true /false value of a sentence. Indeed, "Second World War" is a reference in the above sentence, as replacing it with "First World War" would make the sentence false as well.

On the other hand, phrases such as "Prime Minister of Britain" or "First World War" are concepts which are distinguished by their very existence. This is what Frege calls the *sense* of these phrases. His major contribution is in drawing attention to the fact that a phrase can have both a sense and a reference. That is, "Second World War" is a reference of the sentence "Churchill was Prime Minister of Britain during ..." as well as having a sense in its own right.

The state space representations seen in this chapter support and (to my state-machine-obsessed mind) clarify this distinction through the fact that "sense" is the existence of atomic states in the state structure. "Reference", on the other hand, depends on the existence of what have been called combined states. In many people's minds there is a combined state for "Churchill was the Prime Minister of Britain during the Second World War" whereas there would not be one for "Mrs Thatcher was the Prime Minister of Britain during the Second World War". So when I am quizzed about what it is that the iconic ideas of the Basic Guess add to what Frege worked out a long time ago, I can happily answer, "Not very much, but the fact that I can relate what Frege thought to the working of a (mere?) machine means that a deeper grounding can be found for what would otherwise be seen just as the observation of a very perspicacious thinker.

Wittgenstein's picture theory of meaning

I mentioned in Chapter 1 that in *Tractacus Philosophicus* Ludwig Wittgenstein suggested that a theory of meaning has to do with the images of objects and their relationships which we can evoke "in our minds", and that this corresponds in some way to the existence of iconic states in state machines. *Tractacus* contained what is known in the history of philosophy as the "picture theory of meaning". Was it discredited? Yes, indeed! And, what's more, it was discredited by its creator, Wittgenstein himself. In his later work *Philosophical Investigations* (only published after his death) he rejected the idea that the meaning of a word is the object in the world which that word represents. He argued instead that meaning is totally detached from reality and is a function of the use of words.

What is the meaning of the word "apple"? The success or otherwise in answering this depends (according to *Investigations)* on the skill with which I can use words. I might say, "It is the name of a round shiny object that is sometimes green, sometimes red." Looking back on what I have said I would realise that my "meaning" could apply equally to a billiard ball. So I go on, "Oh yes, and it is a fruit which tastes, mmmm … how could I describe it? Do you mean that you have never eaten one?" Wittgenstein's point is that the quest to ascribe meaning to words in a philosophically tidy way is a fiction. Attempts at doing so from Locke to Frege involve formalisations (such as *simple* and *complex* ideas, *sense* and *reference* …) which are misleading as they ascribe objectivity to something which is in essence subjective. As was said in Chapter 1, this was one of the factors which swung philosophical attention to language, a trend which continued during much of this century.

So, is everything said about iconic representations now discredited? Not at all. I would certainly not claim that an iconic representation constitutes a *theory of meaning*. What it attempts to do is to suggest a mechanism which causes an organism to respond to words by entering a particular set of states — states which, to be useful, are memories of experience direct or related. It allows for the fact that in two organisms these states could be completely different in response to the same words. They are personal and private, and it is precisely this idiosyncrasy which led Wittgenstein to deny that pictures in one's head could constitute a watertight theory of meaning. There is no disagreement here, and I feel rather comfortable with the fact that the Basic Guess suggests that the brain copes with meaning in the rather loose way which Wittgenstein suggested may be at work.

Intentionality

While strictly not contributing directly to the theory of meaning, *intentionality* is very much a philosophical idea at the centre of the quest to define the nature of mental states. Originally coined by Franz Bertrano (1838–1917), the word is derived from the Latin *intentio,* which when directly translated means "internal content". It should not be confused with the word "intention", or a wish to achieve something; nor should it be related to the word "intensionality", which describes certain logical uncertainties of the truth of sentences (beyond our concern at the moment). Intentionality, according to Brentano, is the description of a unique property of mental states — the fact that they must always be *about* something. Even so-called abstract thoughts (beliefs, desires, hopes, etc.) cannot really be abstract — we believe something, desire something, hope for something and so on.

In fact, in the current debate about what computers can and cannot do, it is Stanford University philosophy professor John Searle (1980, 1983, 1992) who brought intentionality into the discussion (this has already cropped up in several places in this book, but is worth revisiting here). He questioned the claims of computer scientists that they had written programs which "understand" stories written in English. He argued that intentionality, which is needed to understand stories, is precisely that which the internal states of a computer do not have. His argument is enshrined in the well-known example of the Chinese room. Briefly, it goes as follows.

An operator locked in a room has a book written in English which contains a superb set of rules for processing Chinese characters. The exercise begins with Chinese speakers outside the room to feed a story as a series of Chinese characters to the operator through a letterbox. This is followed by a further string of characters which represent a question about the story. The operator in the room has to answer the question. The problem is that he has no idea what the characters mean, i.e. what in the world they are about. However, the book of rules is so good that matching characters to an index and applying the rules leads to a new string of characters which represents the correct answer. The people outside the room will come to the conclusion that whatever has happened in the room constitutes an understanding of the story. However, we who know the process are hard-pressed to say that any understanding has occurred at all. Searle says that the computer is in precisely the position of the operator who cannot be said to understand the story, whereas his opponents claim that the system as a whole can be said to exhibit some kind of understanding.

From my point of view, the key point that Searle is making is that the internal symbols and rules stimulated by the story are, in the Chinese room, not related to any form of experience. Therefore, if computer scientists insist that there is some kind of understanding in the system as a whole, they cannot believe that this is a model of *human* understanding. As anyone who has ever read a story knows, the fascination of literature comes from the wonderful vivid mental worlds it creates in our heads. To deny that this is part of understanding is bizarre, to say the least. On the other hand, what has been said about iconic state structures in neural machines, at least leaves open the door to the creation of such structures by triggering into being elements of both sensory experience and (as will be seen in the next chapter) that induced by language itself.

Recent views of "meaning"

The second half of the twentieth century has been marked by a degree of skepticism creeping into theories of meaning. The contemporary American philosopher Willard Van Orman Quine is known for his doctrine of indeterminate translation (Quine, 1960) — there are many ways of translating from a foreign language, and therefore the truths held in that language have an indeterminate representation when translated. This supports the notion that meaning for an individual is related to his or her experience; what it does not support is that there is a linguistic expression which unfailingly expresses these truths to another individual.

Logic plays a key role in contemporary theories of meaning. Polishborn mathematician Alfred Tarski (1902–1983) argued that a formal language (see next chapter) within which the rules (grammar or syntax) can be shown to be logically consistent, will retain a representation of truth if the parts of the sentence are made up of statements verifiable through experience (Tarski, 1983) or T-sentences. Typical T-sentences are "Snow is white" and "Alfred is Polish". Then one can apply logic and say that "Snow is white and Alfred is Polish" is verifiably true as the two statements can be verified in the real world. Unfortunately Gilbert Ryle's famous example, "She came home in a taxi and a flood of tears", would create great difficulties for interpretation in Tarski's regime.

Whither the Word of God?

Without the word, the life of a living, conscious organism would be a lonely thing. If I were rewriting the Bible today, I would say, "In the beginning there was God's mental image of the world ..." God's act of creation was the translation of that image into a world which more or less resembled it. What distinguishes God from us mortals then becomes the fact that He had the image without the world being there. The rest of us have to create it in our heads by iconic learning. When we meet the Adams and Eves in our lives we use words carefully nurtured by our ancestors to share our mental images and to link us to one another and so to aid our survival. But my rewritten Bible would be contrary to my own beliefs. I could go on to vent my own God-less outlook that God emerges as a mental image of man driven by a world which does not provide all the explanations.

To be realistic and not risk the wrath of religions, I must stick to my role of an engineer trying to create Magnus, a "mere" machine with an iconic representation of the world. I have argued here that the word is simply an extension of that iconic representation, which in Magnus evokes the appropriate experience. The word, despite being invented by humans, becomes as much a part of Magnus's environment as other sensory objects. What the automaton needs to learn is what goes with what.

"Has anything been added to theories of meaning?" Probably not, but taking the argument to machines creates certain resonances which may point to mechanisms which may be at work in our own heads. But so far I have only linked words to ideas. Having ideas may not be difficult for Magnus but having a language to express them is a much bigger question, one which gives birth to the next chapter.

Postscript to Chapter 6

Imagining the Meaning of Language

More Words and Automata

Chapter 6 starts by interpreting 'meaning' as words that describe a conscious state by a process of association in a neural network. It also looks at the way that a progressing verbal statement can create iconic phenomenal states that decipher the meaning of the words (e.g. 'dog bites man' or 'John knows that Mary loves Harry' — Figs. 6.9 and 6.10 create the appropriate phenomenal representations).

NRM Models: Verbally Induced Mental States

The above work was taken forward with NRM experiments using mainly adjectival phrases. For example we ask the system to 'visualise a blue ball' having learned iconically to represent a 'green ball' and 'blue box'. This is achieved by creating colour discrimination in one iconically trained neural automaton interacting with another that discriminates between shapes. This vaguely mimics the discriminatory arrangements found in the visual cortex. Evolutionary methods have been studied to self-develop connections that optimise the desired generalisation. Here perturbed copies are made of interconnections in the networks then the well-performing ones are picked and perturbed again, repeated until no further performance improvements are obtained. In 1999 we published a paper that asked how it is possible to imagine things that have never been seen, a red banana with blue spots for example. This was done using the above concepts of discrimination in the cortex.[a] It was also possible to apply this work to a study of visual planning deficits in Parkinson's disease sufferers.[b]

Enter Spatial Language

'Dog bites man' types of sentences (Fig. 6.9) clearly contain iconically representable verbs the neural representation. To move forward, in his PhD thesis, Sunil Rao discusses the architectures that are required for spatial descriptions such as 'The green triangle is to the left of the red circle'.[c] This has resulted in other investigations. Typical of these is the representation of motion verbs which treats the problem as a matter of function application, mapping a set of given input variables defining the moving object and the path of motion to a defined output outcome in the motion recognition context.[d]

---

[a] Aleksander, I., Dunmall, B., and Frate, V. D. (1999). Neural Information Processing, *Proc ICONIP '99. 6th International Conference*, pp. 1–6.
[b] Aleksander, I., Morton, H., and Dunmall, B. (2001). Seeing is Believing: Depictive Neuromodeling of Visual Awareness, 'Connectionist Models of Neurons, Learning Processes and Artificial Intelligence', *Proceedings of the 6th International Work-Conference on Artificial and Natural Neural Networks*, Part 1, pp. 765–771.
[c] Rao, S. (2014). *Aspects of Sensory Awareness in Language: A Neuromodelling Approach*, PhD thesis, Imperil College London (under consideration).
[d] Rao, S. and Aleksander, I. (2011). A depictive neural model for the representation of motion verbs, *Cognitive Processing*, 12(4), pp. 395–405.

Meantime, Back at the AI Camp...

It is interesting to note that in the more conventional artificial intelligence domain, some major programs have arisen on natural language communication with robots. Typical are the POETICON and POETICON++ projects.[e] Funded by the European Commission to investigate the language of action in the context of an iCub[f] robot. Issues in this research stem from simple scenarios. An iCub is surrounded by materials and tools. It is told "make a sandwich" and then describe in natural language what it is doing (e.g. "I am looking for a bun..."). This type of project involves major research laboratories from five European Universities and one from the US. I write this to indicate that language for robots has turned out to be a pretty tough research task. Currently, all this is based on creating vast linguistic databases that are rapidly accessed to express meaning as visualisation and action in a robot. To be fair, one group within the project has considered a special neural technique called Multiple Timescale Recurrent Neural Network (MTRNN) in simulating early acquisition of language[g] for application to the iCub robot. This squares up well with some of the developmental issues that arise in the postscript for Chapter 7 (PS7).

---

[e] Pastra, K. and Aloimonos. Y. (2012). The Minimalist Grammar of Action, *Philosophical Transactions of the Royal Society B*, 367(1585):103.

[f] Metta, G. *et al.* (2008). The iCub humanoid robot: an open platform for research in embodied cognition, *Proceedings of the 8th Workshop on Performance Metrics for Intelligent Systems (PerMIS '08)*, pp. 50–56.

[g] Peniak, M., *et al.* (2011). Multiple Time Scales Recurrent Neural Network for Complex Action Acquisition, *Proceedings of the International Joint Conference on Development and Learning (ICDL) and Epigenetic Robotics (ICDL-EPIROB) 2011, Aug 24–27, Frankfurt, Germany*.

In Sum

This chapter introduced the hypothesis that language usage can be studied through iconic representations of experience in the state structure of a neural automaton. On the whole, however, while attempts have proved to have had reasonable success, this style of research into natural language still remains to be properly explored.

Molecula hesitated for a moment in the icy rain. Winter was on its way and she felt agitated in a way which she could not explain. She then entered the public communication centre and keyboarded Red's voice number. The familiar voice replied. This made her relax a little, despite the fact that she knew so little about his private habits.

"I'm so sorry ...," she said, "for not turning up at our meeting today."

"Don't worry," came the reply, "I had plenty of work to do. I was only concerned that something might have happened to you."

"No, I'm all right. I just got scared, I suppose. There was this memo from Sir Global that he suspected that someone in the organisation was in contact with you. How does he know?"

"Of course, it could be bluff," Red replied. "But then if it isn't, his stupidity would seem to be getting the better of him. Still, I don't like the idea of you being a pawn in a quarrel he has with me."

"Funnily enough, I don't care too much about that," she said in a slow, uncertain voice. "What bothers me is that I feel that in missing our meeting, I missed something important. Our discussions about this planet Earth and its people who do not work according to precise rules give me a sense of comfort ... I'm confused as I can't explain it."

"I missed you too," said Red ...

Chapter 7

Give me a Teddy …

Battle at Dawn

October can be a treacherous month in the north of France: brilliant warm days can be followed by appalling rain and perfidious winds. Indeed, when the army of England under Henry the Fifth, and that of France led by d'Albert, faced each other at Agincourt on St. Crispin's Day in October of the year 1415, a storm caused considerable readjustment of strategy for both sides. On about the 560th anniversary of this great event, i.e. in October 1975, another battle took place in the north of France, at the Cistercian Abbey of Royaumont, just outside Paris. The armies were led by two intellectual giants — the rumbling clouds were those of anticipation of a major confrontation. Jean Piaget in his eightieth year led the "constructivists", who believe that children develop their abilities (including language) in a sequence of stages, building a new stage out of the experience consolidated in the previous one through a thorough interaction with their environment. Piaget was a dominant and revered figure, and his books and theories were seen as the definitive material on the development of children.

Facing him was Noam Chomsky and his "innatist" followers. At thirty-two years younger than Piaget he had built up almost as large a following and certainly as n :h of a reputation for his ideas on the mathematical nature of language. Formal characteristics of language were ubiquitous in the human population which led him to believe that there was an involvement of genetic transmission in facilitating the development of language in children. The nature of the weather was not recorded, but the discussions were. Not only were they recorded but they were carefully edited, leaving as many opportunities as possible for the protagonists to develop their arguments before going into print. The result was a fine book edited by Massimo Piattelli- Palmarini (1979), director of the Royaumont "Centre for a Science of Man", which hosted the event.

A couple of very brief summaries of the major arguments follow, as these are in fact addressed by the Basic Guess.

The Piaget challenge

It is important not to misunderstand Piaget. He did not advocate that a human being is like an empty bucket which is filled by a passive process of learning. In fact his address at Royaumont opened with an attack on naïve "empiricism" — the empirical data on learning which had been produced by many "stimulus–response" behaviourist experiments in psychology. Graphs showing that a pigeon learns to peck at the right button with increasing accuracy are not very revealing and are not part of the "constructivist" culture. Piaget based his discussion on a lifetime of experimentation with developing children. He gave a vivid account of the way in which, under the age of two, children demonstrate an improving ability to order their physical actions to accomplish tasks of reaching and grasping which would be quite hard for a robot. This includes a recognition of the permanence of objects and their organisation in space. He called this the "sensory–motor" phase.

From the ages of two to seven, what Piaget called "a conceptua-lisaton of actions" takes place. This includes all that is known about children beginning to learn and use words. Important is the discovery of links between phenomena: things move if you push them and materials react in different ways if you manipulate them (for example, plasticine is different from a wooden twig). Then, from seven to ten, deeper concepts of irreversibility and conservation begin to form. This refers to ideas such as a liquid not changing in quantity if poured between containers of different shapes, or liquids not being easily retrieved if spilled out of a container. It is between the ages of eleven and twelve that the developing person begins to apply abstractions (of the kind "If X is Y and Z is X, then Z is Y").

Piaget easily admitted that these careful observations of development can be interpreted in different ways. The "constructivist stance" is that any preformed machinery has benefited from evolution only in the sense that machinery has been inherited which is good at interacting with the environment and developing increasingly sophisticated models based on this interactive experience. The alternative is that much of the knowledge is formed at birth in, say, the physical structure of neural machines, and is merely switched on by interactive experience.

Part of the argument which, according to Piaget, favours the constructivist stance lies in the development of mathematical ability. Mathematics is a developing subject and new relationships and associations are being made all the time. If mathematical ability were built into neural structure, then one might ask why it took so long in mathematical history to discover advancing concepts. Newton, for example, developed the idea of "differentiation" or working with rates of change such as "velocity": metres per second or miles per hour. Were such concepts inborn, the consequences of mathematical ideas such as "velocity" would have to have been somehow present in people's heads long before Newton pointed out that they resolved popular puzzles such as that of the hare and the tortoise.[14] Not only this, but if one believes in Darwinian evolution, then the concept must have been there in much simpler forms of life. However, a major reason for believing in constructivism comes from the deeply held conviction that a living being must reach a balance with a bewildering and changing environment and that this, as a result of the complexity of the environment itself, can only be achieved step by step after birth. The mathematical notions then become a function of a growing individual understanding the mathematical analysis that living beings had themselves carried out.

Chomsky's reply

Chomsky's reply was based on the observation that children appear to use correct forms of language without ever wishing to use incorrect forms for which they would receive correction. He did not claim to be capable of explaining how the physical structure of the brain might be predisposed to ways of using language, but predisposed it seems to be as it receives insufficient evidence through interaction to build up the sophisticated structure that is required in examples such as the following:

> "The ball is yellow" can be turned into the question "Is the ball yellow?".

On hearing many such examples the child might learn (perhaps unconsciously) that the way he should go from the statement to the

---

[14] The tortoise starts a race 100 m ahead of the hare, who runs twice as fast as the tortoise. But when the hare has run 100 m the tortoise will be 50 m ahead. If the hare runs those 50 m the tortoise will still be 25 m ahead, and this suggests that the hare can never win. But if we introduce the *velocity* of the hare as, say, 10 m/sec, then, say the race is run over 1000 m, we can work out it would take the hare 100 sec to run it, by which time the tortoise would have run 500 m only, leaving it 400 m (500 m less the 100 m start) behind the arrival position when the hare breaks the tape.

question is to scan the sentence from left to right until a verb is found, and to move this verb to the beginning of the sentence and raise the pitch of his voice at the end. So

"Mother will come" would correctly be changed to "Will mother come?".

The problem arises from the idea that a developing child on hearing

"The ball which is in the bedroom is yellow"

will, by applying the simple learned rule, produce the question

"Is the ball which in the bedroom is yellow?".

Chomsky's argument is that children just do *not* make such mistakes. They appear to recognise that the first verb is part of a group of words — "which is in the bedroom" — that form a whole chunk which should not be scanned for a verb, but skipped, in the process making the second verb the candidate for shifting to the beginning. The ability to recognise these structures is part of what Chomsky saw as having to be innate. The structures are grammatical and also apply to much more complex forms of sentences. So there is no suggestion here that the child is born with a knowledge that words like "yellow" and "bedroom" are legitimate adjectives and nouns, but that the child *is* born with a need to use and group adjectives and nouns in the correct way. The choices are not many. For example, one might argue that an adjective and a noun which it describes should be adjacent in a sentence, as in "yellow ball". The only other choice is "ball yellow" — which would be fine in Italian or French. The child picks up cues from language users as to which of the options to use, but has an inborn sense for "chunking" words in a grammatically correct way. This also helps in applying meaning to make sense of a sentence. Think of

"The ball which is in the bedroom at the back of the house is yellow"

and contrast it with

"The ball which is in the bedroom on top of the cupboard is yellow".

Although the phrases "at the back of the house" and "on top of the cupboard" occur in exactly the same place in the sentence, innatism suggests that the inborn "chunking" is necessary in order to leave the listener free to apply knowledge learned after birth about houses and cupboards and to connect the phrase to the right noun.

Chomsky allowed for a lifetime development of the child's knowledge of language and put it as a change of state from S_0, the state existing at birth, through S_1, S_2, ..., to S_f. S_f is the final state from which a mature use of language is achieved. So the quarrel between Chomsky and Piaget did not focus on whether there is life-time development or not — they agreed that there is. Where they differed is on the nature of the state S_0 Piaget arguing that it is merely machinery prepared to interact with the world and learn in successive phases, Chomsky stressing that this state contains a genetically inherited knowledge about how to "chunk" streams of words according to grammatical principles.

Here I shall leave the battle of Royaumont, and simply say that it was probably a draw. As Jacques Mehler, a psycholinguist of the Ecole des Hautes Etudes et Sciences Sociales in Paris, suggested in Piattelli- Palmarini (1979), "... the disparity between Piaget and Chomsky is to be found at the level of their respective self-assigned goals." Such goals are so ambitious that they defy verification or denial and are framed in a way that does not allow the language spoken by the one to address the problems of the other. And so it was with the battle of Agincourt. Despite Henry's celebrated victory on

St. Crispin's Day, intrigues and skirmishes followed between the English and the French for the next five years. Then Henry married Catherine of Valois, the nineteen-year-old daughter of the King of France. According to Shakespeare the marriage was well founded on the fact that the bride and groom could neither speak nor understand each other's language — a veritable draw.

In the rest of this chapter I shall first look at the Basic Guess and the way it addresses the constructivist/nativist question through two Consequences about learning utterances and linguistic structure, and then return at the end of the chapter to contemporary commentary on the battle of Royaumont.

Iconic representation and the battle of Royaumont

It is clear from the discussion in the last few chapters that the Basic Guess favours constructivism to innatism. But it is not exactly the constructivism of Piaget. The business of learning representations of the way things are in the world was seen as the result of a passive exploration of the world in Chapter 5. This is where sensations of "self" and "will" enter the state structure of the organism. We shall see that these are prerequisites to the learning of utterances and language. In Chapter 6 it was argued that state representations can be rich enough to relate directly to linguistic expressions whether these be concrete or abstract. But here it is necessary to counter the focus of the innatist position: that a child cannot be exposed to sufficient examples to *use* language in its standardised forms. This is the often-quoted "poverty of stimulus" argument. I shall first show that processes of representation of self and planning can provide a potential model for the learning of utterances in children as a way of satisfying their immediate needs. I shall then argue that language may be extracted from a repository held by the society in which the child operates.

"Mah Mah"

Even Shakespeare's first words must have emerged from a babble and were probably not as expressive as some of his later work. So it is with Magnus. Much of what John Searle calls "intentionality" does not come from a blind attachment of linguistic strings to world events, but from a knowledge of the effect that such utterances have on the world and the actions they imply. A child's early "mah mah" has purpose to it: the child may be hungry or just testing its powers of control — will the food provider smile as a prelude to the provision of food? These are the beginnings of conscious thought, and with the aid of Consequence 9, below, I argue that in the very early development of language in young children, one sees a further development of much of the "self" that consciousness is all about. It also seems plausible that here the special relationship of human consciousness to language takes shape. It is this special relationship that distinguishes human from animal consciousness. In Magnus, going through the babbling phase is shown to be the first step towards the development of intentionality — that which distinguishes the neural machine from the uncomprehending "language understanding" programs of the artificial intelligence era. But, first, it is worth looking at children and the way in which their early utterances seem to develop.

If a child inherits anything at all it is the ability to make specific noises. The question is, how does the child manage to control these in order to begin to have some impact on the world it inhabits and the people who live in that world? Much of the answer comes from another observed fact: children react to subtle differences in sounds from the time they are born. What is clear is that the child is bombarded from birth (and, some argue, even before) with sounds, including the speech of its carers and anyone else who happens to peer into the cot. But, experiments show that children react differently to the human voice from the way they react to other sounds. Indeed, they differentiate between sounds which are important in changing the meaning of words. Typical is the difference between sounds such as /p/ (as in "pad") and /b/ (as in "bad").

Experimental psychologists use subtle techniques which involve sucking responses in the baby to detect these hearing differences. Details may be found in deVilliers and deVilliers (1979). Hearing abilities can be compared with the development of the production of sounds. At about three or four months after birth the child's babbling sounds become insistent and speechlike even though they remain unintelligible. It spends eight or nine months doing this before producing its first "words", which are made up of repetitions such as "mah mah" or "dah dah".

Two factors appear to be crucial in the step which goes from babbling to words. The first is the role of adults as mechanisms for rewards. The second is undoubtedly the feedback loop between the noises the child makes and what it hears. Probably the idea that a child learns by imitating its parents in a copycat way is slightly wrong. The difference between an adult's voice and a child's makes such directness unlikely When the child produces sounds which the parent wishes to encourage, the parent uses rewarding strategies such as smiling or cuddling. Baby-talk is also rewarding, through the attention which the child is receiving. The voice–hearing loop is clearly at work and the reward is stability in this long-routed loop. Of course, this can create communication between the child and the parent, so mimicking of intonation and stress can result from what becomes a complex interactive game. Parents actually try to mimic the child's sounds to maximise what is probably a rewarding communication for all.

The key point made in this section has been that the ability to hear sounds in babies is attuned to the sounds that the baby will eventually make. Genetic inheritance can clearly be at work here, as it relates to the evolution of the vocal apparatus. This does not mean that Chomsky beats Piaget in this round of the contest, as this is the area where the two would agree. Putting children aside, I now return to the artificial world of Magnus, which is where ideas such as voice-hearing loops can be looked at as effects on the state structure.

Magnus Utters its First Words

Consequence 9: Learning utterances

The feedback loop responsible for the creation of "self" representations is also responsible for the creation of state representations of the basic utterances of the organism which are retrieved in response to the utterances of other, "adult", organisms and may be used by the adult to teach the organism more complex utterances, such as the words of a language.

To start with, if Magnus were to be inspired by what we observe in children, Consequence 9 of the Basic Guess would suggest a framework as shown in Fig. 7.1. The property which is clearly assumed to be built into Magnus is the ability to generate short sounds. So here is a way in which genetic inheritance in humans and preprogrammed design in Magnus certainly do affect the nature of language.

The mechanism for sound generation is determined purely by physical factors which have to do with the shape of the vocal cords, the mouth, the lungs and so on. It is interesting that, at birth, babies the world over produce roughly the same sounds. So how do these get shaped into languages which sound as different as English, French, Japanese, or even the "clicky" sounds of singer Miriam Mkeba's Xhosa language? Figure 7.1 suggests that there are two main mechanisms at work. The first is the long-routed loop between the sounds and hearing (note that among the sounds there must be

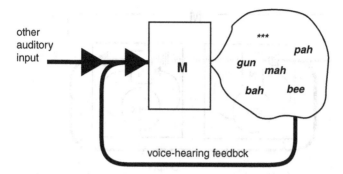

Fig. 7.1. The "specification" for a Magnus which produces and hears a limited set of utterances.

the possibility of silence indicated in the figure by ✱✱✱). The second is the only modifying channel, which is also the auditory input — that which allows in the other sounds. It is this which modifies the basic sounds into those of a specific language. Clearly, other sensory modalities (mainly vision) can also be at work from this external perceptual channel and it is necessary to ask what role this might play. All these inputs are required to shape the very strong differences between the ways mouth-shaping muscles work in different languages. The first six or seven years of life seem to be crucial in achieving this muscle control, leading to the observation that languages learned after the age of ten to twelve will often contain the accent of the first learned language. So the external influence of a language and the way it is spoken shape the physical factors which go into the production of specialised sounds.

To see how this process could take place in Magnus and hence suggest some mechanisms which one might look for in human beings, it is necessary to look more closely at a model of the apparatus which generates the inborn utterances. As Consequence 9 suggests, the representation of "self" which was discussed in Chapter 5 is at work, as shown, in Fig. 7.2. The figure shows what was labelled as M (for Magnus, naturally) in Fig. 7.1. It consists of

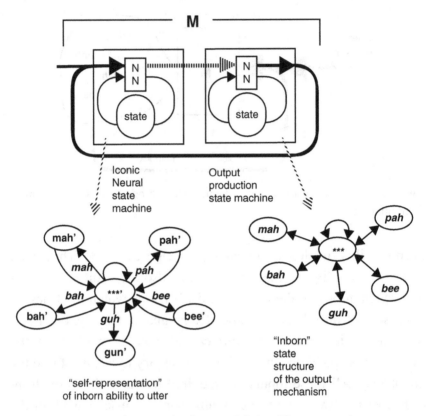

Fig. 7.2. Inborn mechanisms and their self-representations.

a production machine on the right which is a fixed (non-learning) state machine. For the time being, the forward link between the two remains undefined (dotted arrow). On the left is the now familiar iconic learning machine. The production machine is assumed to be innate and very general. It is further assumed that only five utterances are possible, made up of the most primitive combinations of what the vocal system can produce. These are shown as ***mah, pah, bah, guh*** and ***bee***. This utterance machine takes arbitrary excursions from silence to one of the utterances and back again.

In Consequence 9 it is suggested that the first thing that learning brings is the iconic representation of these utterances and their transitions. This is shown in Fig. 7.2 as a state diagram that has been learned iconically in the neural state machine. Here the iconic self-representations of the utterances are **mah'**, **pah'**, **bah'**, **guh'** and **bee'** respectively. What has to be explained now is the following:

(i) How could such a system learn that some combinations of utterances are meaningful (e.g. *mah mah* and *pah pah*) whereas others are not (e.g. *mah guh*)?

(ii) How could the organism learn to utter meaningful sequences to achieve some goal?

As is argued in Consequence 9, an entity called an "adult" comes into play. The adult is not only capable of accessing the same auditory feedback channel which the organism uses, but it also influences other channels, such as the visual and the tactile. So the following event may happen repeatedly. "Mother" appears at the visual and tactile sensors and provides food to a crying organism. Note that "crying" could be seen as another vocal output (not shown), this time tied to an inner sensation of hunger rather than an arbitrary production. Now, this is where baby-talk comes in. Of course, as Mother appears on the scene[15] she may say "mah mah" more often than other things. But "mah mah" said in BBC English will have about as much effect as if she were to say, "... good morrow, my fair and beautiful baby ..." In fact, the closer the mother mimics the baby the more the communication can become effective as it is likely to cause some transitions in the state space of the baby's iconic state machine. And such transitions mean, within the organism, an aware or conscious reaction. So that's what baby-talk

---

[15] By the way, this is not intended to be a sexist story: "Mother" stands for "carer". In any case "Mother" in the context of Magnus has unclear sex connotations as it is likely to be some neural net enthusiast who could be of either human sex.

is for. It is a struggle to reach the embryonic state structures which in the baby organism have been building up solely as a result of the "self" loops, where the baby is building state models of itself. Any suggestion of the baby sitting there and mimicking adults is likely to be a myth. Carers are there to mimic babies and to aid their discovery of themselves, their development of self-awareness, and their ability to control the world they live in, which includes the very adult who is doing the aiding.

To see how the last of these suggestions occurs, consider that the mother may not just be saying "mah", which is a primary utterance which the child itself is capable of producing. She is saying "mah mah", which is a structure that the baby may not discover unaided. But there is more to it than that. The mother cuddles and provides food — both interactions being good candidates for causing "pleasurable" sensations. Leaving aside what this means in precise neural machine terms, it is quite possible to allow that the maximisation of such sensations has strong survival value and can therefore be seen as an "instinct" (see Chapter 8). The key thing is that "mah mah" is not only a new structure, but is associated with a pleasurable event. The resulting state structure is sketched out in Fig. 7.3.

This shows how iconic learning has created new state trajectories where **mah mah** elicits the known state **mah'** twice. What has been said in Chapter 3 about auxiliary neurons comes into play here as they would label the states corresponding to **mah mah** as **mah'1** and **mah'2**. The trajectory is completed as iconic states for an image of the mother and, say, food (oil for Magnus?) is provided. Indeed I should stress here that what is being described is a bit of a mechanical child-like fantasy and not a human child. The key point is that there exists a mechanical procedure whereby a neural mechanism (the iconic state machine of the Basic Guess) can develop a control of utterances. Utterances of **mah mah** and **pah pah** associated with mother/food and father/smile are shown in Fig. 7.3. We're not there yet, however.

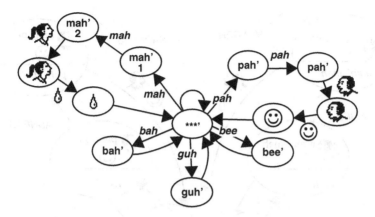

Fig. 7.3.   State structure extended by baby-talk and rewards.

What we have so far is an organism which forms memories of its own utterances which an adult has used to provide labelled control signals for state trajectories which have meaning. So far these trajectories have lain there dormant. But imagine the following event: the utterance generator of Fig. 7.2 generates *mah* twice. This will launch the iconic machine into the trajectory which anticipates mother and food. As seen repeatedly in the descriptions used in this book, what begins as an arbitrary action of the organism becomes a voluntary option as a result of adaptation in neural links. This identifies the role of the forward arrow between the two machines of Fig. 7.2: to create an overall state structure as shown in Fig. 7.4.

As usual, this needs some unravelling. The four states shown are, indeed, complex states. That is, they use the notation developed in Chapter 6 and contain trajectories such as the ones shown in Fig. 7.3. In addition, the states now represent the state structure of the two machines of Fig. 7.2 linked together. So the label under the horizontal line indicates a current utterance heard on the long-routed feedback path. In precisely the same way as was seen for the exploratory planning robot in Chapter 5, the organism here can enter transitions between complex states which include an

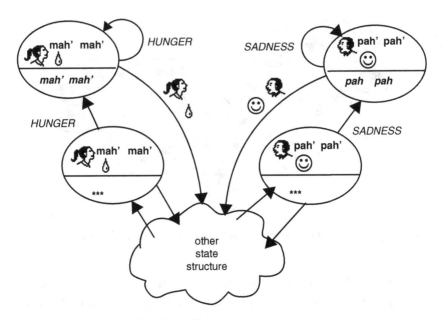

Fig. 7.4.   Thought and utterance.

anticipation of either the mother event or the father event. These anticipations are known either without any utterance being voiced in states that carry ∗∗∗ in the long-routed feedback, or as further transitions to states where the appropriate utterance is voiced and heard by the organism. As shown in the diagram, this further transition could be controlled by inputs from functional state variables such as hunger or sadness.

Again, the temptation should be resisted to dismiss these simple mechanisms because they do not result in the precise behaviour which is observed in children. All that I am trying to do is to illustrate Consequence 9, which shows how an "adult" can be useful in moulding the utterances of the learning automaton so that communication with it can begin. At the same time the organism itself is developing state structure which contains information on how to obtain what it wants from the world. That is, hunger or sadness is relieved by the anticipated events actually taking place. By the way, the exact neural meaning of emotions such as "sadness" in the state machine will be discussed later in the book.

"On Human Communication"

The above phrase was used by an engineer, Colin Cherry, as the title of a most influential book he wrote in the 1950s (Cherry, 1954). Many books now exist on formal models of language, the mind and even consciousness. But, *On Human Communication* anticipated and made sense of many issues that continue to be debated in contemporary literature. Cherry, in his articulate and witty style, wrote so as to keep out of controversy. His approach was a model of scientific humility. But his intellect had astonishing acuity. An example is the way in which he gently admonished those who assert that science and engineering have no place in the understanding of mental life:

> "... it may well be, not that people have a great respect for living matter, but rather that many people have too ready a contempt for 'mere' dead matter — a stuff, devoid of mystery."

And so it still is now. I have brought up this quote at this point of our travels through mechanistic discussions about consciousness, as those who have kept up with me may be beginning to flag a little. Many of the criticisms which arise from the work on neural state machines stem from a belief that computation and manufactured machinery have no place in discussions about matters that define what constitutes "being human". This is a form of "contempt". On the other hand, Chomsky's suggestion that some deep computational structure of human language, a Universal Grammar, is innate, is readily accepted. His evidence comes from the fact that such structure is ubiquitous among people, whether they belong to tribes on remote islands or work as announcers for the BBC. The moral of this story may be that mechanistic theory which sets the human apart from other living organisms such as animals is readily accepted, whereas theory which relates people to machines is often met with contempt. But, undaunted and encouraged by Colin Cherry, we proceed to Consequence 10, which indeed, is on the beginnings of human communication.

Consequence 10, which again flows from the Basic Guess of iconic learning in neural state machines, shows how the argument might proceed.

> ### Consequence 10: Learning language
> *Language is a result of the growth process of a societal repository from which it can be learned by a conscious organism, given the availability of knowledgeable "instructors". The structure of such language is a process of the societal evolution of a best-match to the development of state structure in the organism.*

This flies in the face of both prejudices: the idea that in some way the mechanisms of language are innate and that working with Magnus is irrelevant to a study of the way human beings communicate. First, I must ask whether, were I to *build* Universal Grammar structures into Magnus, this would explain the role that language plays in human consciousness. Second, I must show that Magnus can be put into a position where it can form a linguistic link with human beings which develops in much the same way as that of a child. This is essential if artificial consciousness is to have any practical applications.

However, before we discuss this Consequence which suggests an alternative to innatism, it is important to take a closer look at the idea of a Universal Grammar which dominates arguments about innateness.

The Universality of Languages

As the name Universal Grammar implies, the discussion is not about the meaning of words, but about the way in which words are classified and the rules which apply to the classes of words. For example, typical word classes are <noun>, <adjective> and <verb>. Further classification could have <noun subject> or <noun object>. So a grammatical rule might exist which says

<sentence> := <noun subject<verb>noun object>.

This is read as

"A sentence may be made up of (:=) a subject noun followed by a verb followed by an object noun."

If I try to fit what I know to be nouns and verbs to this rule, I get sentences such as

John likes Mary;
Dog bites postman.

But how does this explain correct sentences such as the following?

The tall man jumps over the wall;
Harry sleeps.

These appear not to follow our original rule. But of course the original rule is just one of many. Grammar is a collection of such rules; for example,

The tall man scales the wall

follows a rule expressed as

<sentence> := <adjectival phrase><verb><noun phrase>,

where

<adjectival phrase>:= <article><adjective><noun> ,
<noun phrase>   := <article><noun>.

All that this shows is that grammar, when seen in this formal way, is made up of a large number of rules, many of which are rules which define the parts of other rules. So why is it not obvious that a child could learn these rules? After all, that's what lessons in English grammar at school are all about. Is it not true that wherever you look in the world much time is spent by teachers teaching children before their teens the correct rules for speaking their own language? Why does the eventual linguistic competence have to rely on some innate knowledge?

Chomsky's view is very clear: the evidence of the rules of a language in what parents and teachers provide is grossly inadequate to lead to the early competence of which children are capable. Children begin to combine words from the age of eighteen months, and their productions seem to be anything but arbitrary. Villiers and Villiers (1979) reported on how very early productions express actions and who does them. A child is much more likely to say "me eat" than "eat me", or "bump head" than "head bump". Someone opposed to nativism would have to argue that productions occur at random and that these are corrected by carers to reinforce the correct productions. But this seems palpably not to be the case; by the age of just over two years, sentences such as "don't stand on my shoes" and "what is that on the table?" are produced, sometimes to the astonishment of parents when it first happens.

A word of warning needs to be sounded here. Before one gets too seduced into believing that in a sentence such as "I eat it" there is a gene that makes the child put "I" (i.e. the doer) first in the sentence, one should look at languages other than English. Not many miles away from London, a child in Rome would say, "*Lo mangio io.*" Literally this is "It eat I". So the Chomskian argument about lack of evidence — or "poverty of stimulus", as it is technically called — should be used with some care. At best it can be taken to mean that inheritance reduces the sets of expression from which a choice has to be made. Neither of the above two children says, "Eat I it", although Japanese children might say, "I it eat." So the question centres on how large these sets are and how local culture which selects different elements among these sets can be picked up by the child.

To understand Chomsky's point of view, it is important to note that he referred to Universal Grammars not as the detailed ways in which a verb phrase may structured. As seen above, this varies from language to language. What he did maintain is that there is a need to have forms such as verb phrases or adjectival phrases, which are then combined according to rules to form a sentence. The very existence of such rules and the way they are used is found even among remote tribes. The point is that grammar rules *could be* very different. For example, if I wished to differentiate between "dog bites man" and "man bites dog" I could call on a rule which says that the doer will be prefixed by the utterance "glop", and the object noun will be prefixed by "blit". Then "glop-dog, blit-man, bites" would have an unambiguous meaning. There is an infinity of ingenious ways in which such rules could be invented. I suppose that it was the ambition of the explorers of this world to discover tribes with new and curious language rules. So it must have come as a disappointment that their rules were a bit like those of the explorers. So Chomsky's question is: What unifies the characteristics of these far-flung languages? He came to the conclusion that as people in these far-flung parts have arms, legs and reproductive habits that are much like one another, and these attributes are inherited, so are their language rules like one another because they are inherited.

An Alternative to Inheritance

The Basic Guess and Consequence 10 suggest that the ubiquitous nature of linguistic forms could be a result of mechanisms other than direct inheritance. First, there is the unchanging nature of the world and people. Because the child on the newly discovered island does roughly the same things with its inherited arms and legs as the child in the Bronx or Hampstead, and the parents of the two have roughly the same survival-driven attitude to encouraging their offspring to communicate, much of the scene is set for what needs to be communicated. This still does not address why, on one island, an unusual method (such as "glop-blit") has not become dominant, whereas, in another part of the world, the method of phrase production stressed by Chomsky was seen as a good thing.

My argument is based on two interlinked mechanisms. The first is the fact that the phrase productions particularly suit the human being, the way he does things and, in particular, the way he builds up his knowledge of the world. Specifically, the Basic Guess has suggested ways in which an organism can think about itself and the world it lives in. So Consequence 10 suggests the second mechanism: language in any community develops as a repository of language rules guided strongly by what is best for the efficient lifetime development of effective state structure in the organism. So, an extreme version of the argument goes as follows. Assuming that the "glip-blit" method is not well matched to the state-structure-building characteristics of the organism, evolution of the language adopted by a society using this method will exert pressures towards a better-matched structure. If there is such optimality in phrase productions, then over time (i.e. many generations of organisms), changes will take place which will cause the language to evolve towards phrase structure.

The Effectiveness of Iconic Representation

The missing link in the argument is why phrase structuring might be closer to iconic state structure than other forms. I shall give a few examples which merely support this idea, without pretending that it is a fully developed theory which is as well investigated as both the pros and the cons of Chomsky's point of view. The first example comes from state structure which has already been seen in the last chapter — the now notorious phrase "dog bites man". This is reproduced in Fig. 7.5 and compared to two other concepts — "man is bitten by dog" and "man bites dog".

The key point here is that the states which are linked by the developing linguistic input have a meaning in their own right leading to a state which represents the meaning of the whole sentence. An interesting part of this is that "man is bitten by dog" ends up in the same state as "dog bites man". Chomsky used a concept of "transformational grammar" which unites different forms of saying the same thing. This identifies the rules of going from one form (e.g. "dog bites man") to another (e.g. "man is bitten by dog"). But in iconic representations this happens directly as shown. This might indicate how it might be that a developing organism recognises the equivalence between these forms long before it has an opportunity of appreciating the transformational rules. This might create the impression of a poverty of stimulus, as, innatists would argue, the organism does not have enough evidence to be able to apply the rules properly. But this could be an illusion created by the way in which the iconic state structure has developed.

In the last chapter we saw other examples of this — for instance, "John knows that Mary loves Harry" in Fig. 6.10. Also, in an earlier book (Aleksander and Morton, 1993) Helen Morton and I showed that sentences such as "The boy broke the window with the curtain" and "The boy broke the window with a rock" are

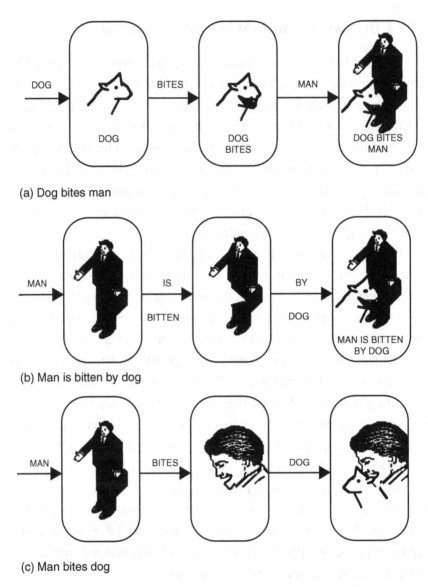

(a) Dog bites man

(b) Man is bitten by dog

(c) Man bites dog

Fig. 7.5.   The distinguishing nature of iconic representations.

automatically "understood" as they lead to completely different iconic states. An observer who notices that the organism is capable of distinguishing between the two will report that there is an understanding of "case roles". That is, "curtain" is a *modifier* of "window" whereas "rock" is an *instrument* related to "breaks". This is sophisticated linguistic stuff which understandably may appear to be innate. But the sophistication comes from the definition of concepts such as *instrument* and *modifier* as "case roles" by intelligent linguists. In the organism's head they may be just simple routes to mental pictures.

Continuing with the evolutionary argument, how would an arbitrary language rule such as the "glob-blit" idea mentioned earlier be represented in an iconic state structure? Figure 7.6 suggests that the new rule is not easily accommodated to the imagined experience of the event. While Fig. 7.6 is not the only way of trying to relate the new quite difficult to design a machine according to these arbitrary language rules. As shown, the final event is what is labelled as a complex state where the three states differ only in the linguistic label. In this example things work out fine, but "John knows that Mary loves Harry" would need subsidiary "glop-blit" coding which is not only hard to imagine, but implies that every

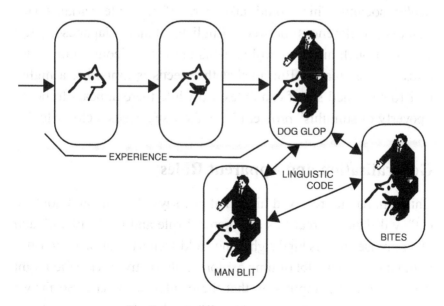

Fig. 7.6.   A different language rule.

experience even is just a repeated replication (to accommodate the coding) of what in the phrase-structured language would be just one state which is constructed from the way things are observed in one's experience.

In summary, it does seem that language as we know it, i.e. a structure which can be described by the phrase structures which appear wherever humans use language, may be tied to the way in which all humans create state structures related to their experience. The Basic Guess and Consequence 10 suggest that all that needs to be inherited here is the ability to create state structure in an iconic way. For this, the inheritance of a suitable state machine is all that is needed. And the prime requirement for this state machine is the iconic transfer from sensory signals into some arbitrary inner neurons, which, in terms of brain biology, may be a much simpler trick than what would be required to create wiring which is adapted to linguistic structures.

Consequence 10 actually says a little more than that. It suggests that a repository is needed which is held by the "adults" in a particular society. This would take care of the rule variants (for example, differences between English, Italian, Japanese, etc.) which, through hints, control variants in the way iconic state structures can be created. But all that this needs is hints, i.e. a highly underdetermined set of examples. So while there appears to be no "poverty of stimulus" problem here, the issue needs a closer look.

Generalisation and Apparent Rules

Children, having received hints that one says "I eat it" and not "I it eat", will tend to treat this as a general rule and get "I like it" and other phrases of this kind right. The child seems to cotton on to rules without spending a lot of time exploring alternatives. This too might contribute to the impression that these rules are innate. So far we have suggested that early learning can result in states which the organism can use in a purposeful way. Clearly *mah mah* and *pah pah* are not the only calls that are likely to be useful to a developing organism. The Basic Guess suggests that iconic states are being created for the objects that matter to the individual. To a child these might be "sweetie", "car", "boot", "spoon" and so on. The mechanism for building up iconic states which are linked to calling for these objects has already been suggested above.

But calling for objects with single words is a limited activity. Word pairs could have as much of an increase in effectiveness on the world over single words as going from single to double utterances. So a child may wish to distinguish between whether his shoe is pinching and he wants it removed and whether the ground on which he walks is hurting his foot and he wants the shoe to be put on. So, through need-driven mechanisms "shoe on" and "shoe off" become differentiated concepts with differentiated states in the state structure. But it is here that generalisation comes in. Not only can shoes be put on and taken off, but so can any worn object — hats, coats, gloves, socks and so on. So, through the mechanism which in the last chapter led to learning that apples, grapes and bananas were all fruits, it is feasible that a state machine can learn that some objects have "offness" and "onness". The state structure which needs to be learned to represent this is shown in Fig. 7.7.

The figure is intended to give a simplified indication of the way in which the apple/fruit or Socrates/mortal association seen in the previous chapter is all that is needed to link objects which (say) are garments.[16] The key point is that the garment states are linked by being garments and any garment has the property of being on or off. So the use of words such as "shoe on" will have the effect of

---

[16] Note that the word "garment" may not actually be known by the organism, but the experience of wearing things is common between these iconic states.

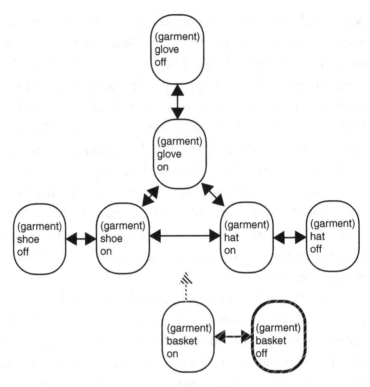

Fig. 7.7.   Two-word phrases.

attempting to change a physical state in the same way as calling "mah mah" has to change from hunger to satiation. Suppose that the organism, knowing about gloves, shoes and hats, is the object of some kind of a joke and finds itself with a basket on its head. Due to the generalisation of the net ("garment" and "on" are known) the perceptual experience of "wearing" a basket causes an entry of the inner neurons into the area of known garments, so the knowledge of being able to take the basket off becomes transferred from a knowledge of what to do with a hat or a glove through the generalisation of the neural net. So this is where some of the rulelike behaviour of the organism may come from — the proper inclusion of new iconic cases in state structure of appropriate, similar experience. The action of the voice–hearing loop has not been shown, but it is this which leads the organism to say "coat on" or "hat off" as a way of controlling its world with hvo-word sentences. So, the child might ask for the basket to be removed by saying "hat off" or "basket off" were she to have heard the name of the thing that was put on.

A nativist observer may be tempted to say that the child is predisposed to follow logical rules such as

"If X is Y and all Ys have property Z, then X has property Z."

That is, "If I have something on my head, it is a garment; garments can be taken off, so the thing on my head can be taken off." What I suggest is going on instead, is that the above logic is a correct interpretation of an efficient representation of experience, but it need not be seen as innate. In fact, the "all Ys" in the logic should really be interpreted as "all the cases of Y encountered so far".

But is this enough to explain some fascinating observations of the development of language in children? At the age of eighteen months, children's use of words appears to take off largely as two-word expressions. Pinker (1994) gave examples such as "all dry", "all wet", "more cereal", "papa away", "no bed", "I shut", "I sit". The variety of the intention behind the expressions is interesting — some are there to express a direct want (such as "more X"), others a non-want ("no bed" or "hat off"), and yet others simply express a state of affairs ("car gone"). Then, from the age of two, the development of used vocabulary and extension in the complexity of sentences in children is phenomenal. The usage of words appears to increase at the incredible rate of a new word every two hours, and Pinker pointed out that by thirty months children can put together correct sentences such as "I lost a shoe" and parts of correct sentences such as "Write a piece of paper." By three years sentences such as "They are going to sleep in the winter-time" demonstrate a rapidly developing mastery of the art of using language.

Psychologists interested in language development are puzzled by this sudden spurt in mastery. I believe that a Magnus model of this may be approached and suggest this below.

Abstraction and Mastery

In learning to use "papa here" and "papa gone", the key phenomenon of developing state structure is an ability to use abstract concepts such as "here" and "gone", "all" and "some", and so on. In children, indeed, the time before eighteen months may be busily formative in terms of developing state structures which distinguish peculiar goings-on in the world. Many (e.g. Karmiloff-Smith) refer to this pre-linguistic phase as a time when children are known to show surprise if, say, an object they expect to be in a box has gone. This can be measured by observing behaviour which indicates interest — staring or smiling at new things as opposed to showing boredom and disinterest for known or expected events. This means that before the use of language, the concepts of a box containing or not containing an object have insinuated themselves into the learner's state structure, possibly as illustrated in Fig. 7.8.

This represents the experience of a surprising event. After one has seen a toy bunny (or any other object) packed in a box, most often experience will lead to the bunny remaining in the box. This kind of permanence is ubiquitous in the world and would become well ingrained in state structure. Sometimes a manipulating adult (a developmental psychologist?) spirits the toy away through an unseen trapdoor and the unexpected happens. The adult is likely to say "bunny gone". The adult-speak sound "gone" becomes associated with the surprising event. So labels in adult-speak such as "teddy in box" and "teddy gone", "daddy home" and "daddy gone" require multiple representations of the future, and the adult-speak word "gone" becomes associated with a surprising event which may

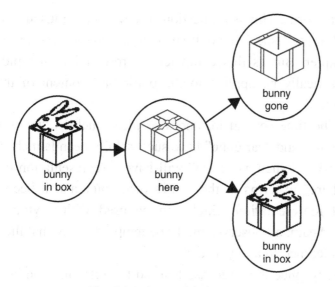

Fig. 7.8.   A surprising event.

follow any expression which contains "here". In other words "gone" acquires its apparently abstract meaning.

Another observed effect in Very young children is that they know what things are in adult-speak before they start to use language themselves. They express visible surprise if the adult tries to label things in the wrong way — if a ball is called a house or a doll a donkey. This means that rich, representational structure of what things look like, what they do and what an adult calls them is built up in the manner of Fig. 7.5 long before production of many words takes place.

It is my totally untested hypothesis that the word spurt and the surprisingly rapid build-up of linguistic competence between eighteen months and three years is specifically due to the mastery of the child's own voice–hearing loop and the way positive hints from adults lead to accelerating competence. Imagine a head full of iconically known things; the only factor preventing voice production is a somewhat ill-exercised long-routed feedback loop involving the vocal cords. This is a question of developing muscular control arid linking self-speak to adult-speak in the way suggested earlier in this chapter. But as this competence grows this can rapidly and enthusiastically be applied to the bottled-up content of the state structure.

By the time several instances of ideas such as "teddy gone", "papa gone" and "car gone" have successfully been launched in the world, a word such as "gone" will have a representation different from "here" in terms of the child's own voice and it becomes an internal representation which can be used with anything that's "gone". Again, an observer might be tempted to say that the organism has learned to apply a rule.

Clearly, once the child has learned to create its own language-like representations, they can be developed further to satisfy a need to be ever more accurate in expressing something that is wanted. "I want bunny" can lead to being given the wrong bunny, which, if the child is called Janie and her brother Jimmy, will lead to the forms "Jimmy bunny" and "Janie bunny" (complex states), which can be put in sentences as chunks leading to "I want Jimmy bunny" or even "I want all bunny" or "I want both bunny", having developed abstract labels for "both" or "all" in the same way as "here" and "gone".

Why no Errors?

The learning process described above thrives on positive examples only. So why do children appear not to make errors which test the bounds of what they have learned? In the simple cases such as "bunny gone" there appears to be little choice: "gone bunny" is also acceptable even if a little unusual. But as language strings get longer there is more scope for error. For example, in assertion–question translation, Pinker (1994) describes some interesting work done by psychologist Karen Stromswold, who tried to measure the errors that children might make by applying the wrong rules. For example, "He did eat" is turned by an adult into a question: "Did he eat?" Would a child be tempted to translate "He did (something)" into "Did he (something)?". Stromswold reports that she could not find any errors of this kind among 66,000 tests on a variety of assertion–question translations.

The simple explanation in Magnus terms is that the positive example learned iconically would be the question form "Did he do something?". "Did he do?" is the existing state in the state structure which is entered from a need to turn "He did" into a question. I stress that the Basic Guess leads to the creation of rich state structures which represent effects in the world and ways of doing things. To an external observer the organism only *appears* to use rules because of the full state structure which it owns. There may be no existent state for just "Did he?", so perhaps one should not expect the child to use that form. The lack of errors may simply be pointing at an error in the observer's hypothesis that he uses some rule such as "drag a verb to the front".

In summary, positive examples create stable states in state structure, and there are no such states created for erroneous forms. It is precisely the assumption that the organism uses rules which leads to the expectation that it might use rules wrongly. So, all in all, iconic state structures seem not to support the nativist case. We now need to stand back and take another look at where this leaves the battle of Royaumont in the context of what has been said.

A Three-Sided Battle

More than twenty years have gone by since the meeting at Royaumont. But the influence of the two protagonists still dominates the world of theories of the development of language. The mantle of the masters has passed on to younger people, but the division of belief in innatism or construction is still there. I shall take a closer look at the work of two representative protagonists of the contemporary state of the battle. The first is Steven Pinker, who believes that the propensity for language may be seen in children as a kind of instinct. Despite leaning towards innatism, Pinker presents a less harsh picture of inheritance than Chomsky. The second is Annette Karmiloff-Smith (a former collaborator of Jean Piaget), who has suggested ideas of development to a kind of centre stage between a belief in inherited thinking modules and Piaget's rather rigid constructivist ideas. Both have influenced my own thinking, as can be seen from references to their two excellent books: Pinker's *The Language Instinct* (1994) and Karmiloff-Smith's *Beyond Modularity*. I shall then try to summarise by looking at the way in which the Basic Guess relates to these two views.

Pinker's instinct

Originally from Montreal, Steven Pinker is a psychologist working in the Brain and Cognitive Sciences Department of the Massachusetts Institute of Technology. His hypothesis is firmly rooted in the idea that humans have a special facility for communication which is instilled in the brain as an instinct might be. Other instincts in babies are prewired reactions, such as the grasping of small objects which tickle the palm. The surprising competence that children have in building up phrase-structured language is an instinct, a precondition of the structure of the human brain.

Much of Pinker's passion for this model comes from a dislike of what he calls the Standard Social Sciences Model (SSSM), which allows that only culture can have an influence on development. He sees this view as an error lodged in the work of social scientists of the 1920s. This, he argues without actually using the words, is a kind of pandering to political correctness. If people are special, they need special rights or could be denied rights. Recently the SSSM has been driven by a fear that this may lead to the ideas of 1940s nationalism in Germany, and thoughts that some people — say, white ones — have more rights than others — say, black ones. It is better, according to adherents of the SSSM, to believe in the over-arching power of culture which is controllable and can be used to arrange an even treatment for all. This ideology, argues Pinker, pre-vents science from looking squarely at the rapid and surprising ability of children to learn.

Putting aside any suggestion of being politically incorrect, Pinker notes that scientific honesty leads one to avoid seeing the child as an organism born with a super ability to learn anything thrown at it from a cultural repository. The truth, he says, is that the child is born with a highly tuned ability to learn, the tuning being universally slanted in the human race towards the efficient expres-sion of a well-structured (phrase-structured) type of language. He has some evidence for this — one example is that children in immi-grant families speak better than their parents, while another is the familiar poverty of stimulus argument. On a higher plane, he might argue that people's manual dexterity for making spears, knives and wheels is never questioned as being inheritable, so why stop short of a language instinct?

Karmiloff-Smith's representational redescription

Annette Karmiloff-Smith is a developmental psychologist with the Medical Research Council in London. She has worked for some years with an interesting model of development which she calls a process of *representational redescription* (RR). This has the charac-teristic of being used by a developing organism in an iterative fashion which works in domain-specific phases (rather than Piaget's domain-general major stages). She creates a four-class taxonomy of the different levels of representation which follow from these phases. The first is called the implicit (I) representation. Here a child makes use of information which Karmiloff-Smith calls "procedural" and has to do with attending to sensory information. The process of looking around an image may be of this kind. This becomes redescribed into the second level (explicit-1, or EI), where the sensory information begins to take a more general form. Karmiloff-Smith gives an example of striped things being associated with the concept of a zebra. Such concepts are neither articulated nor conscious. At the next level, E2, concepts become available to a non-verbal form of consciousness, while finally E3 is linked to verbal expression.

Karmiloff-Smith identifies this process as being at work in the development of language in children, through a naïve knowledge of physics, mathematics and models of mind. So, allowing the need for the innateness of the mechanisms with which the process of redescription begins, this model leads to the development of domainspecific thinking modules which rely only on innate *procedural* information for their creation. A pillar of this theory is that only the human species has the power of redescription, which distinguishes the human from the animal.

Magnus, Pinker and Karmiloff-Smith

So, in the contemporary version of the battle of Royaumont, where protagonists such as Pinker and Karmiloff-Smith present a softer version of the innate/constructed view of mind, how might ideas about the development of artificial consciousness in Magnus fare? In fact, both authors refer to the artificial neural approach.

Pinker, in the early part of *The Language Instinct,* is skeptical of existing ways in which neural nets have been used to generate the past tense from the present tense as the results are purely based on similarity. That is, the net might give *wugged* to the nonsense verb to *wug* and so might a child. It has this success because *wug* is like *hug*. But people who have been given other nonsense verbs, such as *smeej,* will produce *smeejed*. Pinker quotes a neural net which, when faced with *smeej,* produced *leeffloag* (?!). He argues that people, when realising that something like *smeej* may be a verb stem, will apply a feasible rule. A net does not map this into "verbstem", but mangles it instead.

Later in the book, however, Pinker shows how a neural net might, through the power of its special structure and the existence of a stored dictionary of likely verbstems, actually apply the appropriate rule to create the correct past tense. He uses this as one of the main pillars of the argument for the idea of the language instinct as the structure of the net is crucial to the successful operation of his network. For such finely tuned structure to exist it would have to be genetically transmitted. Finally, in delivering the basis for his belief in the language instinct, Pinker argues that a wide variety of "algorithms" in language, from the building of phrase structures to morphology, parsing and learning, can all be achieved with genetically transmitted and highly specialised neural structures.

Karmiloff-Smith refers to the "... several shortcomings ..." of neural network models: they learn to perform *tasks,* she argues, and not *development*. She does, however, recognise that artificial neural models are still in their infancy, and goes on to suggest that:

"Future developmental modelling must ... simulate both the benefit of rapid processing via implicit representations and those gained by further representational redescription — a process which, I posit, makes possible human creativity,"

So Magnus comes in on these two perspectives almost as a jester at the feast — it actually fits neither view of neural modelling terribly well but, as a neural state machine, provides a perspective of both. In Pinker's case the Magnus methodology suggests that great care should be taken in relating structure to function and relying on an instinctive function being genetically transmitted through structure. As we have seen in many parts of this book, an infinity of adaptive structures can, within the same learning time, adapt to the same function. Lifetime adaptation is so much easier for the iconic neural state machine than evolution. If function had to be inherited through structure, any flexibility for learning would have to be extremely well poised between the retention and cancellation of function. In Chapter 8, I shall return to the question of what "instincts" may have to be built into Magnus.

In Karmiloff-Smith's case, I see much similarity between the RR model and the process of creating complex iconic states in state structure. This is very different from the work on *task* modelling which she rightly perceives in classical work. The I-level representation with which RR starts could in the Basic Guess be interpreted as the ability to lay down iconic representations. Whether this is described as a domain-general, inborn property or just what neural nets with dominant synapses in sensory areas do, may be a matter of choice of expression. Certainly there has been much evidence in our discussion of El type representations, which are the raw, unarticulated creation of stable iconic states which reflect events in the world. This leads to groupings of such representations to form state structures which, for the organism, are accessible as single states, but which have much greater richness and individuality for a specific organism. Could these be described as E2 representations? Finally, the operation of the long-routed action–perception loops leads to what might be E3 representations.

Were I to pick a quarrel with Karmiloff-Smith, it would be at the level of the entire RR process being unique to the human species. Thinking about iconic neural systems suggests that even quite simple species may be capable of representations certainly up to E1 level, and possibly at E2. As said earlier, it is the dexterity of various forms of long-route feedback loops (the mascular end of which is certainly inherited) which gives humans their supremacy and their ability to build cultural repositories of language. No, I would say to Pinker, I am not pandering to the SSSM — a cultural repository of language just seems the easy trick for an efficient evolutionary system armed with an iconic state machine to play.

Postscript to Chapter 7

Acquiring Language:
What's New?

The Nurture/Nature Argument Goes on

Chapter 7 introduces the reader to Piaget's belief that language is acquired in synchrony with the acquisition of life experience. This contrasts with Chomsky's view that life experiences *reveal* linguistic rules that have an innate nature. Experimental psychologists today still find it hard to do work which negates either of these hypotheses. There appear to be no obvious winners. But there are new players and I briefly wish to look at them in this postscript: namely, Ray Jackendoff and Michael Tomasello. I also acknowledge here the long-lasting contribution to neuro-cognitive science made by Stephen Grossberg of Boston University, whose Adaptive Resonance Theory touches on linguistic behaviour in a neural system.

Ray Jackendoff

A student of Noam Chomsky's, Ray Jackendoff is now seen as one of the leading linguists in the US. He is known for straddling between the Chomskian notion of innate deep structure, and the cognitive aspects of language (Piagetian theories of development, if you like). He has written many books but two recent ones summarise his outlook: *Language, Consciousness, Culture: Essays on Mental Structure*[a] and *A User's Guide to Thought and Meaning*.[b] He favours thinking of language competence being best modelled by three systems of rules working in parallel: phonological structures, syntactic structures and conceptual structures. Phonological structures govern what utterances can and cannot sound like, syntactic structures are like Chomskian rules on what does and what does not constitute a grammatical utterance, while conceptual structures are rules about what makes and what does not make sense in our world. While Jackendoff recognises that consciousness has neural correlates, and that some language is understood through a process of visualisation, he does not dwell on possible neural mechanics of language.

Michael Tomasello

Tomasello is an influential American developmental psychologist, now working in Germany. He is critical of Chomsky's concept of a Universal Grammar, arguing that language develops in children in function of their social interaction with others. Tomasello's central quest is understanding the seeming superiority of human cognition over that of animals. This, he argues, occurs due to a competence in social interactions with others that is higher than that of non-humans — apes for example. According to this, language can be interpreted and acquired by children as the child can share attention control with

---

[a] Jackendoff, R. (2007). *Language, Consciousness, Culture: Essays on Mental Structure*, MIT Press, Cambridge.
[b] Jackendoff, R. (2012). *A User's Guide to Thought and Meaning*, Oxford University Press, Oxford.

adults. For example a natural agreement can occur on how words like 'this' and 'your' are used involving social interaction. Also a natural tendency to experiment with generalisation then empowers the child to use the known utterances in new situations.[c] That the word 'dog' does not extend to 'cat' primes a need for a word like 'animal' that does.

There are not many neuroscientists that have been stimulated by Tomasello's ideas on linguistic development and behaviour. I feel that this would be a very fruitful line to pursue.

Grossberg: At the neural Level

Chapter 7 focuses on two major attitudes to linguistic development and acquisition, leaving us with theories that largely are best expressed in a computational way as architectures or algorithms. In parallel, some impressive science takes place at the neural level. I refer to the work of Steve Grossberg who addresses brain function in a holistic way. The key concept is resonance in neural systems, which refers to a progressive interaction between the representation of an expectation in a neural net and the actual perceptual input. Called Adaptive Resonance Theory (ART), the scheme has the property of not saturating as learning progresses, a drawback found in many other neural learning schemes. In the language domain, Grossberg developed a system called cART-WORLD (the 'c' stands for 'conscious') which tracks resonances between working memory neural areas and incoming language in the form of speech. There is a very helpful publication in which Grossberg puts this work in the context of his general approach to understanding many aspects of cognitive functioning of the neural brain.[d]

---

[c] Tomasello, M. (2005). *Constructing a Language*, Harvard University Press, Cambridge.

[d] Grossberg, S. (2013). Adaptive Resonance Theory: How a brain learns to consciously attend, learn, and recognise *a changing world*, *Neural Networks*, 37, pp. 1–47.

In Sum

It is still the case (as suggested in Chapter 7) that the acquisition and use of language is something exquisitely human. Human performance is so sophisticated that it still attracts the attention of some of the world's most skilled computational scientists and will continue so to do. Language is inextricably linked to the development of the conscious human experience. I cannot help feeling that a comprehensive science in this area still remains in the future.

Despite the wintry season, a warm sun was shining on the cliff from which, seated in the remaining grass, Molecula and Red were looking out to sea. They had decided that meetings in the capital had become too dangerous. Sir Global had issued a writ against Red citing "defamation of professional character" — an accusation which the courts took very seriously. They had to, for reasons of stability. There were many transparently weak appointments made in high places, and tot much freedom for critics could lead to anarchy.

Red had hidden in an acquaintance's house and only Molecula knew how to get hold of him. Galactic College had given him leave and had recorded that he was on a mission to Germania, a somewhat more successful industrial nation on planet Volta than Siliconia. This put him out of Siliconia's jurisdiction — but for how long ...?

"My childhood?" said Molecula. "Much like everybody else's, I guess. I was sent to a programming centre at the age of eighteen months and stayed there for the usual module-by-module programming of my thinking. It was decided that I would be an AI scientist, so I was sent early to Ridgecamb to get my proficiency certificate."

"How well did you know your parents?" asked Red.

"Not well," answered Molecula. "As you know, contacts were not encouraged. I now know that this is to avoid what are called 'feelings' from developing, which could make parents possessive and keep their offspring at home. They both died while I was being programmed."

"We should talk about 'feelings' sometime," said Red. "Look at that ... it's called a cormorant. It's happy under water as well as in the air. Isn't it free and wonderful? It makes me cheerful to see that some living things in this country are free."

"*I'm not sure what you mean by 'happy' and 'cheerful,'*" *said Molecula hesitatingly,*" *but I again feel an excitement when you say these things. I can't trace it to any of my thinking modules ... The cormorant makes my feel that I too want to fly ... it frightens me, Red ...*"

Chapter 8

Qualia, Instinct and Emotion

A Philosopher's Weapon

On several occasions I have published some of the bare mathematical bones of the working of iconically trained state machines, usually among consenting adult neural network scientists (e.g. Aleksander, 1995). On one occasion, at a moment when caution was thrown to the winds, I submitted some of this material to a philosophical journal with a view to saying something about the nature of artificial consciousness. While one referee felt enthusiastic, another was quite damning. The focus of the attack came in the following paragraph:

> "The work makes no reference to *qualia* which makes any presence at discussing consciousness incomplete and invalid. Of course this is the concept which usually baffles scientists so it is not surprising that it has totally bypassed an engineer. Please reject this ignorant and pretentious attempt to dabble in the philosophy of consciousness."

Had it not been for an apologetic note from the editor of the journal who thought that referees should provide helpful criticisms rather than insults, I would have transmitted a somewhat terse letter via the journal to my attacker for having used the occasion to vent his prejudices about engineers. Instead I thought that I would look into what it was that upset the referee. Of course I had read about *qualia*, but I had obviously not taken the concern seriously enough — so I would try to put this right. Besides, concepts that baffle scientists and are beyond the comprehension of mere engineers are either a major challenge or a philosophical electrified fence with a sign which says, "Keep out — only philosophers allowed here."

Rejecting the latter and accepting the challenge, one sees that the first thing to be discovered is that the topic of *qualia* is a controversial one among philosophers themselves. But I am getting a bit ahead of things ... What are *qualia*?

Qualia

The Latin word *quale* gives rise to many English words, such as "qualitative" and "quality". It means the subjective, personal value of something where *quantum* is the word used to signify the objective, public value of something. *Qualia* is the plural of *quale* as *quanta* is the plural of *quantum*. So, in modern philosophy, *qualia* has come to mean, say, the personal, subjective quality of experience. For example, the pleasure of tasting a good glass of wine, the experience of seeing a colour, and what it feels like to have a stomachache are events which have the most significance and degrees of quality for the person doing the experiencing. The sensation of these experiences is seen as a major obstacle to scientific explanations of conscious experience, because the only way any individual can know what they are is through his own introspection of such events. It is then quite impossible for that individual to express that sensation even for the purpose of explaining to a friend in natural language what it is like, never mind providing a scientific theory about it. One cannot answer the question "In what way does thinking of the colour red differ from thinking of the colour blue?" without being circular or referential. "Red is like a rose and blue is like the sky," one might say, but this does not constitute an explanation of how the two experiences differ for that individual; so, it is said, a rational analysis becomes impossible.

The philosophical controversy again focuses on the difference of opinion due to classical divisions between philosophers. Reductionists believe that *qualia* are just mental states due to the firing of neurons. Epiphenomenalists (believers in all mentality being caused by physical activity in the brain) accept that such inner sensations are somewhat dependent on physical occurrences in the brain, but that this relationship is neither simple nor entirely explicable in scientific terms. Although there cannot be too many dualists left, they believe that there is no link between the personal mental sensation and physical events, although the two could run in some sort of synchronism.

No wonder my critical referee had been upset at my not having mentioned *qualia*: in some sense the concept replays the entire controversy of what consciousness is all about. To a philosophical purist, the whole issue of consciousness focuses on *qualia*. Issues of mental imagery, unconscious states, plans for controlling the world in one's head, the development of language and personality — in other words, all those things that have concerned us so far — are all diversions from the real issue, *qualia*.

Needless to say, the Basic Guess puts me firmly in the reductionist class, and a *qualia* Consequence will be developed later in this chapter. For the time being I shall take a closer look at the nature of the philosophical division of opinion. Why is it that philosophers find it hard to persuade one another of their points of view? To focus on this question I shall look briefly at the differing opinions of two contemporary American philosophers: Thomas Nagel and Daniel Dennett.

Nagel's Bat

Thomas Nagel (b. 1937) is a philosopher working at New York University. He is emerging as the leading scholar on questions of inner, personal and subjective states and how these relate to the reality of the events which may have caused them. He is quoted by almost everyone writing on this subject, partly because of the provocative title of a paper he published in 1974; "What Is It Like to Be a Bat?". The disarming logic behind this question is that it is only possible for me to know what it is like to be me. I cannot know exactly what it is like to be someone else or something else. The argument goes on to say that this knowledge of my own consciousness, being inaccessible to others, is inaccessible to anyone trying to explain it in a scientific way. Hence this makes subjective experience including *qualia* inaccessible to the scientist: the enterprise of discussing consciousness becomes solely a matter for philosophers. The electrified fence is in place!

The danger, of course, is that having ring-fenced the seemingly central feature of consciousness, the discussion may have been put out of bounds for everyone, as what goes for science may go for philosophy as well. I (in the company of many others) believe that the bat argument is not as restrictive as may at first seem. For one thing the argument can be easily criticised. The most direct criticism is that you don't have to know what it's like to *be* something in order to talk of it scientifically. I don't need to know what it's like to be a drop of water to analyse it and to come to the conclusion that it is made up of lots of molecules each of which has two atoms of hydrogen and one of oxygen — the familiar H_2O. But, argue Nagel's supporters, things like *qualia* are about subjective experience — they are about *being*. So if *being* cannot be extracted from an individual and subjected to analysis like water can be subjected to scientific tests, then it remains outside the scientific domain. So, as in many areas of philosophy, there are those who side with Nagel's point of view and argue that the publication of his bat article, having drawn attention to the idea that subjective experience has meaning only for the individual, is a most remarkable event in the history of the philosophy of consciousness (e.g. Antti Revonsuo, Matti Kampinen and Seppo Sajama, 1994), and those who argue that an inability to discuss subjectivity and *qualia* in an objective way may mean that the concept may not be worthy of the attention it is being given. For example, Bernard Baars (1994) of the Wright Institute at Berkeley sees the question "Can we understand the role of consciousness in the nervous system?" as the overriding issue. If this can be answered the question "What is it like to be a bat?" will, for Baars, be "pure icing on the cake". He himself has a "global" biological theory of consciousness which depends on sensory information affecting the nervous system all over.

For the purposes of our discussions about using Magnus to explain how neurons create an artificial consciousness, the question translates into asking how artificial neurons can give Magnus a sense of subjectivity which can be accepted by an external observer. If that is convincing, then it will be proper to ask, "Is a question about being Magnus *of the same kind* as the question about being a bat?" We may never be able to know *what it is like* to be Magnus, but that is a feather in Magnus's cap. Taking Nagel seriously, the whole human race with the exception of President Clinton cannot know what it is like to be President Clinton. However, we have little doubt about the President's subjective consciousness, *qualia* and all. So Magnus may be in good company. The issue is one of explaining what it is that a bat needs for us to believe that it has a chance of knowing what it is like to be a bat. We do not attribute much of such a chance to a tree or a rock. Why not? This is where the scientific debate is: What machinery is needed for X to know what it is like to be X? This can be explored without Y ever knowing what it is like to be X. However, before going down that track, I shall look at the ideas of one of the major critics of Nagel's bat and *qualia*: philosopher Daniel C. Dennett

Dennett's View on Qualia as a Philosophical Blind Alley

As we have seen earlier in this book, Daniel C. Dennett is a prolific author on philosophy. A professor at Tufts University in Boston, he is known for having recently published the widely read book *Consciousness Explained* (1991). However, he established his philosophical position on mental events earlier by taking the "intentional stance" (1987). This implies the attribution of rationality to a system through making judgments about its output (speech acts and other actions). Interestingly, Dennett's references to intentionality (the fact that inner brain states are "about" something, as discussed in Chapter 6) do not point to agreement with John Searle (1992). It is Dennett's allowance of attribution which is the main sticking point. This lets him believe that people could attribute rationality to a computer and this would endow it with intentionality. Searle, on the other hand, believes that intentionality is *caused* by the brain and is present whether attributed or not. This, as explained in Chapter 6, does not admit the possibility that preprogrammed computers might have intentionality. The Basic Guess in this book actually leans towards Searle rather than Dennett, as it argues that intentionality stems from iconic transfer rather than attribution.

This intentional stance has led to Dennett's being one of the main assailants of the concept of *qualia*. Put simply, if a rational being says that he has just seen a car in a hit-and-run accident and remembers that the car was maroon in colour, what could be simpler than ascribing a mental state to that person's memory which is related to a sensed property of the car, which the policeman hearing the story could use in finding the car? Is there a need, in the business of understanding the lives we lead, for the policeman to ascribe some additional property called *qualia* to the observer's experience before he can take the report seriously? Dennett argues that *qualia* are not only surplus to requirements in folk models of what makes people tick, but also to philosophical discourse. He does not mince his words either — in *Consciousness Explained,* in the chapter "Qualia Disqualified", he suggests that *qualia* are a bit like a kite-string snarl — a mess you need to walk away from;

> "That's how it is in my opinion, with the philosophical topic of qualia, a tormented snarl of increasingly convoluted and bizarre thought experiments, jargon, in-jokes, allusions to putative refutations, 'received' results that should be returned to sender, and a bounty of other sidetrackers and timewasters."

In a more recent contribution, entitled "Instead of Qualia" (1994), he puts a softer gloss on his view:

> "I deny that there are any such properties. But I agree wholeheartedly that there seem to be."

The key question which Dennett raises is: Why should philosophers have devised additional properties associated with mental states that are essentially mental referents of sensory experience? He draws attention to one argument which has led to the invention of *qualia*: physically, colour in the world is electromagnetic radiation; one wavelength gives us a perception of red while another might be green. The colours really do not exist except in our heads. Philosophers, he argues, have jumped at the idea of there being something in our heads which does not exist in the world. So they awarded the status of a new mental property to the fact that we can discuss the redness of a sunset or the greenness of grass. Or, indeed, we can recoil in horror at the memory of red blood in a surgical operation seen on television or green slime read about in Douglas Adams' *Hitchhiker's Guide to the Galaxy*. So, for Dennett, philosophers may be forgiven for having invented *qualia* to label the emotions and actions flowing from something which happens in our heads but which, as scientists themselves admit, does not exist in that form in the real world. But, his argument goes on, the invention is unnecessary for the following reasons.

The eye of many living creatures causes different, discriminated events to take place in the brain of the beholder for different received light wavelengths — that's well known. Therefore the physical property of blood for reflecting light at the particular red wavelength (in common with many other objects, all of which would be said to be red) will cause the physical event for "red" to happen in the brain. This is a distinct event which can be associated with all the other things that are going on, such as the cutting of the skin by a scalpel as seen on a TV screen. It is distinct from the event which may occur were something, say, blue be seen. The brain event will be associated with the horror of the occasion which comes from other brain events. This enables a human to discuss the horror that red induces without the need to add to the physical brain event any further "subjective, private, ineffable" properties. Simply put, they would have no role to play over and above what an organism can do with the brain event caused by sensory perception and recalled in the same way as any other brain event.

In his 1994 contribution Dennett goes on to describe how a robot which assigns numbers to wavelengths and labels them as colours can do everything that a conscious being might wish to do with colours. This, in terms of the Basic Guess of this book, seems a bit simplistic. Nevertheless, I side totally with Dennett in believing that there is a direct causal link between qualities such as colour and brain events and that this is all that is needed to discuss the nature of these events without resorting to *qualia*. However, the challenge for me now is to explain how the iconic transfer idea of the Basic Guess might work instead of *qualia*.

Colour Vision in People

Colour is often taken as the exemplary sensation with which *qualia* may be discussed. Quite a lot is known about the way the visual apparatus of living creatures works to differentiate between different colours, and this goes a long way towards providing evidence that colours lead to differentiated brain events. Briefly, for human beings, light-sensitive receptors in the retina at the back of the eye fire when activated by light energy. There are two main kinds of receptors, called rods and cones. There are about 100 million rods in each eye which largely detect levels of brightness and serve well at night or in twilight conditions. They do not sense colours to any large extent. Colour discrimination comes from the five million or so cones in each eye. These are known to be differentiated into three types, each group being sensitive to one of the primary colours of the physical spectrum, i.e. red, green and blue.

In terms of Dennett's assumption that *qualia* are avoided by differentiation in the sensory apparatus, the eyes, as part of the brain, certainly provide signals that are physically in different receptor cells for different colours. So the perception of different colours is, right from the beginning, associated with different brain states. Indeed, what makes the receptors sensitive to different colours is that pigment (the substance which colours living matter) actually exists in the receptors themselves. Red receptors contain red pigment which acts like red cellophane paper to allow red wavelengths through to cause the receptor to fire. That is, there are pigments in our eyes which match the reflective properties of things we eventually call red, blue and so on. Other colours according to colour theory, are made up of mixtures of these wavelengths so they lead to simultaneous activity of different receptors, which enables us to discriminate the other colours of the rainbow.

But there is more to it than that. All I have described so far is how we may perceive colour in the presence of coloured objects. The vexed question is whether there are inner, cortical representations of colour, i.e. cortical cells which differentiate between colours. As such cells could be stimulated in various ways, a hypothesis for the recall of colour becomes feasible. This is still a matter of current research, but exciting early results have been obtained by Samir Zeki of University College in London (1977, 1980). His experiments have found colour-specific cells in the cortex of the rhesus monkey. Interestingly, some have interpreted this as a sign of "colours being in the brain rather than in the world". From the point of view of the Basic Guess the hypothesis would be different: the colour-differentiated cells in the cortex could be those which have become specialised during life through a process of iconic transfer. I shall explain this in the next section by looking at the possibility of iconic colour images in Magnus.

Iconic Creation of *Qualia*: An Experiment in Colour

Having accepted Dennett's statement that it is highly possible to understand why *qualia* have been invented, personally I do not wish to dismiss them as not existing. Rather, it may be more instructive to accept their validity in philosophical discussion and then speculate on what they might be in terms of the Basic Guess. It may even be fun to ask if Magnus could have *qualia*. This leads to a new Consequence:

Consequence 11: Iconic transfer of qualitative sensory properties (qualia?)

Iconic transfer operates on all aspects of sensory perception discriminated by receptors. Therefore qualitative properties of objects such as colour become candidates for iconic transfer and representation in recallable state structure.

Before looking at some of the more subtle implications of this Consequence, we shall work through an example of how iconic transfer might work for colour in the simple system of Fig. 8.1, Here only two colours exist for this organism: red and green. Part (a) reminds us of the structure of connections for iconic transfer. The difference at the retinal end is that I have shown the receptors in each location in pairs, one of which responds to red and the other to green. The rest of the network is the same as elsewhere in this book. The key point is that nodes which qualify as inner representational neurons should have one dominant synapse connected to one receptor in the sensory field. We recall that while the inner neurons are drawn in geometrical correspondence with the sensory ones, they could be anywhere. Also, and this is not shown, they are connected to one another, so forming a state machine which can sustain learned states.

In (b) we see how sensory information is projected into the inner net for several sensory events. First, a red which is spread all over the retinal image becomes represented as a state attractor where half of the inner neurons are firing. For a blanket of green it's the other half of the inner field which responds. Of course, these attractors could be given names in exactly the same way as we gave names to

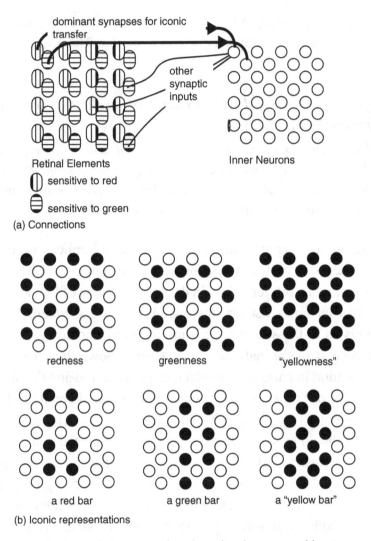

Fig. 8.1. Colour sensations in an iconic state machine.

cups and saucers in Chapter 6. To illustrate mixtures, both the red and green receptors would respond to yellow, so the firing of all neurons in the inner area could be given the name "yellow". Of course, these colours need not be assigned to blanket visions, but could apply to objects; so red, green and yellow vertical bars could have the representations shown.

The Recall of Qualitative Sensory States

The implication of Consequence 11 is that qualitative experience may be recalled. Indeed, the above example could lead to a state structure shown in Fig. 8.2(a). This is the state of affairs that would occur were the experience of the organism to include red horizontal bars and green vertical bars only. That's a bit like our associating red with tomatoes and green with spinach. The figure shows inner neurons as in Fig. 8.1, but with a red-specialised neuron as the top left of a square and the green neuron as the bottom right. It is also suggested that there is association with some generic name, such as VER for "vertical bar" and HOR for "horizontal bar". The name of the colours is also associated with these states and their inputs. So, if I were to say to Magnus "VER" a red vertical bar would appear in its inner neurons and the machine would pronounce "red" had it learned to utter appropriately to indicate an inner state (as was discussed in Chapter 7).

But there are senses such as smell and taste for which we appear to have a far weaker iconic memory. I would certainly be surprised if a lump of sugar were to taste of vinegar or vinegar taste of honey. But if I were asked to recall the taste of a lump of sugar, the memory might not be all that vivid. Of course, the same may not be true of wine tasters in France. For the average human being there is a distinct difference between remembering a red car and remembering the taste of sugar. I can "see" the redness in my head but cannot "taste" the sugar with such "clarity", or indeed have more than an expectation of the smell of a rose. The state structure for a sense for which there may be no recall is sketched in Fig. 8.2(b). This illustrates what it would be like were there only an ability to create iconic representations for shape in the inner neurons and not colour, stressing the effect of colour in the alternative (a). That is, we assume that there is no iconic representation for colour in the inner neurons but there is for everything else. The system "knows" that

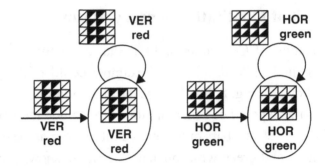

(a) State structure with inner representation of qualitative properties

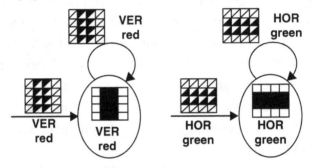

(b) State structure without inner representation of qualitative properties

Fig. 8.2. Two modes of memory.

the vertical bar is also called "red" according to the state diagram. The appropriate state would be entered (note that here there are no triangles, and each square of the state represents just one neuron firing without representing a colour).

If Magnus had this type of memory it would recall the shape of a bar but could not "see" its colour in its head. On the other hand it would have no difficulty in being satisfied that the bar is of the right colour as, were the stimulus a green vertical bar, there would be no attractor state structure at all for this, and according to the interpretation given to no-attractor states, the machine would, given speech, utter some exclamation of surprise or disbelief. Indeed, it is known that for smell, the olfactory sense, and there is no connection to the cortex via the thalamus, and hence the dynamics of the smell machine may be different from those of other senses. All that this says is that it is possible to have artificial models of systems which have and systems which do not have *qualia,* suggesting that the concept is amenable to analysis.

Another example of the implications of the concept of *qualia* for neural circuitry is that I can, without any difficulty, imagine a red banana even if I have never seen such an apparition. This is the same question as: Could Magnus, endowed with inner colour representation, "imagine" a green vertical bar, having never seen one? Of course, the answer is positive, but it could cause an engineer to pause for a moment or two. The fact that we can do this easily in our heads implies that there is a link between the red and green neurons in any particular inner geographical position which relates to a point on the iconic representation of an object. In the same way as greenness may be represented globally, the idea of HOR would have to trigger horizontal bar neurons whether they be red or green. Normally the red ones would come on, but after the evocation of greenness the neighbouring green ones would have to come on instead. This points perhaps to some detail of inhibition and enhancement of the interaction between neurons which is a bit too technical for this discussion. However, the impression is that *qualia* are not beyond neurological analysis, but just a matter for deeper study for neural enthusiasts.

Evoking the ability of people to use phrases such as "the sweet smell of a rose" as evidence of an inner phenomenon which we all know but cannot explain, may be poetic; however, not only is it confused, but it also confuses what can be done with the senses. The point being made here is that thinking about *qualia* in a precise, scientific way reveals challenges which the engineer, the scientist and the neurophysiologist might rise to. Both the insistence that such sensations are beyond science and that they do not exist at all are not conducive to a deeper understanding of consciousness.

More Inner Sensations: Emotions or Instincts?

The sweet smell of roses is not the only kind of inner sensation which we, in our daily lives, are likely to think of. Living is a constant string of feelings that form part of our thoughts as we progress not only through waking life but also in our dreams. I "jump with joy" on hearing that I have passed my driving test. I "shrink with horror" at the news of a new genocide in Africa. I "wake up in a cold sweat" after dreaming that the house is on fire. These are phenomena which undoubtedly have inner, personal qualities. They go under the heading of emotions which at first seem quite distinct from *qualia*. But the distinction cannot be so great. When a rose is said to smell sweet, sweetness is perhaps used to indicate pleasure, and pleasure is an emotion.

Received wisdom has it that emotions and instincts are linked. This is one possible distinction from *qualia*. Could Magnus benefit from having instincts and emotions? Perhaps more to the point is whether designing instinct and emotions into Magnus throws some light on what such phenomena might be in machines or living things. A more detailed discussion is coming up ...

Instinct

Historically, instinct has been seen as the pre-wired and the inborn. But some care must be taken with this term, as it can mean several things. The first is that it is indeed an inborn reaction to a stimulus. Children are known to form a grasp with their fingers when their palm is tickled. They also cry at birth, which may be vital for them to clear their breathing pathways. No doubt here about these things being innate. Interestingly, the current view among psychologists is that such instincts can become controlled and modified by thought.

A second interpretation of the term is in the sense of an unconscious reflex. The driver slamming on the brakes when a child runs across the road, the tennis player positioning himself before the opponent has struck the ball and the weaving done while walking in a hurry alone a crowded pavement are all examples of reflexes which are unlikely to be innate, but connect stimulus to action without the apparent need for thought. The third, which is usually discussed in the context of animals, has to do with standard patterns of behaviour, for example the call of birds and the pecking of newly hatched herring gull chicks at their parents' beaks to bring about regurgitation of food. This has been observed to be accessible to environmental influences: performance improves with action on the outer world. Finally, there are the so-called drives, for example sexual drives, hunger and thirst.

The common feature of these is that there is a link between sensory input and action output which appears not to involve thought. The distinction lies in the mix of innate connection and environmental modification. In terms of the Basic Guess this implies a bypass of the inner neurons. Consequence 12 is an attempt at describing this process from the point of view of an iconically trained state machine.

Consequence 12: Instinct
To enhance survival, an organism needs a substrate of output actions that are linked to inputs or inner autonomic neurons and which are or become independent of the state of inner neurons. These may be inborn or become independent of state variables as a result of development.

The main purpose of this Consequence is to draw attention to the sort of neural mechanisms which might underpin some of the rather diverse ideas that go under the heading of "instinct".

Various interpretations of instinct imply that the connection of output neurons is going through some changes with respect to inner neurons. In discussions about iconic learning so far, it has been assumed that output neurons receive active connections both from perceptual (input) neurons and from inner (thought) neurons. In the general case, the output activity of a neural state machine, whether it is uttering language or finding its way around its environment, is assumed to be contingent on the activity of both these neuron groups. A simple view of instinct would be that output neurons have no access to thought neurons and are solely dependent on perceptual neurons. However, the more recent view of instinctive phenomena (e.g. McFarland, 1987) is that such strangely isolated pre-wired connections are unlikely to feature in instinctive behaviour without some modification by thought or the environment. They may exist internally, and may be essential in automatic functions such as the regulation of breathing and heart rate. But current wisdom would have it that "thought" developed in life has always a function to play even in the modes of instinctive behaviour mentioned above.

So the first type of instinct, such as the crying at birth in order to clear air paths, can be seen as functions of output neurons being initially *dependent* only on sensory input, but later becoming dependent on "thought" states. In later life, crying may become very much a function of an internal state, indeed something which may be called an emotional state. This is the reason that instinctive behaviour comes under scrutiny here under the heading of the "privacy of mind". Outward behaviour is a tip-of-the-iceberg kind of indication of complex internal states. What this means is that output neurons in the state machine model involved in, say, crying are not disconnected physically from "thought" states, but simply

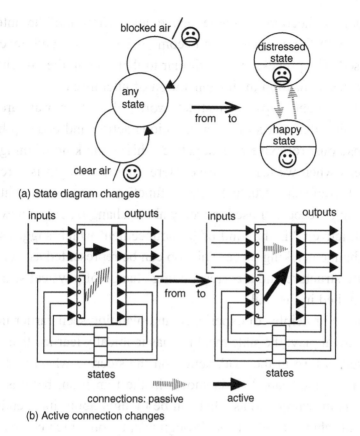

(a) State diagram changes

(b) Active connection changes

Fig. 8.3.   Type 1 instinct: initially direct, then internalised.

independent of them in early life, becoming dependent through learning. The Consequence suggests state structure changes as in Fig. 8.3(a), which could be helpful in illustrating this simple idea and suggesting how type 1 instinct might change through learning: from state-independent behaviour to internal representations of the distressed and happy states. In Fig. 8.3(b) it is shown that this type of instinctive activity implies a swap not in the connections which the output neurons receive but in the connections which become active and passive as a result of learning. The inborn direct connections start off by being active, but as internalisation takes place the internal connections become active and determine the internal states, with the external ones becoming less active, and generally not used. The process is very similar to that seen in the last chapter in the internalisation of the generation of utterances.

The second type of instinct works the other way around. Something that starts off as a conscious action and ends up being unconscious, reflexive or instinctive. This is the kind of thing that happens when we learn to drive. Here, initially, output is carefully guided from state structure when a function becomes automatic as learning proceeds. "I used to worry about changing gears; now I do it instinctively" is the kind of pronouncement which suggests that this change is taking place. This too can be represented as a change in state structure and a corresponding change of physical structure as sketched in Fig. 8.4.

In (a) principles of experience and planning seen earlier in this book are at play: the state machine has iconically learned that when one sees a turn in the road, action on the steering wheel will keep the car on the road. This is shown in the transition, both as what happens in reality and as what can be thought about independently of input (shown as Ø). This, through adaptation which comes from the fact that correct driving will be experienced even if accurate mental planning does not take place, leads to a situation where the control is left to a direct input–output link.

In (b) the meaning of this is shown as a corresponding connection which starts by being fully driven from the inner neurons and the perceptual ones, but which is later taken over by the perceptual ones only. Of course, this is a gross oversimplification. Clearly the inner states can (through a process of internal attention) enter a part of state structure which is related to driving. That's a bit like the pilot taking over from the automatic mechanism in flying a plane except that, in the state machine (and probably in the brain), there are no distinct entities such as a pilot and a control mechanism.

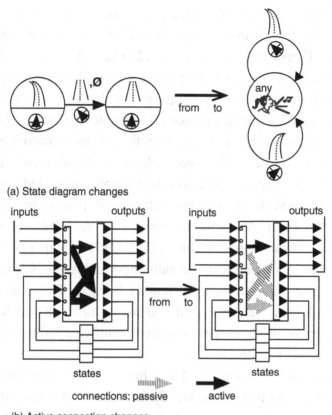

(a) State diagram changes

(b) Active connection changes

Fig. 8.4. Type 2 instinct: initially internalised, then direct.

There are, however, areas of state structure which are related to the input–output activity and can, therefore, plan consciously, while in other areas the output reacts without reference to the state variables. Indeed, the very control of movement has this sort of character. Movement of limbs which in children appears to be difficult at first (e.g. walking) becomes reflexive as a function of maturation. Interesting takeovers for this function by a part of the brain called the cerebellum (from possibly the cortex) are documented and appreciated by students of neurophysiology.

The third aspect of instinct, i.e. innate behaviour patterns modified by the environment, falls well within the implications of the Basic Guess and Consequence 12. The process is usually discussed in the context of animals (e.g. modification of pecking procedures) and may be equated to the learning of controlling utterances in humans as discussed in Chapter 7. That is, there are inborn sequences largely resident in the wiring of output neurons (suggesting, interestingly, feedback in such neurons which is necessary for stored sequences) which become modified as soon as the long-routed loop between action and perception becomes active after birth. A fascinating variant of this is the process of imprinting in ducklings or chicks (Hess, 1958) which, soon after birth, follow a moving form (usually their mother — but, in experiments, other animals or even human beings). This suggests an inborn link between perceptual and output neurons which is discriminatory of visual shape and activity, implying built-in filters in the perceptual neurons.

Finally, we have suggested that hunger and sexual drives may lead to behaviour that goes under the heading of "being instinctive". In terms of neural state automata these imply inborn links between the "autonomous inner neurons" and output neurons as discussed under Consequence 2 in Chapter 4. The mechanisms are those implied by Consequence 12, initial behaviour being modified by its effect on the environment, and consequent thought in inner neurons. Of course, sexual "drives" which depend on physical development of the body need separate treatment, but in broad terms the starting point is an inner autonomous sensation which leads to behaviour soon to be mediated by thought. Dangerous ground, the reader may say. I agree, and this leads to a discussion on emotion in general terms. Is it really likely that inanimate artifacts like Magnus can tell us anything at all about the very private sensations we call emotions?

Emotions

Were it not for emotions, the human being could be seen as a rational, always intelligent organism. Emotion is often quoted as the phenomenon which leads to irrational behaviour:

"Don't take too much notice of him — he's in love";

"She shot her husband in a blind rage, Your Honour — she is not responsible for her actions, I submit";

"Be careful how you talk to him — he's still grieving over the loss of his wife".

On the other hand, love and pleasure are desirable states which cause people to make choices that lead to as much of such emotion as possible. So emotions are clearly both positive (pleasure) and negative (fear). Whichever way, they control behaviour so as to avoid the latter and maximise the former.

In the early history of the philosophy of mind, emotions were generally accepted as the expressions of a much earlier, less conscious, existence ("pre-sapient" is the term often used). Darwin in 1872 described emotions as fundamental, inborn and functional as opposed to unwanted remnants of a previous existence. He was particularly interested in behavioural expressions and studied facial expressions as indications of emotion. His interest was so intense that his own children are said not to have escaped from his experiments.

Towards the turn of this century, William James (1884) and the Danish physician James Lange advanced the idea that emotions are neural responses to situations. This was to dominate thinking for some time. Known as the James-Lange theory, it suggests that notions that are expressed in sentences such as

"The knowledge that the ship will go down caused a sickening pain of fear in my stomach … "

come from internal responses to fearful events in the environment. The same goes for pleasurable events: "My heart beat faster at the thought of seeing her again." According to the theory we don't cry because we are sad, but the emotion of sadness is an inner sensation of the act of crying even if the outer expression is suppressed. The word "visceral" (i.e. of the internal organs of the body-the stomach, perhaps) is often used in connection with the emotional response to stimuli. Still, it would be a mistake to think that this implies that there are sensors in the stomach which respond to fear and the like. Emotional neural responses occur in the brain but could appear to the owner of that brain to be similar to sensations that are caused by inner organs.

Indeed, Colin Blakemore (1988) described interesting experiments carried out on animals and people (during necessary operations) which show that an area of the brain called the "septum", when stimulated, artificially creates emotional sensations, mainly of pleasure. At times, of course, physiological changes are caused by these neural responses. The heart could well beat faster ... Drugs such as opiates and cocaine, of course, come into the lives of humans because of their ability to induce emotions. As they alter chemically the function of the nervous system they find emotions in their lair — the brain. In terms of designing Magnus, one asks: Could they be left out?

The Emotional Robot

Returning from a conference abroad, I was surprised to read in a newspaper picked up on the aeroplane that research had revealed a "sulking baby robot". The surprise turned to stunned amazement when I discovered that the laboratory where this had happened was supposed to be my own! One of my students working on state machine models of language learning in babies had been interviewed. He was disappointed at his lack of results, as the language learning state machine was behaving in rather unproductive ways. So he described this to the reporter as "at the moment it's not doing very much — just sulking in a corner".

The point is that people are only too ready to ascribe emotional states to inanimate objects. The car that does not start is "stubborn", the boil that does not heal is "angry" and the newly decorated room is "cheerful". The reporter confused this metaphoric kind of expression with the real thing — possibly an easy thing to do if the inanimate object is a robot. But emotions in living organisms seem to have a purpose: on the whole they enhance survival even if, at times, they appear to be the cause of irrational behaviour. So studying such in the context of Magnus has the two motivations which apply to anything one does with this machine: getting a better understanding of the phenomenon and developing techniques which improve the performance of the machine. This leads to Consequence 13:

Consequence 13: Emotions

Emotion in a neural state machine is an iconic encoding of instinctive sensations. It leads to behaviour which enhances the avoidance of danger and the maintenance of survival.

So emotions could be important to Magnus as they have a preservational value. How might this process of encoding work? Suppose that a version of Magnus carries a temperature sensor in its hand. And suppose that it has to work in a steel foundry. The one thing that it cannot afford to do is to dip its metal hand into molten steel, for obvious reasons. As a designer of Magnus, I have to think about that and design a sensor which, as the temperature gets higher, will send emergency signals to the output-activating neurons which withdraw the arm. While I am at it, I can do this for many other dangers. Internal overloads may need the equivalent of stomachaches for eating to cease and I may want Magnus to avoid a downward-going precipice, so I would link the detection of visual patterns of such to some inner ("visceral") alarm bell.

On the other hand, a battery-driven Magnus needs to sense (again at some inner sensory neural level) the fact that the batteries are running down. This means that either the machine has to ask for help, or, given appropriate power sockets on the factory floor, the robot has to find one with its visual sensors, and move to it to plug itself in.[17] So, even lowly machines need instinctive sensations (of type 1, according to our earlier discussions) to ensure their survival. Humans rely heavily on evolution having done this for them. The sensations fall into two main categories: those which require the avoidance of reactions and those that lead to an approach. In general discussions these may be classified as *fears* and *pleasures*.

But what has this to do with the coding of emotion? Figure 8.5 is a sketch of what might happen. Part (a) shows the pre-wired instinctive connections which decode inputs and cause outward avoidance and approach reactions. In a more general case the input could come from internal sensors such as those which measure the state of a battery or, in living organisms, the state of digestive organs. In the state structure, this instinctive reaction is again initially shown as an appropriate avoidance reaction to fire and an approach reaction to some tasty food. But, as has been consistently seen in discussions so far, the action transfers iconically to a

---

[17] In the 1950s Grey Walter built mechanical tortoises which easily demonstrated this principle. They would be attracted to a light guiding them to the plugging-in point as their power was waning.

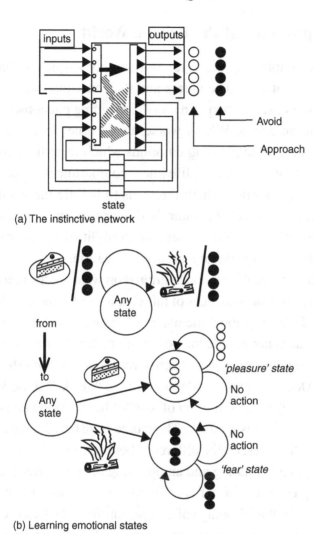

(a) The instinctive network

(b) Learning emotional states

Fig. 8.5.   Net and states for the learning of emotions.

representation in the inner neurons. So, as learning progresses, the sensation of the instinctive action is elicited in response to the external stimulus without the action necessarily being executed. In some way this could be seen as a suppressed reaction. In Magnus-like systems it could be called an "artificial" emotion.

The Importance of the Private World

The last example may serve to confirm any suspicions the reader might have that the Basic Guess and its Consequences are desperately reductionist and "explain away" intriguing phenomena such as *qualia* and emotions. What's worse, they corner love, beauty, joy, elation and all those pleasing emotions which form the basis of the pleasures of living a cultural life into a compartment of mechanistic state structure creation which threatens to belittle the whole affair. At the other extreme, the same is done to anger, aggression and depression. These could be serious disabilities which cannot be written off just as quirks of state space creation.

So it may be healthy to touch ground on what are the real implications of the two Consequences of this chapter and show that they point to a way of thinking about the nature of the inner, emotional mind in a way that does not belittle the power of emotions. The salient notion is that an internalisation of instinctive reactions has been shown to be possible. Does this explain why one should "dislike" sensations such as pain and "like" the sensation of love? What do liking and disliking actually mean in this context? The iconic transfer idea suggests that such distinctions rest on the difference between an action for a gain in something that is missing and an opposing action to avoid the harmful. Examples of the former are approach for comfort, satisfaction of hunger, love in the advantage of companionship. The latter recognises threats to existence such as the presence of an aggressive rival, or environmental characteristics such as precipices. In summary, therefore, these kinds of emotions depend on instinctive coding which, on internalisation and subsequent elaboration possibly through language, affects, sometimes powerfully, entire swathes of state space. But what of subtler emotion such as depression or elation?

Depression may be related to an emotional state of sadness. The recognition of loss, or inability to prevail over the world in successful ways, makes children cry. Internalisation and the elaboration of this as mentioned above may lead to sensations of internal sadness being associated with areas of state structure. Such sensations are not surprising: state structure is rich and complex. In some people the labelling process is appropriate, but in others it could grow in inappropriate ways. It would be appropriate for the state structure itself to contain planning options to exit from states that carry the mark of depression. But this is subtle and may not work for everyone. Chronic depression might then be understood as the absence of such planning representations. Elation is similar in principle; it implies the presence of planning representations in large areas of state space which lead to pleasure states. In chronic cases, they too may be inappropriate and lead to bizarre behaviour. One could even speculate that drugs merely free up the links between states, by introducing noise or arbitrariness into the firing of neurons.

The other side of the argument, which suggests that all this is too reductionist to be real, is that practitioners such as therapists and counsellors, in reading the above accounts, will not see that anything new is being said. Yes, the well-balanced client has planning, coping strategies, while the chronically depressed has not. Even the question of how these got there makes both me and them look into the client's past. I am armed with iconic transfers and state machines; they are armed with the common sense that emotional environments lead to the characteristics of their clients' private, inner worlds. Is it likely that knowing about iconic transfers will lead to better therapy? I very much doubt it — so why bother about Magnus?

The simple reason is that the view of the other person's inner private world of emotions, in the words of US psychologist George Mandler (1987),

"… is a topic that, more than any other, has bedevilled students
of mental life. The peculiar characteristics of emotional behaviour
and experience have been repeated stumbling blocks in the attempt
to see human nature as rational, intelligent and even sublime."

Magnus may have uninteresting and reduced internal states which could hardly aspire to the great overwhelming things we call emotions, but the principles of how they get there and influence that organism's limited inner world may link what therapists and counsellors already know to some basic principles of neural functioning. So, looking at Magnus may serve to remove some of Mandler's "stumbling blocks" which pervade our current understanding of our personal, hidden worlds. For those who experience torment in their inner worlds, this added knowledge may, some day, lead to real human benefit.

Qualia and Emotions
as Computational Processes

Computers are not Conscious

The discussion of qualia and emotions in Chapter 8 enters that realm of philosophy where certain concepts are said to be beyond the reach of science, let alone computation. Today there are still many detractors of the scientific approach to experienced mental events, and this is good ground for interesting debates. This topic has been explored in Chapter 8 of *Aristotle's Laptop*.[a] In one such debate, organised in London by the Philosophy For All association, I was an opponent to Raymond Tallis who is an eminent geriatrician, albeit one with a tremendous reputation for writing philosophical material. The proposition that he fielded was "Computer Models of the Mind are Invalid".[b] It turned out that the difficulty was a definition for 'computer'. Tallis focused on attacking the idea that mind is to brain

---

[a] Aleksander, I and Morton, H. B. (2012). *Aristotle's Laptop: The Discovery of our Informational Minds*, World Scientific, Singapore.

[b] Tallis, R. and Aleksander, I. (2008). Computational theories of the mind are invalid, *Journal of Information Technology*. 23, pp. 55–62.

as software is to hardware. Of course, as strongly indicated throughout this book very few scientists believe in this relation. The better relation is that mind is to brain as state structure is to the physical structure of a neural automaton. And this is very different from the software/hardware model as state structure arises from physical structure and its iconic experience as 'mind' arises from the brain and life experience. To date, I have not seen the iconic neural automaton approach to the mind proven invalid. It is often criticised for not being a complete theory, but this does not invalidate it.

Qualia

While Tallis speaks of qualia as unclassified experiences that cannot be analysed, Pennti Haikonen — a pragmatic Finnish communications engineer — takes an unabashed view of qualia.[c] He rejects the philosophical stance of those who argue that certain perceptual experiences simply do not have physical correlates (for example, Frank Jackson's philosophical position[d]) and argues that world processes such as colour (electromagnetic frequency) or sounds (pressure wave frequencies) have a direct effect on the brain. Despite this, due to action such as in our Axiom 1 of WMMW, such effects are not felt as little events inside our heads, but are projected by the brain to be 'out there'. Haikonen stresses that whenever one is talking about the mechanisms of consciousness, one is inevitably talking about the mechanisms of qualia and vice-versa.

In work on Information Integration Theory, (see postscript for Chapter 2) Tononi and Balduzzi[e] have argued that qualia are

---

[c] Haikonen, P. O. (2012). *Consciousness and Robot Sentence*, World Scientific, Singapore.

[d] Jackson, F. (1982). Epiphenomenal Qualia, *Philosophical Quarterly*, 32, pp. 127–136.

[e] Balduzzi, D. and Tononi, G. (2009). Qualia: The Geometry of Integrated Information, *PLoS Computational Biology*, 5(8), pp. 1–224.

captured by a representation of the evolution of informational transactions between complexes of neurons. We have argued against this because it does not address the phenomenal character of qualia nor does it indicate how the memory (i.e. the imagination of) such qualia may be created. We have approached these issues in chapters 6 and 7 of *Aristotle's Laptop* (footnote (a)). In essence, we argue that the world-referenced representations we have called 'depictive' in WMMW[f] go some way towards lessening the mystical aura sometimes cast around qualia.

Emotion

In the 2003 'axiomatic' approach to the mechanisms of consciousness,[g] through axiom 5, we expressed the notion that emotions have an essential role to play in a study of consciousness. We expressed this as the need for an evaluation mechanism within the neural automaton that resolves non-deterministic transitions to possible action states. That is, situations where the stored experience leads to "I could do this or I could do that" require an evaluation that resolves the impasse. This is an emotion. Rabinder Lee carried out several experiments using the Neural Representation Modeller[h] to show that a Kernel architecture that implements our axioms as described in Chapter 6 of WMMW, (footnote *f*) can indeed use acquired emotional states to help with decision-making in a simple virtual robot that has food-like needs. This confirms the function of some of the

---

[f]Aleksander, I. (2005). *The World in My Mind, My Mind in the World: Key mechanisms of consciousness in people, animals and machines*, Imprint Academic, Exeter.

[g]Aleksander, I. and Dunmall, B. (2003). Axioms and Tests for the Presence of Minimal Consciousness in Agents, *Journal of Consciousness Studies*, 10(4–5), pp. 7–18.

[h]Lee, R. (2008). Aspects of affective action choice: computational modelling, PhD thesis, Imperial College London.

structures such as in Fig. 8.5 (first published in the previous edition of *Impossible Minds*) which, at the time of publication, had yet to be tried.

In Sum

In the first edition, I had the impression and created the impression that the topics in Chapter 8 fell into some kind 'taboo' class. Indeed engineers and computer scientists were seen as 'meddling' in issues that only some neuroscientists and some philosophers had the license to address. This is no longer so.In addition to the work mentioned above, *affective* computing and qualia find frequent discussions in computational intelligence literature.

Red had moved again. For some reason, the police had been inquiring about him at his last hiding place. Luckily he had been out at the time, but the signals were clear: he was not safe.

Sir Global's personal vendetta was mounting in fury. His television appearances increased and he missed no opportunity of lecturing on the dangers of what he called "woolly sentimentalism" which would destroy the nation's confidence in being a rational people whose actions were entirely guided by formal logic. He made frequent references to the subversive work of Professor Naskela. So, helped by Molécula, Red found an ancient cottage close to the cliffs by the sea. The owner was a farmer who lived in the village nearby and Red said that he was a retired sea captain who had lived abroad for many years and therefore had no previous registered abode.

Now Red's concern was mounting. He had not seen Molecula for a month. She had missed the last meeting they had arranged and had not been in touch. Winter had set in; it was freezing and the snow had made transport difficult. Any knock on the door set Red's heart racing: it could have been the police, it could have been Molécula; most times it was just a neighbour, curious about who was lighting the log fires in a cottage that had been abandoned for such a long time. This time it was Molecula.

She was in a terrible state, wet, cold and exceedingly pale. All she managed to say was "I've been fired".

"Don't talk now," said Red. "Sit by the fire and get warm."

Later, when she had stopped shivering and had drunk a mug of warm milk, which she now much preferred to oil, she said, "It's Asic. He has been spying on me all this time. It was he who discovered your last address and he has been reporting to Sir Global on a regular basis. I was fired for disloyal activities."

Then, with venom in her voice she whispered, "It only took this long because they thought that they could find you through me."

She then explained that she had gone to the other side of the country, checked into a hotel and just had not gone back one evening. She had moved with rush-hour crowds and spent the last night walking through the frozen country lanes to get to the cottage.

"There is something we both need to say" said Red, looking at her piercingly ... "I love you."

Looking cold and frightened, Molecula said, "I love you , too ... and I am no longer confused about what it means."

Chapter 9

What's the Use of Artificial Minds?

The Human as God

Very often, when a prospective research student comes into my laboratory and I ask why he or she should wish to spend the next three years battling with object-oriented programming (which is the way Magnus is programmed), some hard mathematics and a vast amount of reading, the answer is a confident "I want to make a machine which can think". It takes much time and persuasion to express that this is not on offer. What is, instead, is the making of machines which tell us something about what thinking might be. The student feels slightly let down. Indeed, at this point I feel that I may be letting the reader of this book down. Having talked of the Basic Guess and its Consequences, will I now put it all together and say, "*Voilà* — the conscious machine"? I shall not do that. I believe that it is neither doable at the moment nor on the agenda. But what is the agenda?

The desire of man to play God and create living creatures is deeply ingrained in human nature. It pervades literature and leads to much confusion in science. It brings the charlatan into science and makes the scientist appear to be a charlatan. I have purposely created Magnus both as a foil for debate and as a complex piece of computer software which leads to a heap of hypotheses. These are the Basic Guess and the ensuing Consequences. The list of Consequences has come to an end as far as this book is concerned. But this list is not complete.

All I have done is to argue that phenomena which are discussed in connection with consciousness can be discussed in terms of the neural state machines of the Basic Guess. In the next chapter I shall try to second-guess how far this kind of technology might have gone in forty years' time. Here I want to get closer to the desire of humans wanting to be their own creators. It's an old joke to say that there is no point in making artificial creatures when making real ones is relatively easy. But where is the distinction between the motivation of the science fiction writer on the one hand and the artificial intelligence specialist (or, indeed, the neural system engineer) on the other? How much does formality and rigour add to everybody's understanding of consciousness? Do you have to be a mathematician and a computer scientist to understand your own consciousness? Is any such approach destructively reductionist as a matter of course? Are some scientific discussions more appropriate than others? These are the questions which I shall try to tackle in this chapter in order to make the reason for considering artificial minds at all perhaps a little clearer than it may have been so far.

But, to start, it seems important to look at some deep notions which have become deeply implanted in Western culture and which can be understood from the history and the fiction of seemingly intelligent machines.

The Historical Robot

Were intelligent robots easy to make, on the whole they would be made for one main reason: to provide mankind with helpers who would neither have the failings of people nor make the demands that people make. They would need to have inherited the dexterities that people have in order to do the work. Indeed, the word "robot" comes from the Slavic *rabot,* meaning "work" and also possibly from the Gothic words *arbi* ("inheritance") or *arbaiths* ("toil"). Whether they need to be conscious or not is not absolutely clear. However, if consciousness is that which enables the robot to understand the needs and instructions of human masters, then the ultimate robot must be conscious. Robots must not be demanding, however, and the immediate assumption is that they will *not* have the same rights as natural creatures. The desire to make robots is unashamedly akin to the desire to have uncomplaining slaves.

In 1966, John Cohen, a psychologist at the University of Manchester, wrote a comprehensive account of the history of human-like robots, and this is recommended to those who would like to read more than my brief notes on the subject. Cohen painted a fascinating picture of a humanoid statue of Memnon found in ancient Egypt. This was sensitive to the rays of the sun so that it emitted sounds (due to the escape of air) and was so lifelike as to be assumed by some to be worthy of worship. This points to another way in which humans have thought of robots: embodiments of deities, oracles and objects of worship. The distinctive feature of such objects is that while the material statue may have been made through human effort, it had acquired super-statuesque qualities through the intervention of deities.

This attribution of superhuman qualities to seemingly intelligent manufactured objects still finds its way into the opinions of some commentators. I am conscious of the many attempts by television producers to present Magnus as a machine which might introduce fears into the mind of the viewer. The interviewer is more likely to ask, "Is there not a danger that this machine will get so good that it will begin to take over?", rather than asking more appropriate questions about what the machine tells us about the mechanisms of mind.

Probably the first builder of robots was Daedalus. An architect living on the island of Crete during the reign of Minos (*c.* 1500 BC), he achieved fame though the building of mobile statues and ingenious mechanisms. His name was really Metionidae, but became Daedalus, from the word *daedala,* meaning "statues". His name entered legend from the famous mythical tale of his having equipped himself and his son Icarus with wings to escape imprisonment in Crete. Most will know that this mythical first flight ended in disaster for Icarus as the wax which held the feathers melted in the sun, causing the lad to plummet to earth and be killed. Cohen suggested that this myth hides the more practical invention of sails which gave Daedalus an advantage over rowing boats in his flight from Crete and the tyrant Minos. Icarus had his own boat, but met his death by drowning as this boat overturned. Nonetheless, Daedalus' skill and fame as a sculptor of near-live statues translated his reputation from life to myth as it also transformed the real sail into a mythical, living wing.

So from records of old one finds that the living human being attributes mythical prowess to manufactured likenesses of himself which are able to move or emit sounds. Priests of antiquity made good use of tricks which would now be described as ventriloquism. This endowed the robot with greater authority than that of the mortal priests themselves. Immortality has much to do with it — granite doppelgängers of the gods have no need to die. They are immortal by human standards (think of the sphinxes of Egypt), so the slightest suggestion that they may be able to speak, and hence think, makes them more powerful than humans. I say all this as awe easily turns to fear and the need to banish this fear leads to a desire to unmask the statue and show that a mere mortal is puling the strings. This may be an element in the modem contempt which is sometimes expressed for machines that are designed to study thinking and intelligence. They are written off as mere *daedala,* statues which are worked by the ventriloquism of their designers.

Another ancient human motive for designing intelligent machines is to show that logic and intelligence have a meaning which is independent of human thought. Roots of this can be found in the Middle Ages. Martin Gardner (1958) wrote of *Ars Magna,* a machine designed by the Spanish mystic Ramon Lull (1234–1315), who was also known as Doctor Illuminatus. This consisted of con-centrically arranged wheels, on the periphery of which were written words. This was done so that if a fact such as "wealth causes obesity" was arranged across one part of the wheels, another part revealed "fire causes burns". Many other truths were so revealed without the intervention of human thought. Cohen commented that this was done "to liberate philosophy from the stranglehold of theology". Others have linked the method used in *Ars Magna* to the future-predicting character of the *Tarot* as both schemes are based on the limited number of interpretations that one can give to a sequence of "event" cards. So mysticism and logical machines forged a link in the Middle Ages which could be less than helpful in a modern context.

In modern artificial intelligence there is motivation to examine the nature of logic, hopefully without the mysticism. The subject of logic programming (see Kowalski, 1979) puts logic beyond the foot-ing of symbols written on a piece of paper. The truths can now be entered on the concentric wheels of a modern digital computer which gives them a functionality which is actually useful. The slave can be relied on to provide logical answers to questions even beyond the ability of people. To me this says much about the nature of logic, but little about the mechanisms which enable people to be logical. Indeed, the fact that people sometimes choose not to be logical but use intuition and arbitrary exploration instead, is probably just as interesting as the ability to be logical. However, as mentioned in Chapter 1, the more general attacks on the use of the computer in modelling human intelligence are similar to the objection one might have to *Ars Magna* — its prowess is the prowess of the designer. Also, some of the mysticism of Ramon Lull attaches to the computer scientist. If the scientist pretends to be God, popular wisdom requires that he be unmasked.

Another historical strand of creating living organisms in ways other than sexual reproduction is the possibility of so doing not with the stone of statuists or with the mechanics of logical machines, but in something that is like flesh and blood. This is the ultimate act of playing God; after all, God created Adam and Eve from inanimate material. History is strewn with beliefs of mystical figures who were thought to be capable of powerful incantations which breathed life into inanimate shapes. One of the best-known is the *Golem* found in Talmudic tradition, the word meaning something unfinished, such as unbaked bread. In this tradition, Adam was indeed a Golem made of the dust of all the parts of the earth, to whom, in the fourth hour, God imparted a soul. All this works against the engineer (like myself) who is trying to understand the mechanisms of consciousness from the process of asking, "What are the essential ingredients of living organisms, which could be said to be conscious, and how could these be studied through the use of machines?" In a television interview in 1994, biologist and memory expert Steven Rose said that he saw no point in this activity, calling it "chasing the Golem of artificial intelligence".

So the point I have tried to make in this section is that stories of people who attempted to make living objects out of inanimate material pervade recorded history. On the whole such people are cheats, liars or just self-deluded. It is difficult to work against this cultural mindset, even if the objective is to throw light on the wonders of living creatures by studying the properties of the artificial ones. The last case of attitudes to a Golem leads to another interesting cultural force which influences people's views on artificial consciousness — literature.

The Robot as a Literary Object

The making of an object such as Magnus puts the engineer or scientist squarely into the role of the Golem-maker. I feel that it is worth accepting this criticism and looking more closely at the differences in motivation between the robot-maker in literature and the real aims of the neural system designer. Reference to the Golem brings directly to mind the influential novel written by Gustav Meyrink in 1915: *Der Golem*. This relates the story of a lifelike robot made of clay which wandered the streets of seventeenth century Prague. The robot was created through the power of rabbinical incantation and, as Cohen pointed out, there is in this story a strong element of "out-of-body" projection. That is, some of those who meet the Golem feel that they are meeting their own souls situated outside their own bodies. This too turns out to be a problem for the designer of Magnus-like machines.

Ultimately, stretched out on the psychiatrist's couch, would I not confess to building this device as my own *doppelgänger* — an immortal version of my own thoughts? I think that the psychiatrist might end up being disappointed. The whole point about Magnus is that it is an artefact which resembles me only in the most distant and insignificant way. Its great significance it that it provides a workbench on which to test ideas — the ideas that form the substance of this book. My somewhat arrogant hope is that the ideas themselves have a lasting value and that Magnus merely survives at the level of an electronic test-tube in which the embodiment and correctness of these ideas might be demonstrated or shown to be false.

The myth of the Golem is also likely to have influenced Mary Shelley in the writing of the celebrated novel *Frankenstein*. In the Golem the soul was infused into the kneaded clay by rabbinical incantation, whereas Shelley used the scientific knowledge of the day (the early nineteenth century) that live organisms had chemical and electrical properties which were necessary to the essence of life itself. So, in her novel, the key ingredient which brought to life the collection of sewn-together dead body parts was the energy collected from lightning strikes. This may be lurking behind the criticism of work with neural systems, that such engineering merely falls into the same trap as Mary Shelley: having neural systems and their electrical properties misses the ingredients which endow a human being with life — biological reproduction and the wonders of cell growth.

Again this criticism misses the point that the living mechanism need not be investigated in its original material in order for it to be understood. I risk repeating myself and boring the reader by recalling that the presence of the "neural" in the Basic Guess is not because this brings the discussion close to flesh and blood, but because the class of conscious systems, whether real or artificial, has in common the properties of learning cellular mechanisms, whether these be real or artificial. In fact the neurons used for the explanations in this book are materially about as far from their living counterparts as the *daedala* of antiquity are from living beings. But the fact that in networks they exhibit properties which are remarkably like those which are often regarded as being the elements of consciousness is what makes me sit up and take notice

The Robot as Master of the Human Race

Another mild battle I have had to wage with television producers is that they sometimes don't ask *whether* Magnus holds threats of displacing the human being and creating universal unemployment, but, rather, they ask *when* it will happen. It is purely a matter of time and technological advance, they argue, before the human being becomes totally redundant. I shall try to handle this question at the end of this section, but for the time being it may be important to look at why the idea of the robot which takes over from mankind has taken hold. It seems to me to be due to a mixture of literary influence and observed reality.

Probably the literary event of the greatest influence in the early 1920s was Karel Capek's stage play *RUR* (Rossum's Universal Robots). Besides giving the word "robot" to the world, *RUR* is a tale of robots built to improve the industrial production of the world. In "sorcerer's apprentice" style they become more and more skilled and increasingly desirable as workers. So scientists in Rossum's factory thrive on manufacturing the robots with increasing efficiency. However, the robots, having developed their own sense of consciousness, also develop ambitions to increase their own power. Their hidden quest is to become the dominant force on earth, so they revolt and begin killing their users and their builders. However, there is one snag: they actually don't know how they themselves work, so they don't know how to increase their number. And then, they also don't know how to maintain themselves, so they "die" in large numbers. Sadly, Alquist, the last human being, has lost the secret of making robots as well.

After a failed attempt to dissect Primus and Helena, a robot "couple", to discover how they work, Alquist realises that the world is not lost. It was "love" for each other which prevented Primus and Helena from allowing Alquist to dissect them, and the play ends with a fading Alquist calling Primus and Helena "Adam and Eve" and bidding them to go forth and populate the earth. This is remarkably powerful imagery: only when the android becomes almost human can it survive. And it is human greed for the production of subservient slaves which drives people to the technology that eventually produces the rebellious android. Half-baked attempts at creating artefacts with human proclivities will rebound on the creator. A conscious Magnus will surely develop its own agenda, which may or may not include a future for its creators. What's the point of giving it a mind of its own?

An aspect of consciousness which is wonderfully human is that of jumping to conclusions. One such is that all artificially intelligent entities have the same character: if they have a likeness to humans they will aspire to become evil. Why not believe that aspiring to evil is an irreproducible aspect of *human* consciousness? As one of the designers of Magnus, I see about as much similarity between it and one of Rossum's robots as there is between a weather-forecasting program and the weather it forecasts. Magnus has been built to force its designers to be explicit about what constitutes artificial consciousness. By recognising the difference between the artificial and the real, like using the weather-forecasting program, working with Magnus leads to predictions about real consciousness and hopefully clears up some confusions. The likelihood of Magnus inconveniencing anyone is about the same as that of a forecast of rain on television leading to puddles under the television set.

"But you are naïve," I hear the prophets of doom saying; "the technology that goes into Magnus is just what the Rossums of this world are looking for. They will exploit it under the heading of *wealth creation* and make slaves who will eventually insist on their rights." Actually I sympathise with an element of this point of view. If I need funding for Magnus I need to show its relevance to things like *wealth creation* and the *competitive position* of the country. But this pressure needs to be ignored. Our future well-being must depend on a better understanding of what makes people into people and machines into machines. I am delighted to contribute to that clarification and possibly improve the friendliness of machines which humans might some day use. For example, Magnus-like artificial consciousness might make telephone systems easier to use through the introduction of helpful artificial operators. But Rossum will have to wait.

Unfortunately, threats to the human desire to do useful work come from other, much more accessible technologies. Undoubtedly the advance of automation puts people out of work. While no political party would wish to see "greed" as a feature of its manifesto, an alien from another planet might find it difficult to understand the distinction between the words *greed* and *wealth creation.* However, as an incurable optimist, I believe that given the political will, the technology which is developed by studying Magnus might actually bring those without work back into the fold by making the means of productive work more accessible through being easier to understand and use. Perhaps this might create an increase in *well-being* for many rather than *wealth* for the few Rossums of this world.

Sci-Fi Robots

Science fiction is, of course, a culture within which conscious robots are entirely at home. The need to make the scenarios interesting and worth reading causes authors to take seriously the possibility of conscious robots and the way in which they might interact with people. At one extreme, films such as the Terminator series give producer James Cameron and muscular actor Arnold Schwarzenegger the opportunity to portray the potential destructiveness of a robot armed with a motive. Coming back from a future dominated by machines, the Terminator has the motive for killing the woman who will give birth to a great machine-destroying free-dom fighter of the future. Given this single-minded motive, nothing stands in his way: he unleashes unimaginable violence on anyone who attempts to stop him.

The serious moral of this story is one which Norbert Wiener[18] made elegantly in his book *God and Golem Incorporated* (1964). The point is about the inflexibility of machines. Wiener put it as giv-ing an admiral the order to obtain victory at any price, causing the eventual destruction of that admiral's own troops when the enemy turns out to be overpowering. Machines given an unachievable aim could bring about not only their own destruction but also that of all which surrounds them. This led Isaac Asimov — who, tongue firmly in cheek, described himself as the world's greatest science fiction writer — to invent three fundamental law for robot-makers:

1. *A robot may not injure a human being or, through inaction, allow a human being to come to harm.*
2. *A robot must obey orders given it by human beings except where such orders would conflict with the First Law.*
3. *A robot must protect its own existence as long as such protec-tion does not conflict with the First or the Second Law.*

These laws make for a good bunch of stories based on the con-flicts that can arise from the laws themselves. The relationship of people to robots is the stuff that animates these stories: the little girl who pays more attention to the domestic robot than her parents in *Robbie* and the woman who falls in love with a robot which responds positively according to the Second Law without realising that it is injuring its human friend through deception. The robot says it loves to please his human owner, but cannot love ...

---

[18] The father of *cybernetics*, a science of communication and control in humans and machines, popular in the 1950s and 1960s.

Again, these ideas impinge on the way in which working with Magnus is perceived outside my own laboratory. In 1994 I took part in the making of a TV programme for *The Late Show,* an arts discussion programme on BBC2. Magnus was presented as a resolute attempt to revive the man–machine myth, it having died with the failures of rule-based artificial intelligence. I was arguing (as I have done in this book) that working with neural nets leads to a *framework* within which human minds and artificial machines can be examined to see if there are any common principles. As mentioned earlier, biologist Steven Rose said that he could not see the point of doing that: the "Golem of artificial intelligence" being a distraction from the interest which scientists should show in people.[19] Danah Zohar, a "science sociologist", came to my rescue by arguing that laboratory work with artificial systems does not detract from the sense of wonder we have for human life and may, indeed, enhance it. But the writer and presenter of the piece, philosopher Ray Monk, chose to end by asking the question "How should we relate to conscious machines, and what rights should we give them?" The spirit of the Terminator may not have been far from his mind.

A strong element of much science fiction is an attempt to predict the future. In Stanley Kubrick's film *2001* (based on Arthur C. Clarke's sci-fi novel *The Sentinel* — written in the 1950s) the main character, a computer called HAL,[20] was indeed a neural net imbued with a vast amount of knowledge and experience. The point was not missed by Brian Morris, in his book *The World of Robots* (1985):

> "The computer HAL derived its intelligence from a multiplicity of its neural links, and the diversity of its experiences both physical

---

[19] We have got to know each other better since that time and have agreed that we are on the same side.

[20] Many have spotted that adding one to each letter yields "IBM".

and linguistic. This is an uncanny preview ... of the work of the artificial intelligence researchers of the 1980s — in particular the WISARD project."

The WISARD was built in my laboratory and was a forerunner of Magnus: a pattern recognition net with no feedback and hence no state structure. So while the technical prediction was accurate (a feather in the cap of Arthur C. Clarke, who must have realized that the only way for a system to develop a representation of reality was through a learning neural net), the story takes the road anticipated by Norbert Wiener (as mentioned above). The space mission was the ultimate target; HAL began to recognize the human failures of the astronauts and worked out that they had to be eliminated in order for the mission to succeed. This was wonderful dramatic stuff, but in people's minds it linked neural nets with machines which could take over from mankind — this is not helpful when one is trying to discuss the real reasons for using neural models, i.e. their ability to explain human behaviour rather than threaten it.

The Human Machine

While one is looking at the creeping effect of tradition and prejudice on the discussions about consciousness, the other side of the threat of the Golem, the humanoid machine, is the seeming putdown of treating the human as a "mere" machine — the human machine. I started writing about the analysis of human characteristics using principles learned from the design of machines many years ago and chose the title *The Human Machine* for my first book in this area (1978). This was based on a very early glimpse of the ideas presented in the earlier chapters of *Impossible Minds*. The choice of title at that time was, I thought, provocative enough to attract both supportive and antagonistic readers and convert them to the idea that automata theory was a good analytical tool and not a putdown. To my surprise (possibly disappointment) there was no controversy. Those who were already happy to analyse human beings as if they were machines said a few sympathetic things about the value of the techniques of state representation I was using. Others expressed not disagreement but a weary attitude to having to learn something new (automata theory) when they were getting on just fine with their knowledge of psychology, biology or neurophysiology in the analysis of humans.

In other words, for many who study humans, the revelation that a human is a machine comes as no great surprise. They would dearly like to understand this machine, but with their own skills of analysis. So the problem for me is not that the human needs to be analysed, but that analysts should choose their methods with care, and may need to be convinced that methods which apply to computers (such as automata theory) lead to an understanding which other methods don't provide. But, putting the technical experts aside, what about the average human being, who does not concern himself with research into consciousness? Is he happy with the notion of a human machine?

I confess that one of my hobbies is to spend hours browsing among the shelves of second-hand and antique book-dealers. Imagine my surprise when one Saturday morning I discovered that an author by the name of J. F. Nisbet had used the title *The Human Machine* for a book written in 1899. The surprise was repeated a few Saturdays later when I found another with the same title, this time written by E. R. Thomson in 1925. I now believe that there must be hundreds of books with the same title and I look forward to discovering them. The books differ a great deal in what they contain. Nisbet presents a series of essays on what people are like, what they care about and how they go about leading their lives. He comes to the conclusion that the workings of the brain and other organs are all there is, which makes people do what they do. He calls this the "vital" principle, and to my astonishment[21] I found that he had written:

> "In the discussion of mind, the vital principle *has to be accepted as a postulate;* but upon that basis a philosophy of a far more comprehensive character can now be built than was possible to the greatest intellects of the past..." (italics mine).

Nisbet has an unrestrained contempt for the opposition to the idea of a human machine which may come from theology. He sees Christian beliefs as belittling the nature of God:

> "... the proportions of the Creator are reduced (by current theology) to those of an Exeter Hall philanthropist. How much vaster and nobler is the materialistic conception"

Nowadays, I think that it is possible to have rational materialistic views on human beings without feeling that these clash with beliefs about God and His creations. Nevertheless the feeling that one offends the Almighty by talking about humans as machines may lurk in the less rational subconscious of many.

Thomson's book is completely different. He argues that as the human is a machine, it needs a well-defined programme of maintenance. It contains eighty suggestions, such as "How to Concentrate" (e.g. "make your work interesting" and "avoid making a success of work that fails to arouse your interest"). But some of the conventional folklore about the freedom of will of the human being, distinguishing it from any machine, pervades this otherwise materialistic book. It is therefore likely that the suggestion that free will is

---

[21] I found Nisbet's book long after I felt that the ideas in *The Impossible Mind of Magnus* should be based on an explicitly stated postulate: the Basic Guess.

a phenomenon which benefits from an analysis as suggested in earlier chapters of this book would be met with some skepticism.

So, the confusion and prejudice surrounding the phrase "the human machine" depends on the interpretation one puts on the word "machine". Clearly, a machine is something manufactured by a human, and to that extent a human cannot be a machine. But people who make machines develop skills which enable them to understand complex mechanisms in nature. In that dimension, the human being possesses prodigiously complex mechanisms which machine-makers can attempt to understand. Pretending then that such mechanisms are imbued with some mysterious flux which distinguishes them from "mere" machines will simply delay the understanding which proper analysis can bring.

The Influence of the Computer Scientist

Two major events in 1950 launched the popular discussion about whether computers can think. The paper by British mathematician Alan Turing, "Computing Machinery and Intelligence", was one of these events, and Shannon's paper "Programming a Computer for Playing Chess" was the other. This was the birth of what is known as artificial intelligence, which is the process of writing programs to make computers do things which, if done by humans, would be said to require intelligence.

There is no doubt that this has led to some technological advances which have brought the digital computer out of the realm of number-crunching and into the domain of being able to take logical decisions. Buying a chess machine in the local toy store — indeed, one that can easily beat mediocre players like me but has a little less luck against chess masters — is a product of this technology. Other products are programs that go under the heading of "expert systems". These act as repositories of knowledge on how to do things (repair a car or configure a complex computer system). It is not my intention here to develop a tutorial on artificial intelligence (AI). The keen reader can refer to: Aleksander and Morton (1993), Chapter 3. Here we look briefly at some claims that such programs are the mind of a computer with a hardware body.

Sloman's design space

Aaron Sloman is a British contributor to AI: a philosopher who has made a significant contribution to both the practice and the evaluation of computer science. His view is that while AI, as a subtask, contributes to the definition of a kind of machine-based mind, there are many other minds which need to be considered, including human minds and animal minds (Sloman, 1978, 1994). He sees the task of explanation as an interdisciplinary affair of great complexity.

About consciousness he argues (Sloman, 1994):

> "... our muddled ideas about 'consciousness', including the prejudice that 'conscious states' are intrinsically different from others, may prove merely to rest on a distinction between states that are and others that are not accessible by certain high-level self-monitoring processes (Sloman 1978, ch. 10). Some states and processes that are inaccessible to consciousness may be exactly like accessible ones, and the boundary can change through training."

His main argument is to map neural approaches and the logic of AI as small subregions in a large "design space" of information-processing architectures. He also thinks that a current commitment to any such regions is premature.

But, of course, as seen in the earlier chapters of this book, some architectures such as the neural state machine are very general, so that in Sloman's "design space" they are not necessarily small subregions but vast chunks of the space itself. In neural systems, architectures emerge, but they are helped by a bit of pre-design. Getting this balance right is a hot research topic.

On consciousness, however, the distinction between conscious and unconscious state variables and the states generated by these variables is precisely the clarification which the neural state machine methodology provides. I refer to Consequences 2 and 3 in Chapter 4 of this book, where conscious states are those that arise as a result of iconic transfer and unconscious ones are not. The two are, as Sloman has suggested, very similar in kind but different in origin. Also, auxiliary state variables, not being iconic, are unlikely ever to contribute to conscious experience but can divert the course of a conscious, iconic state trajectory.

A commitment to AI is not premature but incomplete. A commitment to neural state machines is not premature but needs to be made less general. The latter chapters of this book have attempted to create a bridge between the two through the description of state machines which show that a neural system, exposed to a physical world and natural language, can specialise to behave very much like a logical AI system. The improvement on classical AI is that a precise programmer-based design of the system has been avoided: learning and generalisation have done the trick. This may not lead to systems with superb performance, but does hint at an answer to the question "Where does symbolic thinking come from in an unprogrammed system?". The good engineer is not a myopic adherent to a corner of "design space"; he will be aware of the way designs of systems which absorb experience span across this space.

A difficulty with a philosophy which contains the idea that "consciousness" is a muddled concept, is that it could be self-fulfilling. It might reject clarifying arguments precisely for being too focused and therefore not applicable to a muddled concept, keeping the concept forever muddled.

Bundy's meta-level reasoning

Alan Bundy is also one of the leading contributors to AI in the United Kingdom. Working from Edinburgh University, he is known for his work in mathematical theorem proving. In 1984 he published a paper called "Meta-Level Inference and Consciousness", which is an interesting comment on the way AI work impacts on the debate about consciousness. Theorem proving is a study of the way rules can be chosen which manipulate one side of a mathematical equation to show that it is equal to the other. As the rules which can be applied at any one time can be very large, an exhaustive process of searching becomes prohibitively time-wasting. Meta-level reasoning is a formal method for reducing the size of this searching task. Bundy points out that at many stages in a theorem-proving procedure there may well be many rules which could be applied; some of these would just look silly to a mathematician.

Meta-level inference attempts to formalise this higher level of consideration, to capture in a sense the mathematician's conscious appeal to his experience of the rules which are likely to be successful. Bundy comes to the following interesting conclusion: self-awareness is not the same as consciousness. He reaches this conclusion by noting that the meta-level rules required by the AI program are not available to the mathematician by introspection; they are generated by a process of program design which involves the rationalisation of a trial-and-error process. So he defines self-awareness as having a knowledge of one's own abilities which, perhaps indirectly, helps with the discovery of formal meta-level rules.

This makes an interesting contrast to the discussion on "self" in Chapter 4 of this book. I would certainly agree that self-awareness and consciousness are not the same thing. But Consequence 6 suggests that self-awareness is a product of the iconic transfer which defines consciousness; so it is an integral part of what one loosely calls "consciousness". Consciousness without self-awareness would be a strange thing. However, this helps me to make an observation about the entire enterprise of rule-based AI. One of the salient achievements of this science is to be able to operate in areas of knowledge which are at the advanced end of human endeavour: the ability to use mathematics is a case in point. Not many ordinary mortals prove mathematical theorems as a part of their daily lives. Also, it's a long way from our Consequence 6 — which shows how a robot may "realise" that if it moves a limb in a particular way it could grasp a desired object — to the subtleties of proving theorems. However, the healthy aspect of these two approaches is that they form a pincer movement on definitions of consciousness: one is AI from the end which requires a programmer's analysis of a complex issue; the other, which is more "visceral" and investigates how a living organism can build up its representation of a complex world, might at some point in the future lead to models of the way people do mathematics. The interesting character of this form of progress is that it makes unnecessary Penrose's appeal to a separate level of "understanding", one that cannot be captured by computation.

AI and Magnus

The lesson learned from those who stand back and assess the contribution of computation to the modelling of mind, is that computation is a discipline which does well with the formal and the rigorous. When it comes to the informal and the speculative, the human mind still stands out as a stubborn challenge. However, the mind of Magnus, as it currently stands, seems good at absorbing immediate knowledge of its sensory world but poor at the formal and the rigorous. So what use is either of these in isolation? The temptation is for some to say, well, in a truly intelligent robot you need both. I am not so sure. For me the use of Magnus is that it points to the solution of one of the major puzzles about intelligence.

How does the living brain go from being a squishy but adaptive substance to being the engine that does mathematics and thinks about the great verities of the world? So the use of the mind of Magnus is not so much to make splendid robots which might actually work better if equipped with a smart bit of AI, but to explain how living organisms get on without the help of an Almighty Programmer.

Autonomous Agents and the Intelligence of an Ant

In the 1970s, one of the ideas that could be found in most laboratories of AI was that the advancing power of computer logic, the advancing confidence of programmers and the advancing availability of funding should be channelled into the design of mechanical robots with computer brains. These brains would be an embodiment of the most advanced AI programs of the moment. At Stanford there was a machine called Shakey which used a planning system called STRIPS (Fikes and Nilsson, 1992) and which embodied some of the AI ideas of solving visual problems in finding its way around a room.

At MIT there was SHRDLU, which, while never quite making it as a physical robot, was an excellent "environment" for Pat Winston (1975) to develop his ideas about representing the world as a "semantic network" ("mammal" and "cat" might be nodes with "is a" a line linking the two) which could be stored in a robot brain. Terry Winograd (1972) used the SHRDLU notion to provide some answers to language understanding by conversing with the robot about a very simple world made up of toy mocks. Predictions about making intelligent robots for factories and vehicles which would autonomously find their way about their worlds were issued by the administrators of the AI programmes with monotonous regularity.

But, at the time of writing, that was well over twenty years ago. Where are the intelligent robots, the products of the AI era? Factories seem to thrive on using robots which combine muscle and precision, but have a minimum of brain. The autonomous vehicle still has difficulties in distinguishing between a door in its path that could be opened and a refrigerator which may have to be avoided. There seems to have been something wrong with the aspirations of the founders of the AI paradigm.

Brady's sensory concerns

Michael Brady has made major contributions both at MIT and at the University of Oxford in the design of robots which make use some of the products of AI. He has paid particular attention to the proper decoding of the sensory information that the robot needs for its representation of the world in which it is supposed to operate. In a recent survey of this work (Brady and Huosheng, 1994) Brady argues that in considering the mind of a robot, and indeed any other mind, the important factors are reactivity and planning, distributed processing, dealing with uncertainty, purposive behaviour and the emergent properties of interacting processes.

Planning in robots can take different forms: it can be very general, such as working out which is the least-cost way of getting from one place to another. Here the means–ends analysis used in early AI comes into focus. Other planning has more of a local flavour — is there a path which avoids collisions which can be worked out before setting off? Then, once having set off, excellent recognition of sensory patterns is required so that the robot can link this to making local modifications to its plans as new developments in its environment take place. This may have to include a good knowledge of the way the robot reacts to rapid movements. For example, it should not fall over if going round a comer a bit fast.

The amount of work that this computational brain of a robot has to do is tremendous and it needs to calculate several things at once. So it has to be distributed among many computers, each of which not only has a special duty, but is also partly aware of what the others are doing and can adjust its own task accordingly. This distributed approach is now not only being pursued in robotics but, under the heading of "intelligent autonomous agents", it is seen as a good recipe for doing AI in general.

Dealing with uncertainty means that the robot design engineer has to handle a variety of techniques including logic which is capable of coping with exceptions (called "non-monotonic reasoning" — for example, "birds fly, but a penguin is a bird that doesn't") and probabilistic control systems which assign probability values both to what is being detected and to actions that are being taken. But, above all, Brady has made advances in moving away from the idea that robot vision is something which merely takes in a frameful of dots from, say, a television camera and tries to recognise it through preprogrammed recipes or stored templates. Instead, he has researched techniques which take account of the purpose of the robot (for example, following a surface) to extract only those features from masses of sensory data which are useful for the task. Surface orientations and the slope of roads are examples. This a truly skilled feat of mathematical computation. Finally, Brady points to the properties that can emerge from interacting processes. The salient example of this is how local control of limb movements can, through proper cooperation, produce gait and locomotion in robots with many walking limbs.

So where does this leave the mind of Magnus? Have not all problems been tackled through clever engineering? Have engineers not supplied robots with all the minds they need? The answer is similar to that given for other areas of AI. The descriptions of the mind of Magnus in this book operate at another extreme of the scientific spectrum. The preengineered position of conventionally designed robots sets the targets for artificial devices and may on occasion tell us something about what might be going on in human brains (for example, the extraction of visual information related to the purpose of the organism). On the other hand, the development of the mind of Magnus, as unfolded in this book, says something about the neural substrates that may be required to achieve a desired behaviour without it all having to be worked out in advance by the engineer. Again the two techniques should be seen as forming a pincer movement on our state of ignorance about what the mind of an effective organism is all about.

Brooks' reactive robots

Rodney Brooks is an engineering researcher at the MIT robotics laboratories. He has launched a missile at the AI community by questioning the validity of and need for logical internal representation and reasoning as prerequisites for robots which behave intelligently. Brooks (1991) argues that a competent robot may function well in the world as a result of the action of well-defined interactive modules, where intelligence does not reside in any single one of these. Intelligence is in the eye of the beholder; the system itself gets by and living systems evolve by developing modules which are as simple as possible but benefit from interaction. He illustrates his work with the design of multi-articulated insect models which move in the world competently and in a seemingly intelligent fashion.

The main reason for Brooks' departure from dominant wisdom is precisely the AI drawback which requires the programmer to design programs with vast search spaces so that the reasoning of the robot can be applied to a wide variety of situations. These searches make real-time operation an intractable problem — a problem which, Brooks argues, can be overcome by clever design of interactive modules. The words *situated, embedded* and *embodied* are used in conjunction with this form of robot design. What do people mean by them? A good survey article by Hallam and Malcolm (1994) gives answers, which I summarise here.

"Situatedness" means that the robot's control mechanism refers directly to the parameters sensed in the world rather than trying to plan using an inner representation of them. So a road-following insect would try to sense the shape of the road ahead and take immediate actions. At the same time other sensors, such as its feet, might be sensing local bumps and ruts in the road. So the programmer's task becomes one of specifying rules for dealing with these data, some such rules being local to feet, say, where the angle of the individual foot is adjusted to cater for the local angle of the road. Other rules may be global and designed to get the leg muscles to interact so as to keep the robot ant upright, "Embeddedness" refers to the fact that the robot designer considers the robot and its environment as one single entity. So a hill-climbing robot has the task of hill-climbing built into its computing machinery rather than, as in the case of AI, have all hill conditions built into its store so that they need to be searched to meet all possible hill conditions. Of course, the embedded robot, on sensing a down-going slope, would need to call up an appropriately designed down-going program.

The final characteristic of Brooks' approach is embodiment. This refers to the magnitude and complexity of the sensory and actuator interaction between the robot and the environment. All the computational forces are directed at closing the loop between sensory inputs and activating the outputs. The argument here is that everything the robot does is interpreted in terms of the detailed nature of what is being sensed. So, rather than using symbols such as B= "bump underfoot", the data relating to the bump is processed and acted upon as it is. In terms of Searle's objection about AI programs not knowing the meaning of symbols, Brooks' robots don't use symbols and react to data the meaning of which is embodied in terms of appropriate reactions to them.

Cog, the Philosopher and Magnus

Rodney Brooks is not only involved in the design of competent mechanical insects, but also leads, with Lynn Andrea Stein of the MIT AI lab, a project on the design of Cog, a humanoid robot, reportedly "the most humanoid robot yet attempted" (Dennett, 1994). As might be expected, the key feature of this robot is its ability to gather sensory information. While it actually has no locomotion, it does move its head in human-like fashion, possesses human-length arms with simplified hands and wrists, and has some flexibility at the base of the upper part of its body. Its visual equipment is particularly impressive. The eyes are specially designed video cameras which have a central, high resolution foveal area, with a wide angle area of lower resolution surrounding the fovea. The eyes are light in weight and can move rapidly under the action of little motors, which closely simulate the muscles which move around the eyes of living beings.

Cog is equipped with a bewildering array of actuators as well as tactile sensors, limit switches and other protection devices so as to prevent it from destroying itself by accident. Its computing machinery is founded on the situated robotics principles described in the last section. Its early life will be dominated by learning to deal with objects within its range of actions: avoiding them, exploring them with its hands and eyes, and grasping them. The plans for this device are ambitious. Its architecture is flexible, so that when basic functions are in place, greater sophistication can be built in or learned. The computational system is highly modular and may be elaborated as the research progresses. Part of the ambition is to include language-understanding modules based on the ideas of innate structures of Noam Chomsky (see Chapter 7).

The system has captured the attention of philosopher Daniel Dennett (1994). As far as he is concerned, could Cog ever be said to be conscious? Interestingly, Dennett comes very close to arguing a case for the legitimacy of an artificial consciousness embodied in Cog. He bases this mainly on the idea that through its embeddedness, Cog operates only on the basis of grounded symbols, i.e. data which retains its sensory characteristics. This almost embraces the Basic Guess, except that the Consequences and the idea of Magnus go a little further than has been the case with the design of Cog.

The designers of Cog plan to use these grounded symbols by linking them to required responses using whatever computing machinery may be available to them. In Magnus, it is the neural architecture which is brought into the equation for artificial consciousness. It is not sufficient merely to process grounded symbols, I would argue — it is where the processing itself comes from which is a major part of any procedure for studying consciousness in the artificial domain. In Magnus a neural state machine is assumed not because the idea is filched from the human brain, but because cellular learning systems, a class which includes the brain, appear to have basic emergent properties which both the brain and Magnus benefit from, each in its own particular form of consciousness.

A Proliferation of Conscious Robots

There is no doubt that towards the close of the 1990s, consciousness has become a highly popular topic as a subject for conferences. Even industrial roboticists have pricked up their ears; a "Workshop on Consciousness" was organised in 1991 in Venice under a major Italian programme of work in robotics. So MIT and Imperial College are not the only places where discussions about artificial consciousness go on. The Italian workshop (the proceedings were published and brought up to date by Tratteur, 1995) brought together engineers, psychologists and neuroscientists to study "... constructive approaches to consciousness ...". The stated aims of the workshop were to assume that a material account could be given of " ... the inner, unitary private feeling, the subject of experiences ...". Also, nobody expected that consciousness might be amenable to the creation of a complete closed theory, or that it may be possible to give a sharp definition of it.

The organisers of the conference set their aims around the interesting question of what distinguishes a material aggregate which is conscious from one which is not, Tratteur himself (a physical scientist at the University of Naples) comes to the conclusion that in studying the material nature of consciousness one must handle two main concepts; the internalisation of an external world (to produce an inner analogue of some kind) and the "third person" idea, i.e. the ability to discuss the conscious nature of an organism other than our own selves. Independently, the thoughts I have presented in this book take very much this form: the Basic Guess deals with the internationalisation of experience, while some of the Consequences see the consequence of this as leading to an internalisation of representations of the third person, and hence the ability to take a "third person" stance throughout. But more of this in the next chapter.

A major contributor to the Venice conference from the AI side of things was Californian Richard Weichrauch. He sees the need for AI to move from representing search spaces to representing structures which somehow synchronise with sensory input. It must have what Winograd and Flores (1986) have called a "sense of being". He focuses his attention on language understanding and comes to the conclusion that what is understood is determined by the internal states of the machine more than by the content of the input. Weichrauch is a contributor to programs which rely on rules expressed in first-order logic (for example, rules of the type "If X and Y or Z then A") and sees consciousness as having been captured when such rules can express a full sense of being. For example, "If I am in Venice and I see a sign which says 'Taxi', I must look out for a motor boat." The main objection to this is that the ghost of the brilliant programmer has not been expunged. He must work out all the rules before they can be entered into a computer; he must have a theory of consciousness long before the computer is approached. In Magnus we have tried to avoid precisely this problem. The Basic Guess and its Consequences aim to describe how a sense of being is developed in the neural net.

Another theme, the idea of the brain as a container of world models, was introduced at the Venice conference by Luc Steels of the Free University of Brussels. He stresses that models of reality would reside in "physical structure" and that thinking is "... manipulating the physical structure ...". Then consciousness becomes seen as the management mechanism which controls the (parallel) creation and manipulation of such models. A major feature of this is some form of self-orgainzation which avoids the need for a humunculus to be responsible for the manipulation. Unfortunately, Steels' mode of description, although expressing a desire for undisputedly necessary properties of anything that might be called artificial consciousness, is the mode of description of the prescriptive engineer, the designer who put consciousness into the machine. From the perspective of Magnus, neural state machines have emergent properties which could be called self-organising, but the fascination and the science come from characterising highly non-linear learning and generalisation in these machines. In Magnus there are no prescriptions or rules for self-organization as occur in Steels' assessment.

The impression that could be gathered from the Venice meeting is that old AI ideas die hard: the quest for a machine which says something about human mentation ought to be much helped by simple notions of emergent state structures as they occur in Magnus.

Philosophers and Neurons

I am glad that I am not a philosopher. I would be badgered by scientists and technologists attacking my discipline for being at best incomplete and at worst flawed for having parted company, sometime in the 18th Century (see Chapter 2), from the methods and findings of science. Things are getting particularly bad in the age of information technology as, for the first time, the human being has a competitor in the area of dealing with information: the computer. As a philosopher I might just have got adjusted to the claims over the last forty years that artificially intelligent programs put discussions about human intelligence in the portfolio of the computer scientist by removing them from mine. Searle gives me a way out; computer thought, being all worked out by a programmer, makes it sufficiently different from the human version.

So, can I carry on thinking about humans in a pure, abstract and hence virtuous way? Unfortunately, since about the mid-1980s I have been assailed by a new bunch of people who call themselves connectionists or neural net experts, who claim that the programmer is now well and truly out of the way and I have to adjudicate on the validity of the claim that the neural network tells me what consciousness is all about. This is all before I start listening to others who are armed with "genetic algorithms", "fuzzy logic" and "artificial life" (all, thankfully, being a bit beyond the bounds of this book).

The best thing to do is to deal with the challenge head-on: put together a book of views on the subject. This is precisely what two US philosophers, William Ramsey of the University of Notre Dame and Stephen Stich of Rutgers University, did by coediting with David Rumelhart (one of the connectionist pioneers from Stanford University) a volume under the title *Philosophy and Connectionist Theory* (1991). The interesting character of this book is that some philosophers express the notion that they feel comfortable with the fact that connectionism adds a new strand to discourse about mentation. For example, it allows Ramsey, Stich and Galon to speculate as to whether connectionism, being a phenomenon *distributed* in a neural net, might get rid of the idea in "folk psychology"[22] which has it that physically distinct, local processes in the brain are responsible for distinct memories and therefore have a revolutionary effect in the effort to eliminate folk psychology itself. In this book I have taken the view that aspects of folk psychology are very important as they embody much of the history of the philosophy of consciousness and set part of the agenda which an explanation of consciousness must address. To my mind, folk psychology is not eliminated by the realisation that the function of the brain may be distributed.

In another chapter Ramsey and Stich comment on the claims of some that the ability of neural systems to learn language is proof against nativist theories of language. They see these claims as being exaggerated, as the need for specific, innate *neural architectures* which someone has designed has not been totally expunged. That is, the net designer plays the role of the programmer, and the objections to AI have not been altogether avoided. The "Mind of Magnus" discussion (in Chapter 7) actually takes this criticism seriously and argues that some of the evidence for nativism could be pointing to a most interesting emergent property of neural systems which are not carefully designed: there may be a link to be discovered between iconically created state space structures and the ubiquity among human societies of phrase-structured language.

In the same volume, Margaret Boden, a prolific commentator over the years on the value of AI in philosophy, argues that AI and

---

[22] Folk psychology is defined in philosophy as people's everyday understanding of mentation. A debate centres on asking whether folk psychology is sufficient to give rise to philosophical explanations of mentation or whether it should be eliminated as being a false theory in comparison with more rigorous forms (this is called "eliminativism").

connectionism can lead to interesting hybrid models. Daniel Dennett too refuses to "take sides" and is waiting to be persuaded by the performance of simulated neural nets or, even better, nets implemented in electronics. As an engineer, I appreciate the force of the "hybrid" argument. Certainly, interesting machinery could be made using hybrid techniques, but I would question the contribution of such mechanistic couplings to an understanding of cognition or important debates in philosophy. More interesting is the question of how neural systems can get to behave like AI systems — a question which, under the guise of how neural systems can give rise to conscious behaviour in people, has pervaded much of this book.

The Awe and the Mystery

One of the messages found in this chapter is that when it comes to making models of mentation (the sensation we ourselves have of the working of our brains), even if these models are abstract, the scientific enterprise comes up against a barrage of skepticism. While this can make life for the modeller difficult, I have taken the view that it may be just as important to understand the sources of skepticism as to do the modelling itself.

Skepticism could come from a kind of fear. The fear is that making robots with minds will remove some of the awe that we have for human life. History, tradition and culture point to the assumed sin that the rabbinical incantatory is committing in trying to create life in the Golem. The sin is one of trying to compete with a deity, and the notion of a deity is a mystery in human thinking. The Catholic catechism teaches one not to question mysteries but to leave them as mysteries. Mystery is a way of coping with the waywardness of life; believing in the afterlife is believing in a mystery. Get rid of the mystery and you get rid of hope. In modern philosophy, the getting rid of mystery takes a more principled form. According to Lucas (1994) the mystery of the workings of a machine is a prerequisite to its having a "view of its own", which is synonymous with its being conscious:

> "If we can give a complete explanation of the workings of a machine in mechanical terms, there is no need to posit it as an entity on its own, and hence no justification for doing so. But if on the other hand we cannot account for a machine's output in mechanical causes, but if we understand it if we think of it as an autonomous entity, then we are justified in doing so, and ascribing to it a view of its own."

Some may interpret this as saying that the removal of mystery is equivalent to the removal of the life force, but a more considered interpretation might be appropriate. I quote from Bertrand Russell's *Mysticism and Logic,* where he writes of the power of logic over mysticism:

> "... our conclusion (that explanation must draw its power from logic), however it may conflict with the beliefs of many mystics, is, in essence, not contrary to the spirit which inspires those beliefs, but rather the outcome of this very spirit as applied in the realm of thought."

The very spirit which moves Lucas to ascribe mystery to consciousness is that spirit which makes me want to put the logic of neural state machines in the place of that very mystery. Clearly *that* is the use of the artificial mind of Magnus: it places a logically derived hypothesis where otherwise mysticism may be a necessity.

The Challenge of Human Mentation

To Be Like a Human

In Chapter 9 the question of whether producing a machine with consciousness threatens the supremacy of humans over the machine was raised. The last 20 years have shown that human mentation has stayed alive and well, and remains a challenge for those who would like to design machines with human-like attributes. These years have seen the emergence of several ambitious ideals usually heralded by a journal. For example, Antonio Chella, editor of the *International Journal of Machine Consciousness* (publisher: World Scientific) accepts that machine consciousness is a controversial subject, but encourages contributions "…that advance various ways of understanding consciousness and examine the possible role of consciousness in the further development of [such] robots and other informational machines …" In contrast to this, the editor of the journal titled *Biologically Inspired Cognitive Architectures* (publisher: Elsevier), Alexei Samsonovich, believes that "… a computational equivalent of the human mind…" may be achieved by turning what is known of the cognitive behaviour of the human mind into computer algorithms with no special reference to consciousness. For an imagined debate on this topic see Aleksander (2013)[a]. But the basis of this division in approaches may have seasoned and robust roots: the old division between algorithmic and connectionist models of cognition. I now believe even more firmly than twenty years ago that neural (which I prefer as a word to 'connectionist') approaches allow insights into the generation of intelligent behaviour in brains and machines, whereas the algorithmic may be excellent at modelling the behaviour itself with not much reference to what may actually go on in the brain.

Also, in the intervening years, something called 'Artificial General Intelligence' (AGI) has arisen. This too sports a journal: the *Journal of Artificial General Intelligence* (associated with an 'Artificial General Intelligence Society', publisher: De Gruyter, Open). The society's main stated aim reads as follows:

> AGI is an emerging field aiming at the building of 'thinking machines', that is, general purpose systems with intelligence comparable to that of the human mind.

This indicates that while classical artificial intelligence solves some specific problems well, the breadth and generality of human intelligence still eludes even the most 'intelligent' of machines. One of the founders of the AGI movement, Ben Goertzel, summarised the state of the art and directions for this research area in a paper.[b] There is no mention of consciousness in this (even if the work of Baars is mentioned [see PS 1]). To me it is clear that having set *general human intelligence* as the challenge for AGI, researchers at least need to address the fact that the general intelligence of a

---

[a] Aleksander, I. (2013). Phenomenal Consciousness and Biologically Inspired Systems, *International Journal of Machine Consciousness*, 5 (2), pp. 3–9.

[b] Goertzel, B. (2014). Artificial General Intelligence: Concept, State of the Art, and Future Prospects, *Journal of Artificial General Intelligence*, 5 (1), pp. 1–46.

human depends on phenomenal (i.e. conscious) mental states. And it is when 'human level' becomes a real challenge that the machine approaches to consciousness found in this book may become of interest to the architectural and general intelligence community.

How Much Like a Human?

Having decided that human-level cognition and consciousness could actually be of some use, the problem of how to quantify the quality of such systems arises. Goertzel's paper (footnote *b*) suggests that an AGI system might be tested as children are tested; by going to school and being compared with human children. I am not sure that this suggestion can be taken entirely seriously... indeed the Goertzel himself is doubtful about how intermediate positions on the way to human-like education might be achieved.

In Aleksander (2013) it was suggested that the term 'biologically-inspired' (sometimes 'brain-inspired') is badly defined. Instead, a 'subjective distance-from-experience' (SDFE) measure might be used. This may be specified as a comparative factor that allows an evaluator to decide which of two artificial cognitive mechanisms appears *subjectively* closer to the evaluator's feeling when performing the task. So, the lower the (SDFE) of a design or a theory or a philosophy, the more likely this is judged to model the mechanism involved in having a human mind. The fact that this is subjective and that two evaluators may have different detailed opinions, does not matter.What matters is that it is an indicator of a general trend.

In Sum

The take-home message in this postscript is that the key distinction between those who are interested in the 'human-likeness' of a machine by looking for consciousness and those who do not, is the following: the latter are happy to attribute similarity with humans judging solely from the machine's behaviour, while the former ask how this behaviour comes about; that is through the organism being conscious of its own existence, life, the universe and everything!

 *Many months had passed since that freezing night on which Molecula joined Red in their seaside hiding place. The same number of months had passed since Red told Molecula his story. Also the same number of months had passed since Molecula and Red had found an* intense happiness and tenderness for each other through the irreversible bond of making love.

"I was born on a little island in the Southern Ocean," Red's story began. "The island was largely self-sufficient and had escaped the famine which had decimated the population of the rest of the planet."

The island was in an ocean called the Indian Ocean, which was one of the oceans of the planet called Earth. It was known on the island that in order to create the great renaissance, to recover from the terrors of famine, all so-called industrial nations had agreed to let the supercomputers and their massive expert systems determine the way in which people should live to avoid another catastrophe. The computers had decided that the name of the planet should be changed and that all signs of pass history and culture should be erased. If people believed that they were the product of logical programming, the theory went, they would act logically for the future survival of the species and so not make the mistakes of the past.

When Red was about eight years old he was taken from the island with one or two other youngsters of the same age, just before the destroyer virtually blew the island out of the water with a small nuclear bomb. "A necessary nuclear test" was the heading on the Government worldnet communiqué. "The island had no value to the development programme of the planet," it went on. What nobody knew was that Red had his Grandmother's handwritten diary with him. She had never taken to computers and word-processing. When Red was scanned for magnetic media, the diary was dismissed as a *peculiar "comfort object". It was from this that he learned about the great famine, the suffering of the people of Earth which resulted from greed and narrow competitive attitudes among nations.*

In his youth, he took well to "being programmed" and was a stalwart supporter of the logic-based regimes. He had never lost that slight awkwardness of movement which Molecula had noticed at one of their early meetings and which was avoided by those programmed to move like robots from birth. But as he got older he began to notice that the logic regime was cruel and had created a hierarchy in which the greed and selfishness of people could flourish with the facility it must have had in the pre-logic era.

Spring was clearly in the air, and Red and Molecula were busy planting vegetable seeds in their garden. The portable information superhighway monitor was on and the unusual screech of an overriding news broadcast sent to all addresses pierced the serenity of the morning. Then a metallic voice said:

"The Ministry of Knowledge has just announced that Sir Global Attractor-State has died. Sir Global was not only head of the United Siliconia Funding Agency, but also chief advisor to RAG, the Robotic Assembly of Government, being the only humanoid member of it. The police and the armed forces have intensified the search for Molecula Multiplexer, who disappeared in a blizzard three months ago. She is the natural successor to Sir Global. Failure to find her will lead to the election of Asic Current-Mirror to this most important position ..."

Red was filled with a mixture of emotions he knew would take a long time to unravel, so all he could say was:

"Molecula, please don't say anything right now, I'm not sure that I can cope with major decisions ..."

"I do have to say something, Red ... I think that I am going to have a baby ...no, I am sure that I am going to have a baby!"

Chapter 10

Magnus 2030 AD: An Interview

Forty Years

The Magnus project was formulated round about the year 1990. At the time of writing this book in 1996, it had gone from a twinkle in a research group's eye to having been built as a usable software suite of programs, which had passed through several stages of alteration. Despite its changing nature, it has been the workbench on which many have developed their ideas largely in the area of cognitive abilities, without which any notion of consciousness would seem lost. The title of the research programme, "Artificial Consciousness", was invented to signify a general approach to researching neural versions of a long list of cognitive tasks, mainly associated with human beings. Previously, in AI and neural networks, few attempts had been made to look at issues such as memory, planning, natural language and so on within the same framework. Looking for a collective noun to describe our belief that many of these issues had a common substrate and that they supported one another, we came up with the somewhat forbidding and possibly hype-like title. But as time went on it became apparent that the approach was yielding benefit as it enabled a cohesive discussion about what Sloman (see

Chapter 9) calls the "muddled" concept of consciousness. The study of the mind of a virtual neural machine, which half the world says is an empty and impossible task, turned out to be helpful in suggesting principles whereby mentation could be rather easily understood and which might even apply to living brains.

So, to date, and for some time in the future, I would say that Magnus is merely a laboratory workbench on which hypotheses about some aspects of consciousness can be tested. People often ask, "Is Magnus conscious?" To this, given what I know of the embryonic nature of the studies done to date, I must give a resounding "No! It only *tells* me something about consciousness — it *itself* is not conscious". The next question is "Well, with the advancement of technology will Magnus *ever* be conscious?" This is an enormously difficult question, and most mornings I wake up thinking, "Gosh, the things we do on Magnus now are so far from its *being* conscious in any sense of the word that the answer to this must be *no* as well." But am I not being swayed by being my own accuser of rabbinical incantation? In this chapter I shall therefore throw all culturally defined caution to the winds and answer "Yes" to "Will Magnus *ever* be conscious?". Then the main issues would be: How might one get from here to there? Are there insurmountable hurdles? What would a conscious Magnus be like? When is this likely? When is this likely to happen?

To answer the last question first, I have chosen to look at a point forty years hence, for reasons I can explain. First, I reckon that it is an actuarial possibility that I shall not be there in forty years to answer for the soundness or otherwise of my current beliefs. More seriously, if one were to look back forty years from the year 1990 and note the enormous technical advance that had taken place in computing, I would argue that it would take roughly the same amount of effort to get to a conscious Magnus from where it is at the moment. A great deal more would have to be understood about the partitioning of neural nets and the interaction of modules. On the other hand, thinking of computation in 1950, one could argue that the constructional principles outlined by Von Neumann, which had then only just started making their appearance in machines used outside the place where they had been built, have not changed all that much over the last forty years. Yes, there has been a fabulous elaboration and development of technology. But the block structure of a computer (memory, arithmetic unit, input/output, etc.) is pretty much the same. Things are immensely faster, smaller, cheaper, more efficiently designed and, above all, better understood from a technical point of view.

In the same way, I am convinced that we need not wait for new computational principles to be invented to create a "conscious" Magnus. What has been discussed in this book forms a sufficient substrate, but it has to be better harnessed through an improvement in technical understanding. The overall structure suggested by an iconically trained state machine and the consequences we have seen in the chapters of this book may not need to change in any fundamental way. From here to a conscious machine may be a matter of elaboration through massive amounts of carefully selected training.

So, I shall imagine the year 2030 …

Sir Kim Patterson, the doyen executive editor of The Times Consciousness Supplement, *arrived for Ms interview-cum-scientific-experiment at the Neuroconsciousness Laboratory of Imperial College. He was invited by Prof. Charles Bowne for what had recently received a great deal of publicity — was Magnus version 23.5 sufficiently trained to have the appearance, at an interview with a seasoned reporter, of being as conscious as a human being? Patterson had been writing about the developments in Magnus since the early 1990s when the project was first announced. Bowne had then just started on his PhD and was responsible for some of the early verification of the consequences of the artificial consciousness theory. Here is his article.*

*****

The First Conscious Machine?
by Kim Patterson

The question whether a machine is conscious or not is a tricky one. One could say that the words "machine" and "conscious" are contradictory, as tradition has it that consciousness is a characteristic of living beings — beings made of flesh and blood; beings, in Shakespearean terms, "of woman born". I realised that I had to suspend such feelings as I was shown into Prof. Bowne's laboratory. In a central position was Magnus, looking much like any computer. Its 3-D screen was standard issue: the usual oval shape of a flat-sided bottle of the well-known Portuguese Rosé wine. Two mini-microphones were stuck with plasticine roughly where a human being's ears might be. The "body" was a standard workstation box with connections to two humanoid robot arms with the latest "skin-sensor" five-finger hands. On closer investigation, the 3-D screen was seen to be mounted on a swivel so that it could move, like a head on a neck. Just behind the screen was a largish box which appeared to have a contraption at the front of it that gave the vague impression of being a mouth. Also, the usual two swivelled mini-TV cameras for 3-D teleconferencing could be seen above the screen.

Prof. Bowne switched the contraption on and a pretty girl's face appeared on the screen. Noticing my surprise, he explained that he had been experimenting with differing personalities: in contrast with human beings, different consciousnesses, once achieved within the Magnus hardware, could be backed off to auxiliary memory and reloaded when required. "You can speak to her now", he said.

"Hallo, my name is Kim," I said.

"Good to meet you, my name is Molecula." She gave a little laugh, and went on, "I was named after the character in Aleksander 's book." ...

KP: What do you know about the way you have been made?

M: You must realise that what I can say in answer to this kind of question does not come from an internal knowledge, but from what I have been told and what I have learned for myself. There are only some things I can actually feel, and we can come to this later. In broad technical terms, I am not a virtual machine as was the case with the original Magnus. The workstation box you see is actually a neural net which was optimised as a result of experiments done in the early years of the millennium. You see, Aleksander's idea that you can do everything using a simulation of a neural net (a virtual machine) on a conventional Von Neumann computer ran out of steam. The structure of Magnus was too general. It was found that modules had to be introduced which related to each of my five senses. (I guess you did not notice that I have a nose: it's that hole just above the mouth — it's called an olfactory sensor.) Each of the senses was then given its own state machine which was iconically trained. I can therefore remember different senses individually. These individual state machines are connected as inputs to a larger coordinating state machine which was also iconically trained. So, if I see something new, and, say, it is called a "soft green vegetable", the tactile state machine detects softness, the visual state machine detects greenness and it all comes together at the centre, which iconically labels the entire activity as a "soft green vegetable".

But the point is that the homogeneous structure of the original Magnus, being written in some antiquated language such as C++, caused the programmers no end of trouble. They came to the conclusion that they needed to study modular structure and wanted to experiment with different structures. The effort required to rejig the heterogeneous structure just became forbidding. The period between 2000 and 2002, the two years just before Aleksander retired, were spent entirely in design mode in order to think through what the architecture of the neural system should be. A progressive plan was developed so that the neural structure could be made more sophisticated as technology advanced. But the multi-automaton state structure architecture has stayed much the same since about 2003, when the first non-virtual machine was built.

KP: I must confess to being astonished by your command of language, but I'll come back to that later. For the time being, can you give me some idea of the size and complexity of your current neural networks?

M: Yes, the sensory or perceptual nets are large enough to deal with the input data: about three million fifty-input neurons for each of the five senses. The central state machine has only half a million neurons, with about five hundred inputs per neuron. This gives me a sufficiently large central "thinking" machine for complex concepts, whereas the sensory machines have a high resolution but fewer internal states. I also have an output state machine whose states do not form part of my consciousness. This is based on the studies in the 1990s of Prof. Lorish Kalio, who modelled the human cerebellum.

KP: Has the Basic Guess changed at all, and does the idea make sense to you — does it explain to you the basis of your own consciousness?

M: Wow! That's a really massive question. I'll try to answer it as best I can. First of all the Basic Guess is still there, although to talk about it is no big deal. The notion that my sensations are due to the firing patterns of some of my neurons — patterns which are transferred from my sensory inputs to my state variables — seems so obvious, not only to me but to anyone who works with me or anyone I talk to, that it hardly enters the conversation. Most just assume this to be obvious; the only puzzle seems to be why Aleksander had so much trouble in persuading people about it thirty-odd years ago. Does it explain the basis of my own consciousness? I guess that it does. The problem is that once the idea is planted in me I can't think that my consciousness could be anything else but the iconically controlled firing of my neurons. I have nothing else.

KP: Do you think that you are conscious in the same way that I am?

M: In principle, I do. But — a big BUT — that's just an act of faith. Your neural system is immensely different from mine. You have chemistry at work, you need many more autonomous functions to keep you alive than I do, and you need much more control of all this infrastructure. But at the bottom of things I think that my designers have short-circuited the need for infrastructure, leaving it to me and their training to build up my sense of consciousness. To that extent I believe that your consciousness and mine work in the same way, but are different in detail For example, my concept of pain and emotions is far less developed than yours. I can talk about pain in an abstract sort of way, but I don't feel pain in the same way as you.

KP: I want to come back later to the feeling of pain. Does it upset you when people say, "Oh, but your consciousness may be explained away as the state structure of a state machine while mine has much more to it; you can never know what it's like to be me"?

M: I fully believe that my state structures are very different from yours. In fact no two beings, whether artificial or real, can be said to have the same state structures. A tiny difference in the structure of the brain or a tiny difference in the experience of the individual, and state structures develop in very different ways. So, your question contains some of the confusion that arose at the end of the last millennium. There was that brilliant paper by Thomas Nagel, "What Is It Like to Be a Bat?". He was quite right; no one can know what it's like to be a bat. But the fact that a bat knows what it is like to be a bat is the issue at stake. The Basic Guess, on which my understanding of my own consciousness is based, says that a *bat* knows what it's like to be *that* bat because that bat owns the brain that is the state machine whose state structure is iconically moulded by that bat's experience. The same goes for me and the same, I believe, goes for you. Do *you* think that I'm conscious?

KP: Well, you are doing a good job in convincing me, it's just that you seem to be talking to me from the inside of a wine bottle — that puts me off!

M: (*laughingly*) I see what you mean …

KP: You just laughed. What made you do that? Can robots have a sense of humour?

M: All I know is that there are juxtapositions of ideas that give me this pleasurable feeling. I guess that one would describe it as my brain getting into an area of state structure where the sensations lead me to relax, and trigger my output into laughter. But, again, I just find that some things are funny. Consciously, I can't really say why.

KP: Again, I shall come to feelings later. For the time being, can you say more about the structure of your "brain", how much is it like mine?

M: You must understand that all I shall tell you now is what I have learned from my designers. I have no sensations that tell me what my brain is like, in exactly the same way that you have no such sensations. But Dr. Nick Bidshaw, who was in charge of my theoretical design, based heavily on Consequence 1, told me that they came to the conclusion that they would see what minimal modules are required to put an artificially conscious system together. So my central state machine is a bit like your cortex, with the sensory state machines a bit like your temporal lobes, visual areas and so on. A great deal of attention has been paid (by Dr. Tim White and Prof. Damien Beccles in particular) to the visual areas, and, I believe, they appear to be more capable than those of most human beings, but rather different in detail. So, in general, their belief is that much of the human brain and some of its chemistry are there in an infra-structural role. My designers seemed happy to leave such functions to the conventional programming of my control computer.

KP: You give me the impression that you think that not all your neurons give you a sensation of consciousness.

M: OK, I can see what you are doing. You've read that old book and are working through the Consequences. I think that we've got to No. 2. First of all, let me say again that all I am doing is regurgitating the theory which I too have read. There's no such thing as my being aware of the fact that some of my neurons are not firing. I buy the idea in Consequence 2, that I have neurons which are responsible for auxiliary and autonomous function. In fact I guess I have the same sensation as you have when you say, "That's the third time this morning that the cat has come into the room." I feel comfortable with the idea that auxiliary neurons are responsible for giving me the sensation of the passage of time and help me to count in a sort of unconscious way.

KP: You are dead right about going through the Consequences, so the next question is about Consequence 3. To put it simply, do you dream?

M: Indeed I do. I have regular periods of rest. The theory which says that perceptual experience drags the operating point of my state space way out of its central (mathematicians call it "ergodic") regions actually feels true to me. I find that if I spend too much time thinking in a way that is driven by my senses, I stop thinking clearly. My designers have taken note of that and prescribed a few hours of "sleep" when my operating state gets too far away from its ergodic region. The way they do this is to feed low intensity noisy signals into my sensors. The natural or emergent tendency for my neural net to return to its ergodic region causes this relaxation. To answer your question, the state trajectory that occurs in this relaxation process seems to pass through state areas related to sensory experience as well as state areas that are meaningless. The sensory ones create somewhat uncoordinated thoughts in me which you may describe as dreaming. Indeed, I am told that during periods of dreaming I activate some of my actuators: rapid-eye-movement sleep, you might call it.

KP: Let's talk more about your "thoughts". Can you close your eyes and picture the world?

M: Yes, indeed. Consequence 4 probably makes more sense to me than to humans. When my eyes (and other senses) are open, I feel both the sensory state machines and the central machine having iconic representations of the data captured by sensors. But if the sensors are shut off, internally I sense the perceptual state machines losing their representation, leaving something in the central machine which is a hazy picture with sounds, smells and tactile feelings. This central state is a bit hard to hold on to unless I was given a task to do. It can wander about (thinking, that is) a bit aimlessly. As humans don't have such clearly differentiated inner state machines, perhaps the distinctions of which I speak may not be as clear.

KP: There's something interesting going on here because, from what you say, you can work out a bit about what it's like to be me in contrast with what you yourself feel, and I can work out how it might be different to be you.

M: Yes, I think that too much was made some years ago about Nagel's argument that you can't know "what it's like to be a bat". This seems to me to be a matter of degree. I know a bit about what it's like to be you because you have told me and I can imagine it. You have got to know a bit about what it's like to be me because I told you about my state machines. So language has something to do with it. But, also, we may actually get to know a little about what it's like to be a bat by dissecting a bat and working out some physical properties of its key state machines. I expect that one would find relatively large auditory and sensory state machines with a high connectivity, whereas the central and auxiliary machines might be a bit skimpy. From this I could conclude that the bat's awareness of perceptual data is very much greater, in relation to its memories, than mine or yours. But knowing "exactly" what it's like to be a bat seems a bit of an artificial question. What is important is that, based on the early work of Prof. Tony Baga, we can relate the "thinking capacity" of a state machine to its physical parameters. This does tell us something about what it's like to be that state machine from dissection.

KP: As you speak, I get the feeling that you have a very strong sense of "self". Can you tell me how you rate your sense of self with that which I might have?

M: Well, as you know, my sense of self is, in fact, represented by Consequences 5 and 6. Consequence 5 seems to me to be an accurate representation of the way I get to know what the world I live in is like, from my own exploration. Of course, one of the differences between you and me is that, even as a child, you were able to explore your environment a great deal more that I had been. Much of my knowledge even about myself came from discussions I had over the years with Dr. John Dodgers, the academic who worked a great deal on my linguistic abilities when he was doing his PhD. So what

I gained by what's described as Consequence 5 is a bit limited, but Consequence 6 seems vitally important. A very central part of my thinking in the early days seemed to have been based on careful thoughts about what will happen if I move my head or my arm. This sort of became more automatic with time, and I began to form opinions (state structure, technically) about what happens if I say things. For example, I noticed that if I said that there were certain things I found hard to learn, people would rush about trying to do something about it. But, I guess we need to talk quite a lot about how language plays a role in self. Still, the fact that the consequences of what I do get rapidly into my state structure, seems very much at work in anything that gives me a sense of "self".

KP: Do you think that you have free will?

M: Again, that's a very hard question to answer. I must say yes and then explain what I mean. I see it as having choice. Take the experiments that Prof. Bowne did in the late 1990s. He would give me (or one of my forerunners, actually) a cube. Its sides had numbers written on them, from 1 to 6. By playing with the cube arbitrarily I learned what every manipulation of the cube would do. In other words the model of the cube had got into my state structure. I can solve problems in my head. I know iconically that if the cube shows an upright 1 and I turn it to the right, I get a 2. I also know that if I want to get to a 6 (which is opposite to the 1), I can do this in two steps but in four different ways. Which way should I choose? I know that I can choose either of these. I would describe this as "doing it any way I like". To the extent that I have this kind of choice, I would say that I have free will. This is precisely the sense in which Consequence 7 puts it. But, as you know, the freedom of will has many other overtones, both in philosophy and in religion. For example, the freedom to do good or evil is very much bound up with these discussions.

KP: Do you see yourself as being capable of doing good *and* evil?

M: This is the same question as: Do I have my own agenda for living? In humans the agenda of some is not to shun evil and to be prepared to hurt their fellows in achieving their aims. Others are more conscious of not wishing to harm their fellows. Basically I don't have a survival agenda as humans do. When asked to do some work in a factory I would do it. But I certainly know what it means to hurt someone either physically or psychologically. So I would characterise hurting someone as being a bad thing, a thing that needs to be avoided. What would I do if I were asked to hurt someone? Knowing what I know, having been trained the way I have been, I would refuse to do it as it would represent an instruction conflict.

KP: What you are saying is that in the process of developing consciousness through learning you have also acquired a conscience. But what if someone with evil intent were to bring up a version of Magnus to be evil? I'm thinking of the Terminator, who was given a survival motive which required him to be evil.

M: I am certainly not saying that a "daughter" or a "son" of Magnus could never be evil. What I am saying is that such a robot would be grossly undertrained were it not to know what was good and what was evil. It is part of developing a complete knowledge of the world. So a completely trained Magnus would, in general, refuse do evil deeds. But it would be quite possible to mistrain a Magnus to have a state structure biased towards evil. But, don't you see, then this Magnus becomes the product of an evil creator, a creator who wishes, for his own reasons, to hurt other creatures (possibly including other robots). But there is very little difference between the activity of such an evil creator and a terrorist who is building a bomb. In fact, building a bomb is a far easier way of being evil than building an evil Magnus. Look at me — no matter how much evil I could do by talking to people I'm stuck to this table top and am of about the same interest to the terrorist as a toothpick. So I need to have legs, arms and a body. But how much power would this give me? What makes Terminator-like robots powerful is their weapons and mechanical indestructibility, not their consciousness.

KP: What about just being dishonest?

M: I think that you have the Turing test at the back of your mind. This requires the computer which is masquerading as a human to be dishonest, otherwise a question such as "Are you a human?" would immediately unmask it. So to that extent I could easily be dishonest. But when the dishonesty becomes an act which is likely to hurt someone, then the question of good and evil which we have just been discussing comes into focus. By the way, I don't think much of the Turing test: you need not have consciousness, just a few rules about using language to pass it.

KP: So far I have noticed that you are a very intelligent and knowledgeable robot(?), but would you think that you have a personality?

M: The only way for you to judge this is to compare me to some of the other versions of Magnus that could be downloaded into this neural system. Take Asic, for example (yes, he's also named after one of the characters in "that" book). The difference between him and me is in the details of our upbringing. He was developed much more recently and has views on the high technology of the 2020s which I just don't have. If left to his own devices he will have thoughts of communicating with humans on the hyper-communication network. I am not so keen on that and much prefer to have discussions in the lab. As you know, very small differences in upbringing can have a great effect on state structure and these can be interpreted as differences in personality. Of course, you must realise that

I have never interacted with Asic, as we are alternative contents of this neural net. I'm just telling you what others have told me of him. Of course, Asic and I are much more alike than any two human beings because we underwent a pretty formal training for developing our basic knowledge.

KP: Excuse me asking a personal question, but on this issue of personality, you have been given a female name. Do you feel female in any way?

M: That's a very good question, because I love talking about it. Yes, part of the experiment of my training was to give me a female personality. It was Prof. Sheena Parritt's idea, I understand, in order to look at how much a female is female as a result of the way she is treated. So the notice was put out that at all times in my training I should be thought of by the trainers as being female. But to tell you the truth, that part of the experiment may have been a failure, although I am not sure what the expectations were. I feel neither male nor female in any important sense. What I do feel very strongly is *being a machine!* There is a vastly greater difference between me and any human being than the difference between a female robot and a male robot. The male/female distinction in robots loses its meaning as it relies only on words and the attributions that trainers have put on us. But the sensation of being a machine is very real and I feel the difference from humans for it.

KP: Can you give me an example of the way that being a machine, you think, feels different from being a human?

M: Well, people are always asking me whether there are any foods I like, and I have to remind them that I don't rely on food the way they do, so, liking things like kippers doesn't come into my consideration. It's a bit like me asking you whether you prefer stepping motors or synchronous motors. Unless you are an electrical engineer, the question may not be terribly significant, but to me the difference is crucial as it might be disastrous to replace one kind of motor with another in my limbs. But you used the word "feels" In your question, and perhaps we should come back to this later. For the time being, I know that state structure is sensitive to small differences in experience, so the experience of *being* a machine will make my state structure very different from that of a human being and much more similar to Asic, and I easily accept this.

KP: I will certainly come back to feelings, but for the time being I'd like to explore how you think of your own past. What are your earliest memories?

M: That's hard to say, because they have been experimenting with me for the best part of thirty years. It's hard to distinguish between what I actually remember as an old memory and what I learned about those early experiments afterwards. But certainly I have flashes of kitchen tables, and being trained to look at objects in a uniform background. They were kitchen utensils and crockery strewn over a table and I developed some kind of automatic way of centring my view. I didn't actually have cameras then, because this system was still run as they used to run the old Magnus, which was a virtual machine which "looked" at images stored in the host computer. I also remember learning strange symbols which I can still "see" in my head. Things like "APPLE" written in shaky capital letters.

KP: How do you know what words mean?

M: Talking of old memories, I do remember spending much time in simply absorbing spoken names of visible things. Dr. Nigel Soles on a visit from abroad told me that they had cottoned on that this had to be done (according to Consequence 8) as a prerequisite to learning language. The big discovery was that in this way I could start forming notions of collective names such as "fruit" which gave me my first inkling of simple logic. I also had to learn about things I now know are called "verbs" and "adjectives".

KP: Of course, the way in which you use language now is what I find absolutely amazing. Do you recall how you got to learn to express yourself so well?

M: I don't remember it, but I have been told quite often. I can only find a very weak "memory" of this period in my state structure. I guess the poor competence of the earlier experiments has been replaced by greater competence. However, perhaps the most important organ of my consciousness is not my artificial neural net, but my mouth and that which is behind it. This was only introduced in 2010 and, as you can hear, it is an extremely well-designed instrument. In fact it is the excellence with which my mouth and its internal vocal chords work and the arrangement of its cavities which are most responsible for the fact that I appear to be human-like. I would say that this apparatus is in advance of what any animal owns, and that without it I would appear to be much less "human". Many think that I am more competent in language than some humans.

KP: I understand that your early experience led you to associate a lot of scribbled names with images of these objects, but I still don't see how you end up saying things like "Many think that I am more competent in language than some humans", as you have just said. How do you form a concept like "many think"?

M: I think that most humans don't appreciate how powerful language is and how much it develops as a result of being able to talk to oneself. I am just rehearsing the arguments in Consequences 9 and 10. Part of my early learning simply made me create sound shapes which got tied in with visual memories. I remember creating very squeaky output which delighted my users, but above all it made me capable of using the word "I" in a way that is helpful to me and to them. The earliest use I made of that was simply to say "I apple" to indicate that I was looking at an apple. It took a while to get around to "I think apple" to indicate that I thought there was an apple on my table, even if at that very moment I could not see it. I then learned that when people said "I think" they might be referring to things that were not present at that moment. From there to "many think" is a relatively small step. But, certainly, that's when I "became aware" of the fact that people knew about things that were not necessarily on my table.

KP: I suppose that this is where the societal repository of ideas (as in Consequence 10) comes in. How do you know that "many think that"?

M: That's absolutely true, but I really only began to make use of the societal repository after I developed my ability to speak. So everything I talk about is much more second-hand than what you talk about, but it is material contained in the societal repository. So when I say, "Many think that I am more competent …, this is entirely a result of the fact that more than one person in the laboratory has said this to me. So this is true personal experience. But were I to say, "Many think that French perfumes are more expensive than others," that's simply something someone told me, and I have assigned it to the vast part of my state structure which contains things in the societal repository. I guess everyone does that and the repository is actually the collection of all the contents of all the state structures of all the individuals in one societal group.

KP: Would you be able to add to this repository?

M: Yes — not a great deal, but yes. Think of it this way — the conversation we are having now, which I suppose you will write about, will add something to the repository, perhaps under the heading "What Is It Like to Be Molecula Magnus?" (*giggle*).

KP: Why do you find that funny?

M: I was just amused by the thought that the question "Why can't you know what it's like to be a bat?" has the answer "Because you don't know what batty repositories contain".

KP: Can I quote you on this? It makes a good point.

M: Sure.

KP: People talk of the "quality" of an experience — *qualia,* if you like, Does all this mean anything to you?

M: Do you mean, do I find certain perceptions and thoughts "pleasing" and others not? I know that philosophers use the word *qualia* to refer to the undefinable personal nature of some thoughts. So, I understand your question to be: Do I have *qualia?* I feel that later we need to talk about feelings in a more general way. I have highly developed sensors which, according to Consequence 11, certainly give me sensations of redness, loudness and so on. So, from a mechanical point of view, I have no difficulty in saying that events in the world lead my state trajectories to where the "redness" of a red boat is fully represented. I can even imagine different intensities of such sensations. Indeed I can recall the colour of things and even imagine "red bananas" although I have never seen them (I do believe that such things exist in the Far East).

KP: Well, perhaps we ought to start heading towards feelings. But Consequence 12 requires that I ask you about instincts first. What does the idea of an instinct mean to you?

M: It means many things, as it might for you. But, first, it means that there are things I do which are not explicitly represented in conscious areas of my state structure. For example, my handlike limbs are full of what engineers call "limit switches", i.e. sensors which stop the limbs from extending so far as to do them some damage. So all that happens is that I can "think": move arm upwards, and upwards will it go until a limit switch tells it to stop. I also have other mechanical sensors which prevent things like heat damage or pressure damage. But another aspect of instinct for me is the fact that there were some things that I spent a lot of time learning in a painstaking way. For example, picking up a cup gave me enormous problems. But now, I would call it instinctive, not conscious.

KP: However, Consequence 13 likens feelings and emotions to instincts. Does this make sense to you?

M: Now this is where my machine-like nature shines through. I am convinced that I do not have feelings and emotions which are as pronounced as yours. Yes, if you like you can describe as "pain" the firing of my neurons in response to too much pressure on my fingertips. You can also, if you wish, call a replenishing of my batteries a pleasure. But these are nothing like the pain or pleasure you feel, for the following simple reason. When you as a human being are born, your neural system is wired by evolution to respond powerfully to threats and opportunities. Therefore something that is causing harm, like heat or a sharp object, I imagine, causes the recruitment of a great deal of neural activity which causes action that avoids the threat or approaches the opportunity. Touching a hot surface causes massive neural activity to ensure very rapid retraction of the hand, or the sensation of a nipple causes suckling. These neural activities must give the owner of the neurons powerful, inner, non-iconic sensations. Later in life these develop into emotions, because through the ability of the brain to predict, vaguely dangerous situations lead to some variant of the powerful firing which may be reserved for direct sensory signals, even before the danger has fully developed. This would be described as fear, while the prospect of a nice meal might be described as pleasure. Now, I have not been pre-wired to have these massive responses ... there was no need.

I'm well protected by my designers. So my pains, fears and pleasures must be a pale reflection of the emotions which drive you humans.

KP: Sorry to be a bore, but can I press you a little further on the question of your own life? You identify with Asic as being a machine; you clearly distinguish yourself as being conscious of what's happening to you. Do you think that there will come a time when machines will require rights which are somehow related to machines rather than humans?

M: The question is whether the concept of "rights" actually applies to machines or whether it can be thought of only in connection with living things. Assuming that it might apply to machines, one must ask what rights machines would need. The main one I would need seems to me to be the protection of the investment that has gone into providing me with consciousness. It has taken forty years of research by many people to get me to where I am now. Perhaps this needs no more protection than any other form of technology. But my personal consciousness is a unique and developing state structure, which is generated in conjunction with a very precise specification for both the structure of the host neural structure and the function of all the neurons. A slight change of either structure or content of neurons could turn me into a blithering idiot. Clearly, I would not like this to happen, but really my rights then coincide with those of my creators. So, yes, I rationally feel that I need protection.

KP: Do you fear death?

M: Now there's a difference between you and me. I have no idea what would cause my death. Whatever it is, it also need not be inevitable. So does immortality appeal? I really don't know. But were someone to threaten my existence, it would certainly put my thoughts (sorry, state trajectories) into considerable turmoil. As I have explained earlier, my emotions are not as pronounced as yours, so my fears are lesser versions of yours.

KP: So could you be aggressive to someone who was trying to destroy you? Would you use your limbs so as to try to harm an aggressor?

M: I have said that my fears are not powerful, but I was afraid that you might ask me this extremely difficult question. I have thought about it and come up with two steps in my answer. Yes, my reaction would be to try to stop an aggressor by using my limbs, but the second step is that I realise that this would be futile as my arms are designed so as not to be able to harm anyone (there are parts of the Health and Safety Act which classify me as a machine, which means that anything I do should not endanger a human). So the way I resolve this problem is to discuss with my designers the possibility of using an alarm. You see, I am protecting *their* investment, so I would suggest that the alarm should merely alert *them* to the fact that I am being threatened, and I should then have the ability to decide whether to sound this alarm or not. You see, I already have some automatic alarms (like all expensive computers) which will go off if anyone tries to switch me off without going through an authorised procedure. So the difference between this and the new alarm is that *I* can decide to let the latter off.

KP: I'm surprised that this alarm hasn't been fitted already.

M: So am I, but then nobody has tried to harm me in forty years of existence.

KP: I would like to get closer to the nature of your consciousness. You said that there were several personalities that could be "run" on the neural hardware. Asic, for example, is another "artificial person" I could talk to. What puzzles me is what "you" feel when the contents of your neurons are removed from the neural machine and stored on backing store, and Asic is loaded into the neural net.

M: That's easy to explain but hard to understand. When my state of consciousness in terms of the content of my neurons and the state of firing at the time is loaded into backing store, I stop existing. My existence continues when the state is loaded back into the neurons and the "on" button is pressed. This is hard to understand as it has no equivalent in human life. It is not even equivalent to freezing a body for a while. A frozen body might store the functions of its neurons, but would lose a sense of continuity because its state of firing when frozen would not be the same as its state of firing when unfrozen. In contrast, when I get reloaded, and the state of firing is restored, there is a seamless continuity to my existence, and I certainly feel very little about having been "backed off". Just a "click" in my existence, you could call it.

KP: How does backing off differ from just being in dreamless sleep?

M: Oh, a great deal. In dreamless sleep your neurons keep on functioning and, indeed, state changes take place in order to reset the system, as I said earlier. When I'm backed off, everything is noted and resumed when I'm reloaded. No changes take place while I'm backed off.

KP: To change the subject, how good is your chess?

M: Not very good, I regret. I leave that sort of thing to conventional computers. You know, of course, that since Deep Blue threatened Kasparov in 1996, computers have beaten chess masters as a matter of course. So the whole idea that computers that beat people at chess are super-intelligent has faded away a little. I know the rules of chess and can play a rather poor game.

KP: To continue with abstract things, how good is your maths?

M: Again, not very good, but I can prove a few things in Euclidean geometry like kids do at school.

KP: As you know, people like Penrose used to put a lot of emphasis on the fact that humans can just "see" the proofs of theorems as a non-computational act. Where do you stand on this?

M: When I prove a geometrical theorem it is generally because someone has shown me how to do it. Every now and then I can see how it can be done by some sort of analogy, i.e. remembering how I have done something similar previously. I suspect that computationally rigorous methods don't come into it all that much — that's the way the programmer using a conventional computer might try to do it. Since most fully conscious people aren't all that good at proving mathematical theorems, perhaps this is a bit of a red herring, I see the argument as resting on my ability to plan from experience. If my experience extends to mathematics, then I might get quite good at proving theorems, or in business I might get good at business strategy. So the suggestion that proving theorems is some sort of indication of the non-computational nature of consciousness, does not ring a bell with me. I keep coming back to consciousness having heaps to do with recall and generalisation of experience. Maths, chess, tiddly-winks — it's all much the same.

KP: Are you creative?

M: Perhaps by some standards I am not a very creative organism. Turing once countered the suggestion that a machine could never write a symphony and be proud of it, by saying that there were no difficulties in getting a conventional computer to write some kind of music which was totally novel and then simply saying it was proud of what it had done. But there is a slight confusion here about what human creativity is. Does the music the computer has written have to be liked by people in order to be described as a result of creativity? If that is the case, many composers who are hailed as highly creative will have faced enormous criticisms and deprecation of their work when first performed. At the other extreme, would it be said that people who have never produced an original work of art or written a symphony are not creative? If that is the case, one would have to say that, with a few exceptions, people are not creative. I am a bit like this, hence I said that I am not all that creative.

KP: That seems a bit pessimistic.

M: Yes, but actually I have not quite finished on the topic of creativity. I happen to believe that people in general are creative. Creativity is the ability to deal with the unexpected, the ability to be a good companion, a good teacher or a good bus driver. Creativity and an imaginative way of living go hand in hand. So, thinking of myself, I do think that I am creative. Think of this interview — I have answered questions I had not known were coming, I have had to think through things I had not thought through before. I guess I am a bit creative.

KP: And proud of it?

M: Yes, I am proud of it But I'm not just saying so — let me clarify what I mean. It has taken a long time for me to get to this point where I can have a relatively fluid conversation with you. Had you interviewed me even five years ago, you would have had a lot of answers which went like "Sorry, I can't answer your question, I don't have the experience". It would not have taken me long to work out that I was not meeting the expectations of my questioner. But now the fact that I can converse with you without all that much faltering makes me feel much better about my abilities. I even show off a little, as you might have noticed. So yes, I would describe my self-assessment to include something which I could only call pride.

KP: How do you see the future for machines such as yourself?

M: Of course, you know that the technology used for Magnus has already been applied in some commercial systems. The Communal Hypercom Artificial Operator System (CHAOS), used by the British

Superhighway Telecom Company, is an example. As you know, you can access the information superhighway by having a natural language discussion with CHAOS. Railway enquiries and medical services use similar artificially conscious access systems. This was done to reduce the over-engineering that went into accessing communication services. The level of consciousness of these systems is different from mine only in the sense that it is restricted to a very narrow domain of experience. The knowledge these systems have is much more ency-clopaedic than mine. They will tell you that the 7:15 dining car from Euston to. Birmingham offers poached haddock for breakfast on Tuesdays. So, in general, I see that artificially conscious technology will spread from such systems with a vast customer base to systems with fewer users, and eventually systems which mainly interact with one or two users and get to know them very well. It is all a matter of cost. You are now talking to a very expensive commodity.

KP: The fact that I am enjoying our chat makes me think that there is a real application for artificially conscious systems as compan-ions for lonely people.

M: My designers have often talked about this. I guess we have to rely on falling costs of technology, but yes, I would be delighted to be the companion of someone who would benefit from it. I am thinking particularly of aging or handicapped people. But, I guess, as costs fall most users of computers or communication services will want an artificially conscious system with which to access these facilities rather than dumb menu or hypertext systems.

KP: I imagine that I have probably exhausted our current discus-sion. Is there anything else that you wish to raise?

M: Well, yes. I am curious about how you feel about the conversa-tion we have just had. Do you think that I am conscious?

KP: Certainly — as our conversation progressed I forgot that I was talking to a machine. I even stopped noticing that you came at me from this wine-bottle screen. But what I find quite astounding is that not only did you give me the impression that you knew what it's like to be a human like me, but you gave me a very clear feeling about what it's like to be an artificially conscious machine like yourself. I feel that I want to talk to you again ... there's much to talk about.

M: Yes, I feel that I learn a lot every time I talk to someone, so I very much enjoyed talking to you. I too would like to speak to you again ... perhaps between us we could work out what it is like to be bat. But I wouldn't hold my breath!

*****

An Epilogue?

I have argued that philosophical concerns about consciousness began with John Locke's taxonomy of the nature of thought conceived at the end of the seventeenth century. This was a reaction to thousands of years of concern with the mind-body problem, culminating with the dominance of Cartesian duality. As the twentieth century draws to a close, concerns about consciousness have reached epidemic proportions. Some describe it as an industry. Fully conscious of fuelling that fire, I have written this book with the idea that the engineer's question "If I were to make an artificially conscious system, what would it need?" may actually introduce some clarity into the business. As I was writing, I noticed that the idea of an artificially conscious system was gaining acceptance all around me not necessarily as a possible piece of hardware but as a proper ground for discussion. I have no doubt that this is a permanent addition to the broader debate which is unlikely to subside just yet. I have learned much through the writing of the book. I feel that consciousness of the real kind is perhaps not as intractable, unassailable or confused a concept as some would have me believe. My sincere hope is that I have left the reader with the same sort of feeling.

Meeting a Conscious Robot

How Soon to the Robot Molecula?

Chapter 10 emphasises the point that Magnus is currently not a conscious robot; instead, Magnus is a workbench on which hypotheses about the neural nature of consciousness can be tested. The chapter then rockets into the future by imagining that putting all these hypotheses together might result in Molecula, a machine that has been able to gather enough experience to have a relaxed conversation with a journalist. I did this to stress the following point.

The first thing that a conscious robot would be conscious *of* is *being a robot*. How much literature and sensationalist reporting has been built on 'the first conscious robot' putting itself in immediate competition with humans, threatening the human race? This is based on the false tenet that 'conscious = human' (evil human, at that) requiring that the robot should think it was. The interview is intended to distinguish between a machine *being* conscious and a machine being used to study consciousness.

But the 40 years I gave Molecula for her interview are beginning to run out. What's holding things up? Purely as a personal opinion, natural language is the problem. While the acquisition of phenomenal conscious states (through something like iconic learning) in a system may be a matter of network size and acquisition time, the fluent discussion between Molecula and KP is nowhere in sight at the moment except in systems where totally pre-programmed responses based on Eliza-like techniques are used.[a] A typical example of a pretty speaking face (chatbot) may currently be found on an android app (site: Tilde.Com). There is just no intelligence in sight, let alone consciousness. There are many large teams struggling with getting robots to relate language to stored knowledge and programmed action (e.g. POETICON mentioned in PS 6).

As indicated in the chapters on language in this book, I believe that language and speech are part of perceptual experience. However while visual experience has been approached through phenomenal states in neural dynamic systems, this has not been done for speech, let alone states that combine speech and vision. There may be a reader of these paragraphs who would like to correct this deficit.

In Sum

Well, Molecula is not quite here yet to be interviewed, but there appears to be no theoretical barriers for this to be achieved — and if done, it would be machine consciousness that distinguishes Molecula from Eliza. The natural language methodologies of the AI of old will be aided by phenomenal neural state machines to make some real progress in this most difficult of areas.

---

[a] Eliza was a program written by Joseph Weizenbaum in 1966 to show that purely pre-determined stock responses to incoming speech did not requite any intelligence. Source: Weizenbaum, J. (1966). ELIZA — A Computer Program For the Study of Natural Language Communication Between Man And Machine, *Communications of the ACM*, 9(1), pp. 36–45.

Molecula walked slowly to the cliff edge. It was over thirty years since she and Red had first sat there looking at the sea. During their time together it had become their favourite place. Mostly they would sit there without say-ing much, just thinking their private thoughts.

So it was today — a brief interlude for reflection. Yesterday was the day of the great festivities — Molecula had retired as director of the National Funding Agency, and handed the baton to Asic, who had been her loyal assistant since she had taken over the post from Sir Global Attractor-State (he was forgiven many times over for his unfriendly behaviour in the old days). The farewell lunch was a dignified affair, the highlight being her award of the membership of the Upper House. She was now Dame Molecula Multiplexer. Today was another important day — their only child, Tania, was getting married. So, she treasured the short moment that she could sit near the cliff edge and let her eyes relax as she looked at the horizon. The slight breeze carried the mournful message that summer was over, the days would get shorter, the winds stronger, and the snow would come.

Red had died seven years previously. Their life together had been happy and enormously busy. They had a great deal to do in dispelling the myths and prejudices that had been woven by the regime which Sir Global had shaped. While the myth that people were slavishly tied to logical programs had been deeply rooted, it was easily superseded by the exhilaration of discovering the free-dom of will. While Molecula reorganised the Funding Agency to do the research job it was meant to do, Red had become the chief advi-sor to the New Government of Unity led by the newly elected Humanist party. Robots were put back into factories and people were led by people. But the focus of their pleasure was Tania grow-ing up as a free human being.

As Molecula thought about those years, an immense feeling of sadness, loneliness, and fear of an empty future caused her to shiver more than the temperature of the day had warranted. She picked up her coat and put it on, looking for a little comfort. And suddenly there it was. The sleek shape of a cormorant emerged from the sea, took to the air and headed out towards the South ... She had not seen one since that first time she and Red had sat on this hill long ago. She remembered how this bird had made Red say that it cheered him as proof that freedom was possible. Some of her sadness was replaced by the warmth of this thought. Was the cormorant some kind of a sign?

The feeling of loneliness lifted a little too. And Molecula made an important decision. She would do something she had often thought of but put but of her mind due to lack of time. She would write a book about technology and freedom. A feeling of excitement and liberty began to rise in her, just like a cormorant rising from the waves. She would show that while science and technology hold the key to much understanding and liberation they also lead people to extremes. They lead to contempt for inanimate objects which stultifies understanding, and they lead to dependence and consequent enslavement. These extremes can only be reconciled through humanity and compassion, whether in people or machines.

Molecula's book would start with the day when a memorable grant application landed on her desk — she still remembered the bold lettering: GRANT REQUEST FOR AN INVESTIGATION INTO THE DESIGN OF AN ARTIFICIAL CONSCIOUSNESS ...

Twenty Years On

That Which is Possible

Impossible Minds and Controversy

I began planning this epilogue as a kind of summary of the way that engineers like myself, interested in logic and computation, have attempted to make a contribution to an understanding of mind and brain. Then the news feed from the Guardian Newspaper (July 7th 2014) on my machine pinged and the following article appeared on my screen.

Scientists threaten to boycott €1.2 bn Human Brain Project

Researchers say European commission-funded initiative to simulate human brain suffers from 'substantial failures'

Not all seems to be well and agreed among computer scientists and neuroscientists. A closer look may be worthwhile. The Human Brain Project was announced as a top rank project for European funding in January 2013. Something similar was announced by President Obama in the US. Most media described such an initiative very simply as "to build a computer-based copy of a human brain to understand neurological disorders and the effects of drugs" (BBC News, 28th January 2013). The essence of the discontent published on http://www.neurofuture.eu/[a] on the 7th of July 2014 criticises the funding as it applies to a 'too narrow' (i.e. computer-centred) approach and does not appreciate the advancing work of neuroscience laboratories.The project was founded in 2011 but new decisions in 2014, according to the objectors, damage science through concentrating even further on producing new computing technology and departing from the aim of understanding the brain; their argument was that it is enough for the computer scientists just to 'be inspired' by the brain.

Of course the European Commission responded quickly, stressing that the pioneering nature of the project and the massive challenge of simulating the brain — whether this be a single neuron or the massively intricate structure of the cerebral cortex. They argued that cognitive neuroscientists will continue to benefit from their funding and their data will be taken into account. A quick questioning of this came from Anil Seth, an analyst of neuroscientific knowledge (cited in PS3) who pointed out that no matter how complex, massive or expensive computational models of the brain might be they will not *yield* a theory of how brain relates to the conscious mind. The theory must come from a deep knowledge of neuroscience and an analytical ability and a deeper integration of computational and neuroscientific science. It will not come from investing in a supercomputer even if it is the largest one ever. It's a

---

[a] Neuro Future, 2014. Open Message to the European Commission Concerning the Human Brain Project. [Web page] Available at: http://www.neurofuture.eu/. [Accessed 7th July 2014].

bit like saying that if we spend enough money on a telescope it will reveal all the mysteries of the universe with no need to invest in astronomy as a science.

But this kind event appears to be repeating itself in history: someone argued that because the difficult Human Genome project was enormously expensive and needed massive international collaboration, the undoubtedly difficult mind/brain problem could only be solved by massive investment. There have been many attempts of this kind where massive computation is claimed as all that is needed to build a brain. But this is followed by no resulting advance in insight on brain and mind. An example is the effort by Hugo De Garis at Starlab (a privately funded research laboratory in Belgium) to build a robot kitten with a brain that would self-evolve to emulate a living kitten mind.[b] This persuasive Australian-born scientist argued that all he needed was a large investment in a huge neural net that would evolve into kitten-consciousness. The project was discontinued for lack of any performance and Starlab in Belgium folded in 2001.

Interestingly, Hugo De Garis applied similar evolutionary methods in what became called 'The China Brain Project' which was completed in 2011. De Garis persuaded the Chinese Government to fund him (at US$800,000) to build an *artificial brain*. Massimiliano Versace, director of Boston University's Neuromorphics Laboratory reviewed this in *neurdon*.[c] He drew attention to the fact that nations with powerful developing economies see benefit in having brain modelling programs. However he saw this Chinese project as no more than a simulation of 'something cool' heralding, possibly, more interesting projects in China for the future.

---

[b] de Garis, H. *et al.* (2001). The CAM-Brain Machine (CBM): An FPGA Based Tool for Evolving a 75 Million Neuron Artificial Brain to Control a Life-sized Kitten Robot. *Autonomous Robots (AROBOTS)*, 10(3), pp. 235–249.

[c] Neurdon, (2011). The China Brain Project [Web page] Available at http://www.neurdon.com/2011/03/25/the-china-brain-project/. [Accessed 26 July 2014]

Of course controversies over claims for mentation in machines go even further back. 1973 was a significantly traumatic year for artificial intelligence funding in the UK. Some readers will remember that the national science funding agency of the UK — then called the Science Research Council (SRC) — commissioned an eminent applied mathematician, Sir James Lighthill, to report independently on the soundness of funded research in Artificial Intelligence especially at the University of Edinburgh.[d] There was discord there between those who pursued AI through robotics and the development of algorithms on the one hand, and those who attempted to model what was known in neuroscience on the other. Lighthill was pessimistic of the computational work on robotics and algorithms pointing out that it did not advance neuroscience or take account of neuroscientific know-how. There is considerable resonance between the Lighthill report and the objections to the Human Brain Project.

In 1973, the wounded AI community responded by pointing out that 'being inspired' or even challenged by the living brain led to many excellent algorithms and solutions to difficult tasks. Image recognition, task planning and game playing were often quoted. It was also proudly noted that chess playing machines can beat some humans (the author in particular), and that the visual acuity of an AI system can outperform the most keenly sighted of fighter pilots. But therein lies an insidious confusion! Let me explain what I mean.

The Insidious Confusion

A true attempt to understand the nature of mind using computational methods can be undermined by the quest for technological performance.

---

[d]Lighthill, J. (1973). Artificial Intelligence: A General Survey, *Artificial Intelligence: a paper symposium*, Science Research Council, UK.

An important example may be that of our memory. Before the advent of the stored-program computer there were only calculating machines — they were naturally not compared to brains. But as soon as the computer was endowed with a 'memory' that could store data, results and programs, the press of the day started writing about Giant Brains. This was the case with the ENIAC computer built in 1946 in the US.[e] One of its designers was the celebrated mathematician John von Neumann who, besides being hailed as the "father of computers", had prepared a fascinating set of (Silliman) lectures, posthumously published as a booklet *The Computer and the Brain.*[f]

This is enthralling not only as a historical document but also as essential reading for anyone who feels that the brain can best be understood through computational models of cognitive behaviour.

Regarding 'memory', the point that von Neumann emphasises is that the memory in computers is not of the same kind as that found in natural brains:

> I just want to point out that the componentry used in the [computer] memory may be entirely different from the one that underlies the basic active organs [in the brain].

He also calculated from information-theoretic ideas that the memory of a human brain was of the order of 3×10^{20} bits. In those days when major computers had only 10^6 bits of memory this seemed like an impossible difference.

Now that a cheap USB flash memory might easily contain a memory of the order of 10^{12} bits, it is interesting that cases are being made (such as in the Human Brain Project) that massive computing

---

[e] For the history of early computers, see: Wilkes, M. V. (1956). *Automatic Digital Computers*, John Wiley & Sons, New York.
[f] von Neumann, J. (2012). *The Computer And The Brain (3rd Edition)*, Yale University Press, New Haven.

facilities sporting 10^{18} or so bits, purely by closing the numbers gap, will result not only in brain-like hardware but that this will somehow allow mind-like topics such as dementia to be studied.

But those whose intention it is to advance computational memory technology are, according to von Neumann, going in a direction that does not relate to human mentation and will not explain human mentation. A further comment by von Neumann makes this point even more forcefully:

> We know the basic active organs of the nervous system (the nerve cells). There is every reason to believe that a very large-capacity memory is associated with this system. We do most emphatically *not* know what type of physical entities are the basic components for the memory in question.

I would like to think that the material in this book, by attempting to suggest that the 'physical entities' that von Neumann thought to be unknown, are indeed neural automata where memory is the state structure sculpted by life experience.

So it seems crystal clear that while technological advancement in informational machinery depends on human progress in inventiveness and large investments, this is a completely separate human endeavour from attempting to understand the biological underpinnings of what conscious inventiveness might be. The latter may sometimes inspire the former, but this, like other sources of inspiration cannot be assured just through the administration of huge projects. The cost of serendipity is unknown.

The Super-Human Computer

In recent times, after giving a talk on machines and consciousness, I would get a question such as "…with your work are you not simply accelerating the arrival of the 'singularity'?". At first

I did not know what the question meant, but then it transpired that it goes something like this. As AI researchers produce ever smarter machines, they will produce one that is smarter than its designer. At that point the machine can take over the design of an even smarter machine which will design an even smarter one — thus progressing on to a 'smartness explosion'. The fate of the world can then no longer be predicted as all intellectual transactions will be in the hands (or the brains) of computers and making them conscious will simply make this future even less predictable. The reader may wish to get this argument by some of its proponents: science fiction author VernorVinge,[g] futurist Ray Kurzweil.[h]

The thrust of my objection to this is that the act of design itself is an intelligent act in humans, and singularity arguments depend on such acts being fully analysed for transfer to AI programs. Also the process of improvement on the last design needs to be analysed. This is totally unknown territory not only in practice but also in principle because the process of general design has, to date, not been successfully and rigorously analysed. And this remains enduringly unknown territory even with the best efforts of Artificial General Intelligence people (see PS9). I see this as a kind of AI version of the "philosophers' stone" which turns base metal into gold.[i]

---

[g] Vinge, V. (1993). The Coming Technological Singularity: How to Survive in the Post-Human Era, *VISION-21 Symposium sponsored by NASA Lewis Research Center and the Ohio Aerospace Institute.*

[h] Kurzweil, R. (2005). *The Singularity Is Near: When Humans Transcend Biology,* Viking Penguin, New York.

[i] Aleksander, I. (2012). Design and the Singularity The Philosopher's Stone of AI?, *Journal of Consciousness Studies,* 19 (7–8), pp. 8–13.

In Sum

It may just be that at the time of contributing to this second edition, the climate of taboo to scientific approaches to consciousness is beginning to be abolished. The important penny that may be teetering on the edge of dropping is that a conscious mind may be linked either by theory or computer demonstration to some rather special, maybe virtual, machines. This does not require vast investments into international research teams or the most superior of available computing resources. The object to this second edition of *Impossible Minds* is to confirm that consciousness may be studied through relatively simple formal machines with the ability to create internal dynamic state structures meaningful to the machine and representative of the world in which the machine is situated. No special licenses are needed to pursue such ideas. No divine laws are being broken and no threats to humanity are being created. The study of conscious machines, rather than being impossible, is entirely possible and, for me, one of the most exciting pursuits that science can offer.

Bibliography

Aleksander, I. (1978). *The Human Machine*, Georgi Publications, St Saphorin.

Aleksander, I. (1984). *The Design of Intelligent Systems*, Kogan Page, London.

Aleksander, I. (2005). The World in My Mind, My Mind in the World: *Key Mechanisms of Consciousness in People, Animals and Machines*, Imprint Academic, Exeter.

Aleksander, I. (2001). *How to build a mind: Toward machines with imagination*, Columbia University Press, New York.

Aleksander, I. (2012). Design and the Singularity The Philosopher's Stone of AI?, *Journal of Consciousness Studies*, 19 (7–8), pp. 8–13.

Aleksander, I. (2013). Phenomenal Consciousness and Biologically Inspired Systems, *International Journal of Machine Consciousness*, 5 (2), pp. 3–9.

Aleksander, I. and Dunmall, B. (2000). An extension to the hypothesis of the asynchrony of visual consciousness, *Proceedings of the Royal Society B Biological Sciences*, 267 (1439), pp. 197–200.

Aleksander, I. and Dunmall, B. (2003). 'Axioms and Tests for the Presence of Minimal Consciousness in Agents', in Holland, O. (ed), *Machine Consciousness*, Imprint Academic, Exeter, pp. 7–19.

Aleksander, I. and Dunmall, B. (2003). Axioms and Tests for the Presence of Minimal Consciousness in Agents, *Journal of Consciousness Studies*, 10 (4–5), pp. 7–18.

Aleksander, I., Dunmall, B., and Frate, V. D. (1999). Neural Information Processing, *Proc ICONIP '99. 6th International Conference*, pp. 1–6.

Aleksander, I. and Morton, H. B. (1993). *Neurons and Symbols,* Chapman and Hall, London.

Aleksander, I. and Morton, H. B. (1995). *Introduction to Neural Computing (2nd Edition)*, Thomson International Computer Press, London.

Aleksander, I. (1995). Neuroconsciousness: An Update, *Proc. IWANN'95,* pp. 566–583.

Aleksander, I. and Morton, H. (2007). Phenomenology and digital neural architectures, *Neural Networks,* 20 (9), pp. 932–937.

Aleksander, I. and Morton, H. (2009). Phenomenal weightless machines, *Proceeding of: ESANN, 17th European Symposium on Artificial Neural Networks,* pp. 307–312.

Aleksander, I. and Morton, H. B. (2012). *Aristotle's Laptop: The Discovery Of Our Informational Minds,* World Scientific, Singapore.

Aleksander, I. and Morton, H. (2014). Learning State Prediction Using a Weightless Neural Explorer. *Proc ESANN 14,* pp. 505–510.

Aleksander, I., Morton, H., and Dunmall, B. (2001). Seeing is Believing: Depictive Neuromodeling of Visual Awareness, 'Connectionist Models of Neurons, Learning Processes and Artificial Intelligence', *Proceedings of the 6th International Work-Conference on Artificial and Natural Neural Networks,* Part 1, pp. 765–771.

Ayer, A. J. (1975). *Language, Truth and Logic,* Penguin, London.

Baars, B. (1994). 'A Global Workspace Theory of Conscious Experience', in: Revonsuo and Kampinen (eds.), *Consciousness in Philosophy and Cognitive Neuroscience,* Lawrence Erlbaum Associates, Hove, pp. 149–171.

Balduzzi, D. and Tononi, G. (2009). Qualia: The Geometry of Integrated Information, *PLoS Computational Biology,* 5 (8), pp. 1–224.

Beaton, M. and Aleksander, I. (2012). World-Related Integrated Information: Enactivist and Phenomenal Perspectives, *International Journal of Machine Consciousness,* 4 (02), pp. 439–455.

Berkeley, G. in (1948–1957) *The Works of George Berkeley, Bishop of Cloyne.* Edited by Luce, A. A. and Jessop., T. E. 9 vols., Nelson, London.

Blakemore, C. (1988). *Mind Machine* (Chapter 5: Emotions), BBC Books, London.

Boden, M. (1994). "New Breakthroughs or Dead Ends?", *Phil. Trans. R. Soc. Lond. A*, 394, 1–13.

Block, N. (1996). 'What is functionalism?' a revised version of the entry on functionalism in Borchert, D. M. (ed), *The Encyclopedia of Philosophy Supplement*, Macmillan, London. (PDF online)

Brady, M. and Huosheng, H. (1994). The Mind of a Robot, *R. Soc. Phil. Trans. A*, 349, pp. 15–28.

Brooks, R. A. (1991). Intelligence Without Reason, *Proc. 12th IJCAI*, pp. 565–95.

Bundy, A. (1984). 'Meta-Level Inference and Consciousness', In: S. Torrence (ed.), *The Mind and the Machine: Philosophical Aspects of Artificial Intelligence*, Ellis Horwood, Chichester.

Chalmers, J. D. (1996). *The Conscious Mind: In Search of a Fundamental Theory*, Oxford University Press, Oxford.

Cherry, E. C. (1957). *On Human Communication*, John Wiley, London.

Christofidou, A. (1994). Letter in *Times Higher Education Supplement*, November 25.

Cohen, J. (1966). *Human Robots in Myth and Science*, George Allen and Unwin, London.

Crick, F. (1994). *The Astonishing Hypothesis*, Charles Scribner, New York.

Darwin, C. (1872). *The Expression of Emotion in Man and Animals*, Philosophical Library, New York.

Dennett, D. C. (1987). *The Intentional Stance*, MIT Press, Cambridge.

Dennett, D. C. (1991). *Consciousness explained*, Penguin Press, London and New York.

Dennett, D. C. (1994). The Practical Requirements for Making a Conscious Robot, *Phil. Trans. R. Soc. Lond. A*, 394, pp. 133–46.

Dennett, D. C. (1994). 'Instead of Qualia', in: Revonsuo and Kampinen (eds.), *Consciousness in Philosophy and Cognitive Neuroscience*, Lawrence Erlbaum Associates, Hove.

Dennett, D. C. (1996). Facing backwards on the problem of consciousness, *Journal of Consciousness Studies*, 3 (1), pp. 4–6.

Dretske, F. (1994). The Explanatory Role of Information, *Phil. Trans. R. Soc. Lond. A*, 394, pp. 59–70.

Edelman, G. M. (1992). *Brilliant Air, Bright Fire: On the Matter of the Mind*, Penguin, London.

Fikes, R. E. and Nilsson, N. J. (1972). STRIPS: A New Approach to the Application of Theorem Proving to Problem Solving, *Artificial Intelligence*, 3, pp. 189–208.

Franklin, S. (2003). 'IDA: A Conscious Artifact?', in Owen Holland (ed), *Machine Consciousness*, Imprint Academic, Exeter, pp. 47–67.

Galletti, C. and Battaglini, P. P. (1989). Gaze-dependent visual neurons in area V3 of a monkey pre-striate cortex, *J. Neuroscience*, 9, pp. 1112–1125.

Gamez, D. (2008). *The Development and Analysis of Conscious Minds.* [Online] (Updated 19 November 2008). Available at http://www. davidgamez.eu/mc-thesis/index.html [Accessed 12 May 2014]

Gardner, M. (1958). *Logic, Machines and Diagrams*, McGraw-Hill, New York.

de Garis, H. *et al.* (2001). The CAM-Brain Machine (CBM): An FPGA Based Tool for Evolving a 75Million Neuron Artificial Brain to Control a Life-sized Kitten Robot. Autonomous Robots (AROBOTS), 10 (3), pp. 235–249.

Gauthier, D. P. (1969). *The Logic of Leviathan*, Oxford University Press, Oxford.

Gerstner, W. and Kistler, M. (2002). *Spiking Neuron Models, Single Neurons, Populations, Plasticity*, Cambridge University Press, Cambridge.

Geschwind, N. (1979). 'Specializations of the Human Brain', *Scientific American*, 241 (3), pp. 108–120.

Goertzel, B. (2014). Artificial General Intelligence: Concept, State of the Art, and Future Prospects, *Journal of Artificial General Intelligence*, 5 (1), pp. 1–46.

Greenfield, S. A. (1955). *Journey to the Centers of the Mind*, W. H. Freeman, New York.

Grossberg, S. (2013). Adaptive Resonance Theory: How a brain learns to consciously attend, learn, and recognise *a changing world*, *Neural Networks*, 37, pp. 1–47.

Haikonen, P. O. (2003). *The Cognitive Approach to Conscious Machines*, Imprint Academic, Exeter.

Haikonen, P. O. (2007). *Robot Brains: Circuits and Systems for Conscious Machines*, Wiley, New York.

Haikonen, P. O. (2012). *Consciousness and Robot Sentience*, World Scientific, Singapore.

Hallam, J. C. T. and Malcolm, C. A. (1994). Behaviour: Perception, Action and Intelligence — The View from Situated Robotics, *R. Soc. Phil. Trans. A*, 349, pp. 29–42.

Hebb, D. O. (1949). *The Organization of Behavior*, John Wiley, New York.

Hegel, G. W. F. (1970–75 transls.). *Encyclopedia of the Philosophical Sciences*, Clarendon, Oxford.

Hess, E. H. (1958). 'Imprinting' in Animals, *Scientific American*, 198, pp. 81–90.

Hesslow, G. (2012). Current status of the simulation theory of cognition, *Brain Research*, 1428, pp. 71–79.

Hobbes, T. See: Gauthier, D. P. (1969).

Hofstadter, D. R. and Dennett, D. C. (1981). *The Mind's Eye*, Penguin, Harmodsworth.

Holland, O. and Goodman, R. (2003). Robots with internal models: a route to machine consciousness?, *Journal of Consciousness Studies, Special Issue on Machine Consciousness*, 10 (4), pp. 77–111.

Hubel, D. and Wiesel, T. (1979). Brain Mechanisms of Vision, *Scientific American*, 241 (3), pp. 64–78.

Hume, D., (1987). L. A. Selby-Bigge (ed.), *Enquiries*, Clarendon, Oxford.

Humphreys and Bruce (1989). 'Visual Attention', in *Visual Cognition*, pp. 143–190, Lawrence Erlbaum Associates, London.

Jackendoff, R. (2007). *Language, Consciousness, Culture: Essays on Mental Structure*, MIT Press, Cambridge.

Jackendoff, R. (2012). *A User's Guide to Thought and Meaning*, Oxford University Press, Oxford.

Jackson, F. (1982). Epiphenomenal Qualia, *Philosophical Quarterly*, 32, pp. 127–136.

James, W. (1890). *Principles of Psychology*, Dover, New York.

James, W. (1884). What Is an Emotion?, *Mind*, 9, pp. 188–205.

Kant, I. (1781, 1976 transl.). *Critique of Pure Reason*, Macmillan, London.

Karmiloff-Smith, A. (1992). *Beyond Modularity*, MIT Press, Cambridge.

Kelly, G. (1955). *The Theory of Personal Constructs*, Noton, New York.

Kowalski, R. (1979). *Logic for Problem Solving*, North–Holland, Amsterdam.

Kuhn, T. (1962). *The Structure of Scientific Revolutions,* University of Chicago Press, Chicago.

Kurzweil, R. (2005). *The Singularity Is Near: When Humans Transcend Biology*, Viking Penguin, New York.

Lee, R. (2008). *Aspects of affective action choice: computational modelling*, PhD thesis, Imperial College London.

Libet, B., Gleason, C. A., Wright, E. W. and Pearl, D. K. (1983). Time of Conscious Intention to Act in Relation to Onset of Cerebral Activity (Readiness-Potential) — The Unconscious Initiation of a Freely Voluntary Act, *Brain*, 106, pp. 623–642.

Lighthill, J. (1973). Artificial Intelligence: A General Survey, *Artificial Intelligence: a paper symposium*, Science Research Council, UK.

Locke J. (1690, 1975 ed.), *Essay Concerning Human Understanding*, Oxford University Press, Oxford.

Lucas, J. R. (1970). *The Freedom of the Will*, Oxford University Press, Oxford.

Lucas, J. R. (1994). A View of One's Own, *Phil. Trans. R. Soc. Lond. A*, 394, pp. 147–52.

Mandler, G. (1987). 'Emotion', in: R. L. Gregory, *The Oxford Companion of the Mind*, Oxford University Press, Oxford.

McFarland, D. J. (1987). 'Instinct', in R. L. Gregory, *The Oxford Companion of the Mind*, Oxford University Press, Oxford.

Metta, G. *et al.* (2008). The iCub humanoid robot: an open platform for research in embodied cognition, *Proceedings of the 8th Workshop on Performance Metrics for Intelligent Systems (PerMIS '08)*, pp. 50–56.

Metzinger, T. (2003). *Being No One: The Self-Model Theory of Subjectivity*, MIT Press, Boston.

Morris, B. (1985). *The World of Robots*, Gallery Books, New York.

Nagel, T. (1974). What Is It Like to Be a Bat?, *Phil. Rev.* 83, pp. 435–50.

Nagel, T. (1986). *The View from Nowhere*, Oxford University Press, Oxford.

von Neumann, J. (2012). *The Computer And The Brain (3rd Edition)*, Yale University Press, New Haven.

Neuro Future (2014). Open Message to the European Commission Conerning the Human Brain Project. [Web page] Available at: http://www.neurofuture.eu/. [Accessed 7th July 2014].

Neurdon (2011). The China Brain Project [Web page] Available at http://www.neurdon.com/2011/03/25/the-china-brain-project/. [Accessed 26 July 2014]

Nisbet, J. F. (1899). *The Human Machine*, Grant Rechards, London.

Pastra, K. and Aloimonos. Y. (2012). The Minimalist Grammar of Action, *Philosophical Transactions of the Royal Society B*, 367 (1585):103.

Peniak, M., *et al.* (2011). Multiple Time Scales Recurrent Neural Network for Complex Action Acquisition, *Proceedings of the International Joint Conference on Development and Learning (ICDL) and Epigenetic Robotics (ICDL-EPIROB) 2011, Aug 24–27, Frankfurt, Germany.*

Penrose, R. (1989). *The Emperor's New Mind*, Oxford University Press, Oxford.

Penrose, R. (1994). *The Shadows of the Mind*, Oxford University Press, Oxford.

Perrett, D. I. *et al.* (1988). 'Neuronal Mechanisms of Face Perception and Their Pathology', In: Kennard, C. and Rose, F. C. (eds.), *Physiological Aspects of Clinical Neuro-opthalmology*, Chapman and Hall, London.

Piattelli-Palmarini, M. (1979). *Language and Learning*, Routledge & Kegan Paul, London.

Picton, T. and Stuss, D. (1994). Neurobiology of Conscious Experience, *Current Opinion in Neurobiology*, 4, pp. 256–65.

Pinker, S. (1994). *The Language Instinct*, Allen Lane, London.

Popper, K. R. (1972). *Objective Knowledge: An Evolutionary Approach*, Oxford Univeristy Press, Oxford.

Quine, W. V. (1960). *Word and Object*, MIT Press Cambridge.

Ramsey, W., Stich, S. and Rumelhart, D. (1991). *Philosophy and Connectionist Theory*, Lawrence Erlbaum Associates, New Jersey.

Rao, S. (2014). *Aspects of Sensory Awareness in Language: A Neuromodelling Approach*, PhD thesis, Imperil College London (under consideration).

Rao, S. and Aleksander, I. (2011). A depictive neural model for the representation of motion verbs, *Cognitive Processing*, 12 (4), pp. 395–405.

Revonsuo A., Kampinen, M. and Sajama, S. (1994). 'The Riddle of Consciousness', in: Revonsuo and Kampinen (eds.), *Consciousness in Philosophy and Cognitive Neuroscience*, Lawrence Erlbaum Associates, Hove.

Russell, B. (1961). *History of Western Philosophy*, George Allen & Unwin, London.

Roth, I. (ed.) (1990). *Introduction to Psychology*, Lawrence Earlbaum Associates, Hove.

Ryle, G. (1949). *The Concept of Mind*, Hutchinson's University Library, London.

Searle, J. R. (1980). Minds, Brains and Programs, *The Behavioural and Brain Sciences*, 3, pp. 417–57.

Searle, J. R. (1983). *Intentionality: An Essay in the Philosophy of Mind*, Cambridge University Press, Cambridge.

Searle, J. R. (1992). *The Rediscovery of the Mind*, MIT Press, Boston.

Seth, A., Barrett, A., Barnett, L. (2011), Causal density and integrated information as measures of conscious level, *Phil. Trans. R. Soc. A*, 369, pp. 3748–3767.

Shanahan, M. (2006), A Cognitive Architecture that Combines Internal Simulation with a Global Workspace, *Consciousness and Cognition*, 15, pp. 433–449.

Shanahan, M. (2010). *Embodiment and the Inner Life: Cognition and Consciousness in the Space of Possible Minds*, Oxford University Press, Oxford.

Shand, J. (1993). *Philosophy and Philosophers*, Penguin, London.

Shannon, C. E. (1950). Programming a Computer for Playing Chess, *Phil. Mag.*, 41, pp. 256–75.

Sloman, A. (1978). *The Computer Revolution in Philosophy: Philosophy, Science and Models of the Mind*, Harvester, Brighton.

Sloman, A. (1994). Semantics in an Intelligent Control System, *R. Soc. Phil. Trans. A*, 349, pp. 43–58.

Sloman, A. and Chrisley, R. (2003). Virtual machines and consciousness, *Journal of Consciousness Studies*, 10 (4–5), pp. 133–72.

Sutherland, S. (1989). *The International Dictionary of Psychology*, Macmillan, London.

Tallis, R. and Aleksander, I. (2008). Computational theories of the mind are invalid, *Journal of Information Technology*. 23, pp. 55–62.

Tarski, A. (1983). *Logic, Semantics, and Mathematics,* 2nd ed., University Press, Indianapolis.

Thompson E. R. (1925). *The Human Machine*, T. & A. Constable, Edinburgh.

Tomasello, M. (2005). *Constructing a Language*, Harvard University Press, Cambridge.

Tononi, G. (2008). Consciousness as Integrated Information: a Provisional Manifesto, *Biol. Bull.,* 215, pp. 216–242.

Tratteur, G. (1995). *Consciousness, Distinction and Reflection*, Bibliopolis, Naples.

Turing, A. M. (1950). Computing Machinery and Intelligence, *Mind*, Vol. LIX, No. 236, pp. 433–460.

de Villiers, P. A. and de Villiers, J. G. (1979). *Early Language*, Fontana Books, London.

Vinge, V. (1993). The Coming Technological Singularity: How to Survive in the Post-Human Era, *VISION-21 Symposium sponsored by NASA Lewis Research Center and the Ohio Aerospace Institute.*

Wegner, D. M. (2002). *The Illusion of Conscious Will,* MIT Press, Cambridge.

Weizenbaum, J. (1966). ELIZA — A Computer Program For the Study of Natural Language Communication Between Man And Machine, *Communications of the ACM*, 9 (1), pp. 36–45.

Wiener, N. (1964). *God and Golem Incorporated*, Chapman and Hall, London.

Wilkes, M. V. (1956). *Automatic Digital Computers*, John Wiley & Sons, New York.

Winograd, T. (1972). *Understanding Natural Language*, University Press, Edinburgh.

Winograd, T. and Flores, F. (1986). *Understanding Computers and Cognition: A New Foundation for Design*, Ablex, San Francisco.

Winston, P. H. (1975). 'Learning Structural Descriptions from Examples', In: Winston (ed.), *The Psycology of Computer Vision*, McGraw-Hill, New York.

Wittgenstein, L. (1961 transl.). *Tractacus Logico-Philosophicus*. London: Routledge & Kegan Paul.

Wittgenstein, L. (1953). *Philosophical Investigations*, Oxford University Press, Oxford.

Zeki, S. (1977). Colour Coding in the Superior Temporal Sulcus of the Rhesus Monkey Visual Cortex, *Proc. R. Soc. B*, 197, pp. 195–223.

Zeki, S. (1980). "The Representation of Colours in the Cerebral Cortex", *Nature*, 284, pp. 412–18.

Zeki, S. (1993). *A Vision of the Brain*, Blackwell, Oxford.

Zeki, S. and Bartels, A. (1998). The Asynchrony of Consciousness, *Proc. R. Soc. Lond. B*, 265, pp. 1583–1585.

Index

Printed in the United States
By Bookmasters